THE SINGAPORE BLUE CHIPS

The Rewards & Risks of Investing in
Singapore's Largest Corporates

THE SINGAPORE BLUE CHIPS

The Rewards & Risks of Investing in Singapore's Largest Corporates

Nandini Vijayaraghavan

Umesh Desai

World Scientific

EW JERSEY · LONDON · SINGAPORE · BEIJING · SHANGHAI · HONG KONG · TAIPEI · CHENNAI · TOKYO

Published by

World Scientific Publishing Co. Pte. Ltd.
5 Toh Tuck Link, Singapore 596224
USA office: 27 Warren Street, Suite 401-402, Hackensack, NJ 07601
UK office: 57 Shelton Street, Covent Garden, London WC2H 9HE

Library of Congress Cataloging-in-Publication Data
Names: Vijayaraghavan, Nandini, author. | Desai, Umesh, 1967–   author.
Title: The Singapore blue chips : the rewards & risks of investing in Singapore's largest corporates /
    Nandini Vijayaraghavan, Singapore, Umesh Desai, Thomson Reuters, Hong Kong.
Description: New Jersey : World Scientific, 2016. | Includes bibliographical references.
Identifiers: LCCN 2015048993| ISBN 9789814759731 | ISBN 9789814759212
Subjects: LCSH: Investments, Foreign--Singapore. | Corporations--Valuation--Singapore. |
    Blue-chip stocks--Singapore. | Finance--Singapore. | Industries--Singapore.
Classification: LCC HG5750.67.A3 V55 2016 | DDC 332.63/22095957--dc23
LC record available at http://lccn.loc.gov/2015048993

British Library Cataloguing-in-Publication Data
A catalogue record for this book is available from the British Library.

In-house Editor: Shreya Gopi

Typeset by Stallion Press
Email: enquiries@stallionpress.com

Printed in Singapore

ABOUT THE AUTHORS

Nandini Vijayaraghavan is a corporate finance professional with extensive experience in researching Asia Pacific corporates. Nandini's twin interests are promoting financial literacy and translating Tamil works of literature into English. *The Singapore Blue Chips* is her maiden corporate biography.

Nandini's first publication is an English translation of Kalki R Krishnamurthy's Tamil classic, *Sivakamiyin Sabadham* (*Sivakami's Oath*). This is a four-volume novel, the book and Kindle versions of which are available on Amazon and Flipkart.

She holds postgraduate degrees in Economics and Finance from Tufts University and London Business School respectively and is a CFA charter holder.

Umesh Desai writes on companies and economies in Asia Pacific, providing a debt perspective for clients of Thomson Reuters. His coverage has extended from power to property and on subjects ranging from primary markets to bankruptcies. He has also been a speaker at various public forums across the region, talking to financial market professionals at events in Hong Kong, Singapore, Tokyo, Beijing, and Kuala Lumpur.

He has been with the company for 18 years, prior to which he was a credit analyst with ICRA, which has Moody's as its largest shareholder. A chartered accountant by training, Umesh started his career as an equity research analyst.

ACKNOWLEDGEMENTS

We would like to thank the following companies for providing inputs to and confirming factual accuracy of the company specific chapters.

Temasek Holdings, Golden Agri Resources, Wilmar International, Olam International, The Singapore Exchange, Keppel Corporation, Fraser & Neave, Sembcorp Industries, ST Engineering, CapitaLand, CapitaLand Mall Trust, Ascendas Real Estate Investment Trust, Global Logistic Properties, StarHub, Singapore Telecommunications, DBS Group, United Overseas Bank, and Oversea-Chinese Banking Corporation.

The following companies either did not object to be included in this book or failed to respond to our requests to confirm factual accuracy.

Genting Singapore, Marina Bay Sands, SIA Engineering, ComfortDelGro and Singapore Airlines.

A big thank you to our student interns from NPS International School, Singapore for assisting us with the research, particularly the Milestones and stock returns sections of this book:

Aadhar Agarwal, Ashwin Kumaar, Bhawna Sharma, Madhura Shirodhkar and Vijay Siddharth.

ENDORSEMENTS

"This was an information packed book where even relative experts will glean new information and the more casual reader will find it a great reference. Despite rising to such prominence, there remains strikingly little information on corporate Singapore, an omission that Vijayaraghavan and Desai have stepped in to correct by writing a piece that is sure to be a reference for years to come."

Associate Professor Christopher Balding
HSBC Business School, Peking University

"The 22 companies featured in this informative and insightful book are some of those that stand out in the Singapore corporate scene. They are relatively large, established businesses with experienced management and strong track records of growth and profitability. Their profiles and success stories, taken together, form a formidable tome for anyone with interest in the Singapore business scene. This is a book for businessmen as well as investors: big and small; casual and professional. I hope you would enjoy and gain from it."

Mr Mano Sabnani
CEO, Rafflesia Holdings Pte Ltd
Singapore

"Well done on a well-constructed book and you have clearly put a lot of effort in to this project.

Overall, I believe that this is a well-crafted and thoughtful addition to the guides available to investing in Asia, and Singapore in particular. There is sufficient detail and insight to engage with an audience that includes both professional and personal investors. It also provides a credible history of the companies profiled and places these in an overall context of Singapore's remarkable economic development. I particularly appreciate the breadth of the companies included and the grouping of these companies according to industrial sector. At the same time, you have highlighted the differences within sector so that investors can understand the idiosyncratic aspects of each opportunity. Rather than gloss over the challenges that many of these companies face, you have highlighted the current difficulties resulting from cyclicality and global factors. You also identify limitations due to local factors. This adds to the credibility of the review and presents a platform of opinion that will serve investors well in the future."

Mark Konyn
Group Chief Investment Officer
AIA Group

CONTENTS

1

CURTAIN RAISER

When we thought of writing a book about Singapore corporations, a journalist joked, "Are you writing about Singapore corporates?! You only have to cover MNCs, GLCs and PLCs — multinational companies, government linked companies and poor local companies." The implication was that the corporate sector in Singapore comprised overseas companies that chose to make Singapore home because of its investor friendly climate, local companies that flourished because of government backing and a host of small and medium scale enterprises that barely survived.

The statement set us thinking. Was the Singapore corporate story so boring and uni-dimensional? Are there no lessons global investors can learn from this prosperous island state that rose from "Third World to First World" in less than 50 years? In this day and age how can an economy thrive by just being an MNC hub and home to a bunch of GLCs that depend heavily on government gratis? But as we delved deeper, a fascinating story emerged. It was that of a forward looking nation that constantly questioned its relevance in a dynamic global environment — re-positioning itself as a world-class financial centre willing to open its borders further to global commerce while showing it innovative capacity by leveraging on its skilled workforce.

In its Doing Business 2016 report, The World Bank ranked Singapore first globally for ease of doing business. Neighbouring city state Hong Kong is ranked fifth, despite having China as a hinterland. World Bank ranks countries in terms of the ease of doing business on ten parameters — starting business (Singapore is ranked 10th), dealing with construction permits (1st), getting electricity (6th), registering property (17th), getting credit (19th), protecting minority investors (1st), paying taxes (5th), trading across borders (41st), enforcing contracts (1st) and resolving insolvency (27th).

Transparency International ranks Singapore as the eighth least corrupt country in the world, after Denmark, Finland, Sweden, New Zealand, Netherlands, Norway and Switzerland. It is the only country in Asia to feature in the ten least corrupt nations. However, Singapore's ranking has slipped to eight in 2015 from seven in 2014. Its score slipping from 87 in 2012 to 85 in 2015 is a cause for concern.

Singapore's corporate tax rate is 17% which is marginally higher than Hong Kong's 16.5% and more attractive than the Asian average of 21.91% and the global average of 23.68%. Singapore is a member of the Association of South East Asian Nations (ASEAN). Corporate tax rates in the other member nations are Indonesia (25%), Malaysia (24%), The Philippines (30%), Thailand (20%), Brunei (18.5%), Cambodia (20%), Laos (22%), Myanmar (25%) and Vietnam (20%).

According to the Business Environment Risk Intelligence (BERI) 2014 report, "*Singapore enjoys the highest ranking for labour force in terms of workers' productivity and general overall attitude; as displayed by superior business performances with advanced technology and low labour unit costs in relation to the value of goods and services produced.*" Singapore's labour force evaluation score is 92, while USA is ranked a distant second at 80.

Singapore has essentially put together all the ingredients for a vibrant corporate sector — state of the art infrastructure, business friendly environment, low corruption, low tax rate and a high quality labour force. This has resulted in this 716 square km city state leading the 2014 foreign direct investment (FDI) rankings. In 2014, 409 greenfield projects were launched in Singapore with an aggregate capex of USD11.38bn creating 2,732 jobs through 390 companies. Following Singapore were the capitals and financial hubs of much larger economies like London (ranked 2ⁿᵈ), Shanghai (3ʳᵈ), Dubai (4ᵗʰ), New York (5ᵗʰ) and Hong Kong (6ᵗʰ).

Ever since the city state secured independence in 1965, the economy has been among the most open in the world. This openness and has not only encouraged Singapore's home grown corporates like DBS, CapitaLand, Keppel Corporation, Fraser & Neave, Singtel, ComfortDelGro and a host of others started acquiring and establishing overseas businesses within years of being incorporated but also the city state has served as a gateway for corporates in other ASEAN and Asian nations.

Singapore is the headquarters of agri-business companies like Golden Agri Resources, most of whose plantations are in Indonesia and Wilmar International, whose plantations are located in Malaysia and Indonesia. Singapore's International Enterprises (IE) invited the agricultural and industrial raw materials supply chain manager, Olam International, to move its headquarters to Singapore from London. Olam acquiesced and expanded to become a significant global agri-business player and was a constituent of the Singapore Stock Exchange's (SGX) flagship index, the Straits Times Index (STI) till September 2015.

Does this imply that Singapore is a corporate utopia, whose companies are unlikely to be unaffected by global economic turmoil? Certainly not. The corporate sector faces multiple risks at the current juncture including an uncertain global macroeconomic environment that includes a slowdown in China, growing pessimism about the European Union, and rising corporate debt levels. At the corporate level one has to contend with low crude oil prices that benefits companies for whom fuel is an input but affects suppliers to oil companies who face shrinking order books amid reduced capital expenditure, thinning margins and slowing revenues. Human resources problems are mounting with labour mobility constrained by tightening immigration laws and amid inadequate gender diversity on company boards.

But these risks should be assessed against the backdrop of the dominant market positions, competitive advantages, performance and financial muscle of large corporations. The following chapters provide snapshots of some of the largest Singapore corporates, challenges these companies face and takeaways for novice investors or just business observers. The final chapter discusses challenges common to Singapore's corporates and provides a summary of the stock performance of the listed companies covered in the book against the backdrop of these challenges.

The flagship stock index of the Singapore Exchange (SGX) is the Straits Times Index (STI). The STI comprises thirty companies, both domestic and overseas, and operate across a wide spectrum of industries. We have covered twenty companies in this book, sixteen of which are STI constituents. The four non-STI constituents are Temasek Holdings, Fraser & Neave (F&N), Marina Bay Sands (MBS) and Olam International.

The Singapore government-owned investment company Temasek Holdings, as the controlling shareholder of several STI constituents including Singtel, DBS, Olam and Keppel Corporation, has played a very strategic role in shaping Singapore's corporate landscape. Erstwhile STI constituent, F&N was purchased by the Thai conglomerate Thai Beverage, which subsequently became a STI constituent. This acquisition among several others is a testimony of the openness of Singapore's economy that facilitates two way capital flows.

The unlisted MBS along with the STI constituent Genting Singapore Plc (GENS) enhanced Singapore's attractiveness as a tourist destination. The two integrated resorts (IRs) operated by GENS and MBS, Resorts World Sentosa and Marina Bay Sands, are among the ten largest in the world and have transformed Singapore into the second largest gaming market in Asia Pacific after Macau within five years of starting operations. Olam, as mentioned earlier, relocated its headquarters to Singapore from London following IE's invitation and has played a role in transforming Singapore into ASEAN's agribusiness hub.

We have chosen the following companies as we believe that these companies best represent the Singapore corporate sector's successes, opportunities, challenges and threats. These sixteen listed companies have a combined market capitalization of SGD311 billion, representing

Company	Industry	Ownership		Market Capitalization	
		Major Shareholder	% Stake	SGD Million (a)	% of Singapore Total Market Cap
Golden Agri Resources	Agri-Business	Massingham International Ltd.	36.50	5,520	1.18%
Olam International	Agri-Business	Temasek Holdings Pte. Ltd.	57.17	5,658	1.21%
Wilmar International	Agri-Business	Kuok Brothers Sdn. Bhd.	18.34	22,540	4.82%
DBS	Bank	Temasek Holdings Pte. Ltd.	29.45	44,734	9.56%
OCBC Bank	Bank	Lee Foundation (Singapore)	19.39	38,079	8.14%
United Overseas Bank	Bank	Wee (Cho Yaw)	8.12	33,615	7.18%
Singapore Exchange Limited	Financial Services	SEL Holdings Pte. Ltd.	23.33	7,823	1.67%
Keppel Corporation	Conglomerate	Temasek Holdings Pte. Ltd.	20.65	9,908	2.12%
SIA Engineering	Engineering	Temasek Holdings Pte. Ltd.	77.49	3,833	0.82%
Sembcorp Industries	Engineering	Temasek Holdings Pte. Ltd.	49.45	4,826	1.03%
ST Engineering	Engineering	Temasek Holdings Pte. Ltd.	49.79	10,554	2.25%
Genting Singapore	Gaming	Genting Bhd	52.54	11,731	2.51%
CapitaLand	Property	Temasek Holdings Pte. Ltd.	40.71	13,165	2.81%
CapitaLand Mall Trust	REIT	CapitaLand Limited	30.00	6,909	1.48%
Ascendas Real Estate Investment Trust	REIT	Ascendas-Singbridge Pte. Ltd.	19.82	6,675	1.43%
Global Logistic Properties	Property	GIC Private Limited	35.73	9,979	2.13%
Singtel	Telecom	Temasek Holdings Pte. Ltd.	52.29	61,724	13.19%
StarHub	Telecom	Temasek Holdings Pte. Ltd.	55.78	4,987	1.07%
Comfort Delgro	Transportation	BlackRock Institutional Trust	5.98	5,434	1.16%
Singapore Airlines	Transportation	Temasek Holdings Pte. Ltd.	54.86	11,998	2.56%

Figure 1

Source: Thomson Reuters & Yahoo Finance
(a) As of November 30, 2016

35% of the Singapore Stock Exchange's total market capitalization of SGD905 bn.

This book is a bird's eye view on some of Singapore's largest corporates, on each of whom a book may be written. It is meant to give those who do not have a background in finance but an interest in investing, a perspective of these companies performance, market position, earnings potential and risks so that investors may make informed decisions. We have tried to restrict financial jargon to a level that is absolutely necessary as avoiding financial jargon in a book of this nature is a near-impossible task. A glossary is provided at the end of this book.

Singapore has four public sector investors — the central bank Monetary Authority of Singapore (MAS), Central Provident Fund (CPF), Temasek Holdings (Temasek) and GIC Private Limited (GIC). Temasek has invested in several Singapore-based and overseas companies. GIC is tasked with managing Singapore's foreign exchange reserves.

As GIC predominantly invests overseas, and in some instances in conjunction with Temasek and entities like Global Logistic Properties, its direct impact on Singapore's corporate sector is limited.

So, we decided to present Temasek as the first company specific chapter in this book to provide a context for the significance of its investee companies in the STI and also explore the commonalities and differences between the Temasek Portfolio Companies (TPC) that are featured in this book.

We hope the readers find reading the book as enriching an experience as we found putting the book together.

2

TEMASEK HOLDINGS

Temasek Holdings ("Temasek"), Singapore's investment company, is not a listed entity. But it has played a pivotal role as an investor in large Singapore-based corporates and a dividend paying corporation to its shareholder, Singapore's Minister for Finance, a body corporate under the Singapore Minister for Finance (Incorporation) Act (Chapter 183). The company is designated a Fifth Schedule Company under the Singapore Constitution along with Singapore's central bank, the Monetary Authority of Singapore (MAS) and the company responsible for managing Singapore's foreign reserves — GIC Private Limited (GIC) .

Temasek was incorporated in 1974 to commercially manage an initial portfolio, consisting of shares in companies, start-ups and joint ventures previously held by the Singapore Government. *"This move enabled the Singapore Government to focus on its core role of policy-making and regulations."* Temasek's investment strategy focuses on four investment themes — transforming economies, growing middle income populations, deepening comparative advantages, and emerging champions

Our analysis of Temasek is limited by the investment company's not so detailed disclosures of portfolio and financial performance; a trait fortunately not shared by its investee companies. Temasek's portfolio valued at SGD354 million in 1974 consisted exclusively of

Singapore-based corporates. The company over the years has expanded and diversified its portfolio to include overseas investments. Over the forty one year period — 1974 to March 31 2016 — Temasek's investment portfolio has grown by over 580 times to SGD242 billion. Temasek's investment portfolio is quite granular, with the top 10 listed investments accounting for about 46% of its portfolio as of March 31 2016.

We have presented below in pictures Temasek's performance during the last twelve years (FY04[1] to FY15) for two reasons. First, certain fundamental changes have occurred in Temasek's investment philosophy during the past decade that has implications on the company's long term return. Second, readers would be able to understand the impact of the 2007–08 Global Financial Crisis (GFC) on Temasek's portfolio and deduce the likely impact when the next global downturn occurs. All figures reported are consolidated figures for Temasek Holdings.

Performance in Pictures

Temasek's assets as reported in its balance sheet are a combination of assets reported at their historical acquisition costs less accumulated depreciation and assets reported at their market value. Temasek's 'portfolio' is its core investment portfolio reported at its market value. Temasek's portfolio is a subset of its total assets. In the last twelve years, FY04 to FY15, Temasek's portfolio and total assets have more than doubled (Figure 1).

A fundamental change in asset composition has accompanied Temasek's asset growth in the last twelve years (Figure 2). The company continues to allocate at least a quarter of its assets to liquid assets such as cash. These have been categorized as current assets. Financial assets accounted for 21% of total assets as of 31 March 2016 (FY04: 7%), while investments in associates, joint ventures and partnerships accounted for 19% (FY04: 9%).

---

[1] Temasek's financial year ending falls on March 31. FY04 refers to the period 1 April 2004 to 31 March 2005

Market Value of Portfolio & Reported Assets

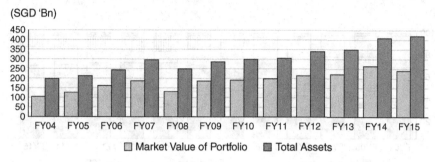

Figure 1

Source: Temasek Review 2005 to 2016.

Asset Composition

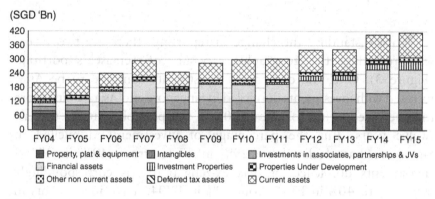

Figure 2

Source: Temasek Review 2005 to 2016.

Temasek changed the classification, for the purposes of reporting, of the geographic composition of its portfolio in FY10. Prior to FY10, the company used to report assets domiciled in Singapore, Asia excluding Singapore, Organisation for Economic Co-operation and Development (OECD) members and others. From FY10, the OECD category was replaced by assets domiciled in North America & Europe, Australia & New Zealand, Latin America and Africa, Central Asia & the Middle East.

Geographic Exposure

(%)

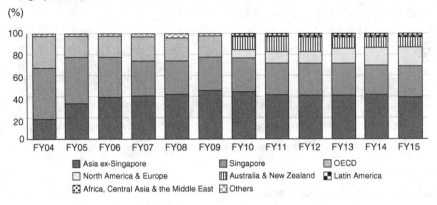

Figure 3
Source: Temasek Review 2005 to 2016.

Notwithstanding the change in reporting, there are two takeaways regarding the geographic exposure of Temasek's portfolio (Figure 3). One, the company's investments continue to be Asia-focussed with investments domiciled in Singapore and Asia ex-Singapore together accounting for about 70% of the portfolio during the last twelve years. But the percentage of investments domiciled in Singapore has declined to 29% in FY15 from 49% in FY04. Investments domiciled in Asia ex-Singapore has correspondingly increased to 40% in FY15 from 19% in FY04. Two, investments in mature economies exceed investments in growth economies. As of March 31 2016, the ratio of investments in mature economies to growth economies was 60:40.

As seen in Figure 4, Singapore Dollar assets continue to dominate Temasek's portfolio, accounting for 58% of the portfolio as of March 31 2016.

In terms of the industry composition of its portfolio, the share of financial services in Temasek's portfolio has declined to 23% of its portfolio in FY15 from a peak of 40% in FY07, telecom, media and technology to 25% from 33% in FY04 and transportation and industrials to 18%

Currency Denomination

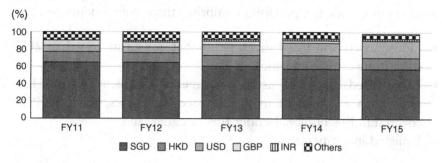

Figure 4
Source: Temasek Review 2005 to 2016.

Industry Exposure

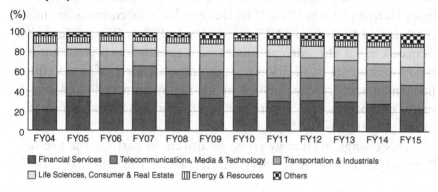

Figure 5
Source: Temasek Review 2005 to 2016.

from 27% in FY04. The share of life sciences, consumer and real estate in total assets has grown to 21% in FY15 from 8% in FY04. The movements in Temasek's portfolio composition have been driven by multiple factors including accelerated growth in exposure to certain sectors such as transport and industrials, change in marked to market value of assets and some re-categorisation of assets. An examination of the industry-wise exposure of Temasek's portfolio in Figure 5 reveals that the portfolio is now more diversified across industries than it was in FY04.

Temasek also reports the liquidity profile of its portfolio. The investment company's portfolio comprises three components —

- Liquid assets and listed investments that constitute less than 20% stake in investee companies,
- Large listed blocs i.e., listed investments in which Temasek has more than a 20% stake in the investee companies. All the TPCs covered in this book fall under this category, and
- Unlisted investments

The share of liquid assets and liquid investments that constitute less than 20% stake in investee companies has grown to 31% in FY15 from 18% in FY05. Similarly, the share of unlisted investments in Temasek's portfolio have grown by 1.8x in FY15 to 39% in FY15 from 14% in FY04. The share of large listed blocs has more than halved to 30% in FY15 from 68% in FY04. It is evident that Temasek is, at the current juncture, focussing on private equity-type investments in addition to its traditional forte of listed equity investments, a strategy pursued by many government linked investment companies and sovereign wealth funds (SWFs) across the globe (Figure 6).

This change in strategy could be driven, in part, by the pressure Temasek's returns have been under since the 2007–08 GFC.

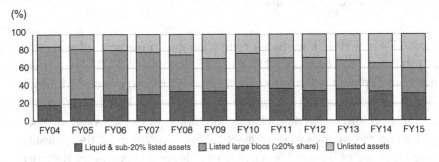

Figure 6

Source: Temasek Review 2005 to 2016.

Rolling Shareholder Returns

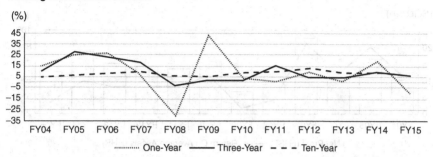

Figure 7
Source: Temasek Review 2005 to 2016.

The company's one year, three year and ten year total shareholder returns in SGD terms are depicted in Figure 7. The ten year rolling shareholder returns have ranged from 5% to 13% in the last decade. However, the one year and three year rolling shareholder returns since FY10 are lower than the pre-GFC levels.

In FY15, Temasek's one year return was –9% on account of the share price declines in Temasek's listed asset portfolio. This is the second time Temasek has generated negative one year return in the last twelve years after the -30% reported in 2008.

Temasek states that its shareholder returns include dividends paid. But the exact computation of this ratio is not disclosed. To obtain an independent view of Temasek's performance we computed the return on average assets (ROAA) based on reported data. The ROAA is defined as the ratio of net income to average total assets outstanding at the beginning and end of a financial year.

From Figure 8, it is evident that Temasek's ROAA is lower than the pre-GFC levels. The FY15 ROAA at 3.07% is again the second lowest in the last twelve year period after the 2.55% generated in FY09.

While Temasek's diversification into unlisted assets seems justified against the backdrop of lower ROAA, only time will tell whether the returns from its unlisted portfolio compensate the investment company for the additional risks it has undertaken.

Net Income & Return On Average Assets

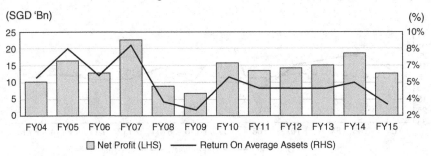

Figure 8

Source: Temasek Review 2005 to 2016.

Temasek has issued SGD, USD, EUR and GBP bonds with maturities ranging from 10 years to 40 years and at competitive coupons. These bonds have been assigned the highest possible ratings of AAA and Aaa by the international credit rating agencies Standard & Poor's and Moody's respectively.

Temasek used to report the EBITDA interest coverage and net debt i.e. total debt less cash. Using these two figures, we estimated its ratio of net debt to EBITDA for the period FY04 to FY14. Starting FY15, Temasek began reporting the ratio of recurring income to interest expense.

We estimated Temasek's EBITDA assuming Temasek's depreciation and amortization, as a proportion of its revenues, was maintained at FY14 levels. Temasek's EBITDA interest coverage i.e. the ratio of EBITDA to interest expenses has been healthy ranging from a minimum of 7.7x in FY08 to a maximum of 14.6x in FY14. In FY15, the estimated interest coverage continued to remain healthy though it declined to 8.80.

Our estimates indicate that Temasek's financial leverage, as measured by the ratio of net debt to EBITDA, has traditionally been low and has ranged from 0.33x in FY13 to 1.20 in FY04 (Figure 9). The significant decline in financial leverage in FY13 could be, in part, because of the SGD 5 billion capital injection Temasek received from the Ministry of Finance that might have resulted in an increase in cash and liquid assets in end-FY14.

Financial Leverage & Interest Cover

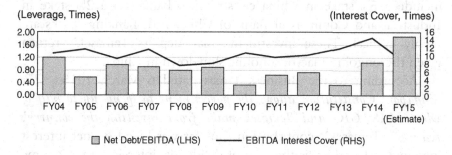

Figure 9
Source: Temasek Review 2005 to 2016.

In FY15, we estimate financial leverage, while still moderate, spiked to a twelve year peak of 1.87x, both on account of the 36% increase in net debt over FY14 to SGD44.4 billion in FY15 and the weaker EBITDA generated in FY15. The impact of the higher debt raised in the form of higher investment may be evident from FY16.

During the twelve year period FY04 to FY15, Temasek's net debt has ranged from a minimum of SGD9.0 billion in FY13 to its second highest level of SGD33.8 billion in FY07, before the FY15 maximum of SGD44.4 billion. We believe the company has borrowed and pared down debt in the past in line with the available investment opportunities and excess cash accumulation. Hence the spike in FY15 net debt was likely driven by investment opportunities than an increase in risk appetite.

Challenges

Regaining earnings momentum, while maintaining an appropriate risk profile, is Temasek's key long term challenge. Temasek's rising investments in unlisted assets and Latin America (2% of portfolio as of 31 March 2016) are attempts to kick start the earnings momentum. The success of these investments may be evaluated only in the medium term.

According to data by SNL Financial, Temasek is the single largest investor in Chinese banks, followed by Vanguard Group Inc and

BlackRock Fund Advisors. Major investments in Chinese banks include a 5% stake in China construction bank and a 2% stake in Industrial and Commercial Bank of China Ltd. Banking stocks are highly cyclical. These investments may depress Temasek's return given the ongoing macroeconomic slowdown in China.

According to the Business Times dated 6 March 2015, "*The Singapore Constitution allows the government to spend up to half of what MAS, GIC and Temasek make from investing the country's reserves*". Temasek's contribution thus far was based on net interest income (NII), which is the sum of dividends, interest, other income and net interest from loans. The NII is actual/realized income. In the 2015 Budget, the basis of Temasek's contribution was changed to net investment returns (NIR), which is the sum of NII and unrealized capital gains less inflation. Hence, the NIR framework includes an element of expected returns.

Temasek in its media communication dated 3 March 2015 stated, "*First, the Net Investment Returns (NIR) Framework does not affect Temasek's approach to investment. Our investment strategy remains unchanged and we will continue to seek sustainable long term returns. Second, while the NIR framework will enable the Government to spend on the basis of Temasek's expected returns, it has no impact on Temasek's dividend policy, which is based on profit. We have a dividend policy which balances a sustainable distribution of profit to our shareholder with the retention of profits for reinvestment to generate future returns. We also take into account our responsibility to protect Temasek's past reserves.... Temasek recognises that the Government's NIR Framework smooths out the volatility and provides a stable and more predictable basis for Government spending through economic cycles. This can be especially important during an economic downturn, when the need for Government spending may be higher while annual returns may be lower....*"

Temasek's reported financials indicate that the company has adopted an appropriate funding policy to grow its assets. But as the subsequent chapters in this book indicate, TPCs have among the highest dividend payout ratios among their peers. Should the government require Temasek to upstream a higher quantum of dividends,

Temasek in turn may require its investees to further increase their dividend payouts. This could lead to a reduction in TPCs' liquidity and a further increase in their cash flow leverage i.e. the ratio of net debt to EBITDA.

The impact of a macroeconomic slowdown in China and the government possibly requiring Temasek to pay higher dividends is exacerbated by the company's relatively small size. Temasek is ranked 39th globally in terms of total assets.[2] The four Singapore public sector investors' (GIC, MAS, Central Provident Fund and Temasek) combined assets amount to USD969.8 billion, which is equal to approximately 25% of the USD3,889.3 billion assets of the world's largest public sector investor, People's Bank of China.

Takeaways

Temasek's ability to rise to the long term challenges lies in its track record of being guided by commercial principles, a prudent asset selection process and a willingness to invest in and divest assets with a view to sustain long term returns. While the dividend payouts of TPCs are the highest in their respective industries, Temasek has enabled its investees to function professionally and there has been minimal intervention in matters of management, strategy and operations of TPCs.

Also, there is a level playing field for TPCs and their competitors. This is evident from instances such as the land transport company SMRT, in which Temasek has a 54.19% stake, being a distant second, to the private sector player, ComfortDelGro.

Temasek generated a negative one year return for the first time in seven years in FY15, due to the poor performance of its listed asset portfolio, a reflection of global macroeconomic conditions. Three year and ten year rolling shareholder returns in FY15 also moderated to 6% each. The FY15 investment performance is a reflection of the

---

[2] Business Times dated 22 May 2015 "Global public sector investors favour real estate, infrastructure"

global financial markets and the inherently cyclical nature of an investment company's performance.

It remains to be seen if Temasek is able to sustain its historical performance going forward given the global macroeconomic uncertainty, the macroeconomic slowdown in China and the recent vintage of its unlisted and Latin American investments. However, the sound performance and prospects of its seasoned investments and liquid and lowly leveraged balance sheet should enable Temasek to generate meaningful and sustainable returns in the long term.

3

AGRI-BUSINESS COMPANIES: AN OVERVIEW

SGX has several agri-business companies listed on it such as Bumitama Agri, First Resources, Golden Agri Resources, Olam International and Wilmar International. One uniform characteristic of agri-business companies is that they are price takers as they are engaged in the commodities business. Hence, agri-business companies' profits are driven by their cost effectiveness.

Agri-business is a very wide term and encompasses several businesses such as:

- Cultivating the agricultural product, alternatively known as upstream production,
- Processing the agricultural output into products that may be used by consumers, as inputs for the food & beverage industry and a wide range of manufacturing industries, also known as downstream production, and
- Supply chain management i.e., transporting the raw materials from the farm/plantation to the processor and transporting the processed products from the processor to the end consumer

It is rare to find a pure play agricultural commodity cultivator, processor or supply chain manager. Most large agri-businesses are

19

engaged in two or more of the above listed activities. Companies engaged in both upstream and downstream production are known as integrated operators/businesses. A company's business model determines its profitability, its cash conversion/working capital cycle and the quantum of its borrowings.

A large scale cultivator of agricultural commodities/plantation operator with a demonstrated track record and an established clientele is usually very profitable and has a low requirement of debt to fund the normal course of business. But these companies' revenues are closely correlated to the volatile commodity price cycle, and during times of a supply glut/decline in demand face heavy losses on account of the perishable nature of the commodities they produce.

An integrated operator whose processing capacity is adequate to meet the company's agricultural output earns lower profit margins from processing than cultivation. Hence, an integrated operator's profit as a percentage of revenues is lower than that of a pure play cultivator. These companies hold sizable inventories to ensure uninterrupted production of downstream products. As these companies access substantial debt to fund their inventories, their debt levels tend to be higher than plantation operators.

Companies engaged in supply chain management, characteristic of trading companies, earn narrow margins and hold sizable inventory on account of which their financial leverage tends to be high.

Of the five agri-business companies listed on SGX, Bumitama Agri is predominantly a cultivator of oil palm, while First Resources is a relatively small scale integrated producer of oil palm. Golden Agri and Wilmar are large scale integrated companies and the supply chain management of multiple agricultural commodities is Olam's primary business.

A large-scale integrated player is able to create a limited degree of end-product differentiation in the otherwise homogeneous commodity space and benefits during periods of low commodity prices from lower input costs. But as a pure plantation operator expands and attains a critical size it becomes essential for the company to embark on downstream operations, so as to independently create a market for its output and eliminate dependence on other integrated operators.

4

GOLDEN AGRI RESOURCES

Two of the largest oil palm plantation companies in the world — Golden Agri Resources (GAR) and Wilmar International (Wilmar), are listed on the Singapore Exchange (SGX). Of these two companies, GAR's business model is relatively simpler as its oil palm business is the largest contributor to its revenues and margins and its China-based soybean and deep sea port businesses are much smaller. GAR, Wilmar and Olam International (Olam) are three agri-business companies listed on the SGX. The three chapters covering GAR, Wilmar and Olam will enable readers to understand the different types of agri-business companies i.e., whether an agri-business company is engaged in upstream, downstream or integrated operations and/or supply chain management, and the impact of the business model on profitability, capital structure and stock returns.

The ideal climatic conditions for cultivating oil palm are found in the areas lying five degrees north and south of the equator. Indonesia and Malaysia, driven by their location and early mover advantages, lead the global oil palm industry. According to the United States Department of Agriculture, global oil palm output for 2014 was 62.44 million metric tonnes (MT). Indonesia (53% of global production) and Malaysia (33%) together account for 86% of global oil palm output. Global imports of oil palm for 2014 were 41.04 million metric tonnes (MT). The major global importers of oil palm are India

(22%), the European Union (17%), China (15%), Pakistan (6%), and Bangladesh, the USA and Egypt (3% each).

Companies that dominate the global oil palm industry include: Malaysia-based Sime Darby Berhad, Felda Global Ventures, KL Kepong Berhad and IOI Group; Indonesia-based GAR, First Resources, Bumitama Agri and Astra Agro Lestari, Indofood Agri Resources, and Wilmar, whose oil palm plantations are located in both Malaysia and Indonesia

Oil palm is one of the most widely used and versatile vegetable oils in the world. Its attractiveness stems from not just its high yield per hectare and low cost (Figures 1 to 3) but also the numerous end uses it can be put to. Oil palm is used as cooking/frying oil and as an input for shortening, margarine and confectionery fats. It is also used extensively in the non-food sector in the production of soaps and detergents, pharmaceutical products, cosmetics, oleochemical[1] products and biodiesel.[2]

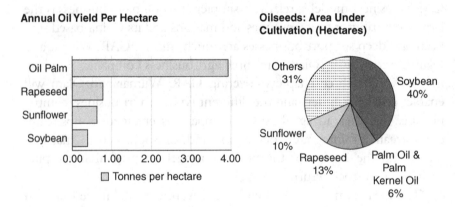

Figure 1

Source: Sime Darby's Palm Oil Facts & Figures, April 2014.

---

[1] Chemicals derived from animal and plant fats used as a substitute to petrochemicals

[2] Biodiesel is a vegetable or animal fat based diesel fuel. Biodiesel may be used alone or blended with petrodiesel. Biodiesel is meant to be used in standard diesel engines and as heating oil.

Vegetable Oil Price Trends

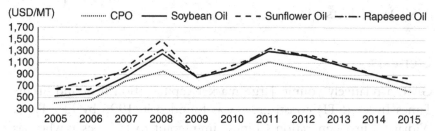

Figure 2
Source: World Bank Commodity Pink Sheet.

Crude Oil & CPO Prices

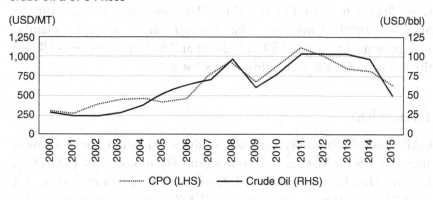

Figure 3
Source: World Bank Commodity Pink Sheet.

However, there are several environmental and social issues associated with oil palm cultivation. Environmental issues include biodiver-
sity loss including loss of rare and endangered species e.g. orang-utans,
tigers, elephants, and rhinos; pollution of soil, air and water; soil ero-
sion, greenhouse gas emissions and climate change and the loss of key
ecosystem services. Social issues related to oil palm include land grabbing, loss of livelihoods, social conflicts and forced migration. To
ensure that widespread cultivation of oil palm does not result in irre-
versible environmental and social damages, consumers are encouraged

to demand that manufacturers use certified sustainable palm oil (CSPO) products.

Genesis

GAR, a relatively young, large market capitalisation firm and Straits Times Index (STI) constituent, was founded in 1996 by Eka Tjipta Widjaja, a first generation Chinese immigrant to Indonesia, who has become one of the wealthiest men in Indonesia. Other businesses promoted by Widjaja include Asia Pulp & Paper, Sinarmas Land Limited, Smartfren Telecom and Sinar Mas Multiartha, a financial services provider. Eka Widjaja's son Franky Oesman Widjaja is the current Chairman and CEO of GAR. The company was listed on the SGX in 1999. Currently, the Widjaja family vehicle, Flambo International Ltd holds a 50.35% direct and indirect stake in GAR and the public holds the remaining 49.65% stake.

Evolution

GAR's oil palm business is mostly conducted through several subsidiaries — PT Sinar Mas Agro Resources and Technology Tbk (SMART), PT Ivo Mas Tunggal (IMT),PT Sawit Mas Sejahtera etc., of which SMART is the largest. As of year-end 1998, the year preceding GAR's initial public offering (IPO) on the SGX had 239,500 hectares of land under cultivation. GAR's area under oil palm cultivation almost doubled during the sixteen years after its listing i.e., by year-end2014 to 472,800 hectares. In addition to growing its plantation area, GAR strengthened its downstream capabilities, benchmarked its oil palm cultivation practices against the Roundtable on Sustainable Palm Oil (RSPO) and the United Nations Global Compact (UNGC) and other international standards, diversified into soybean processing and entered into joint ventures with global shipping companies to operate customised tankers to transport its oil palm products.

GAR'S downstream products include cooking oil, margarine, cocoa butter substitute, specialty fats, shortening and frying fat produced in Indonesia and China and sold globally. These products are sold under the brand names Filma, Menara, i-soc, Kunci Mas, Palmboom, Pusaka, Delicio, Mitra, Palmvita, Palmvita Gold, Goodfry, Masku, SmartBaker, Red Rose and Paloma.

Please refer to Table 1 in Appendix 1 for the key milestones in GAR's evolution.

Financial Review

In 2006, almost 75% of GAR's revenues were from sale of palm oil based products and the balance from sale of soybean products. The company's businesses not only grew in scale but also diversified during the last decade to include four divisions — plantation and palm oil mills (the upstream business), processing and merchandising of palm-based products (palm and laurics), processing and merchandising of oilseeds based products and production and distribution of food and consumer products in China and Indonesia (categorized as others in Figure 4 below).

Despite GAR's revenues registering an impressive 21% average annual growth rate during the period 2006 to 2015, EBITDA per metric tonne (MT) of CPO produced has declined since 2012 due to the declining trend in CPO prices (Figure 5).

Inventory days have ranged from 50 to 60 days since 2006 (Figure 6).

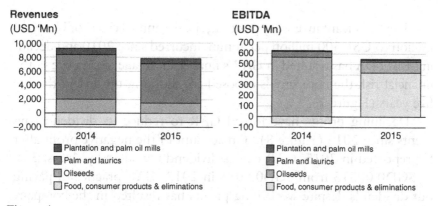

Figure 4

Source: GAR Financial Statements, World Bank Commodity Pink Sheet and authors' calculations.

Revenues & EBITDA

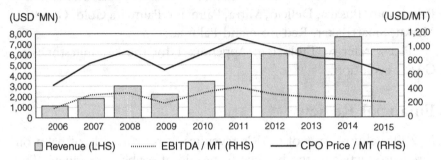

Figure 5

Source: GAR Financial Statements, World Bank Commodity Pink Sheet and authors' calculations.

Days Inventory

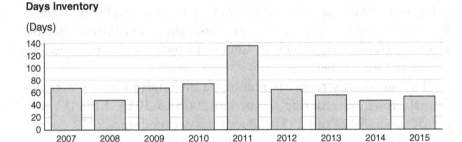

Figure 6

Source: GAR Financial Statements, World Bank Commodity Pink Sheet and authors' calculations.

The significant inventory position, sizable annual capex of USD 300 million to USD 500 million per annum incurred since 2010 and declining EBITDA has resulted in GAR's financial leverage, a measure of the financial risk the company is exposed to, shooting up during the last five years (Figure 7).

Declining profits have forced GAR to reduce its dividend payments since 2013 (Figure 8). On account of the negative profit after tax reported in 2015, GAR cut its dividend per share by almost 54% to SGD0.00515 from SGD0.0011 in 2013. GAR practice of paying out dividends despite weakening profits has resulted in the company reinvesting a lower proportion of its earnings in its business and this practice is a concern for long term investors.

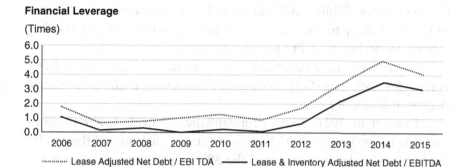

Figure 7

Source: GAR Financial Statements, World Bank Commodity Pink Sheet and authors' calculations.

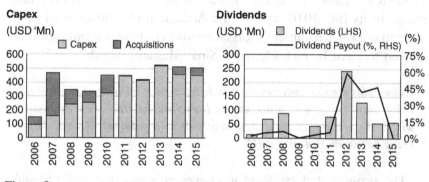

Figure 8

Source: GAR Financial Statements, World Bank Commodity Pink Sheet and authors' calculations.

Challenges

The key challenge facing GAR and the CPO industry in general is the impact of the prolonged low price environment, namely higher leverage and lower liquidity, though CPO prices have staged a recovery in 2016. While CPO continues to be the most competitively priced vegetable oil, the bumper soybean harvest in the US, one of the largest cultivators of soybean, has driven down soybean oil prices and the price differential between CPO and soybean oil has narrowed. The situation has been exacerbated by low crude oil prices. As oil palm is an input in biodiesel, oil palm and crude oil prices have been historically closely correlated. The low crude oil prices are exercising downward pressure on CPO prices. While GAR and other low cost integrated producers of CPO are likely to weather the low price environment, profitability is likely to decline till CPO prices recover.

Lower profits have resulted in the financial leverage of most CPO companies including GAR to increase, exposing them to a higher degree of financial risk.

However in 2016, CPO's fundamentals, namely lower production due to the impact of El-Nino, exports holding up and the resultant lower stock levels, supported the 38% rally in prices since January 2016 to USD783 per tonne in December 2016. The higher CPO prices should enable CPO plantation and processing companies to strengthen their financial profiles.

GAR's expansion and diversification has not been without challenges. In its July 2010 report[3], the Amsterdam headquartered non-governmental environmental organisation, Greenpeace International referred to GAR by its trade name Sinar Mas and stated:

> "*Sinar Mas group is notorious for its destruction of millions of hectares of Indonesian rainforest, peatland and wildlife habitat. Two divisions within the group lead the destruction: pulp and palm oil. Recently, the group has diversified into coal.*"

This prompted global food and beverage majors including Nestlé, Unilever, Burger King and Kraft Foods to stop buying GAR's oil palm products. These aforementioned companies constituted less than 3% of GAR's sales. Working together with NGO stakeholders, the company launched a pioneering Forest Conservation Policy which committed the company to no deforestation and respecting community's rights embodied in the principles of Free, Prior and Informed Consent (FPIC).

The company also intensified its efforts to have its plantations certified as sustainable by the Swiss-based organisation, RSPO. RSPO's members include plantation groups, bankers, traders and environmental campaigners.

---

[3] Source: http://www.greenpeace.org/international/Global/international/publications/forests/2010/

In 2011, GAR's largest subsidiary engaged in the crude palm oil (CPO) business, SMART was the first to obtain RSPO certification followed by two more subsidiaries — RJP and BWL. That year Unilever and Nestlé resumed purchasing oil palm products from GAR. Running a large scale CPO business without endangering the environment and complying with regulations is a challenge not just for GAR but the entire industry. Since GAR launched the Forest Conservation Policy (FCP) in February 2011, there have been an increasing number of producer and consumer companies making similar FCP commitments, referencing the high carbon stock methodology first developed by GAR, Greenpeace and The Forest Trust. In February 2014, GAR made further advances with its pioneering FCP by extending it to downstream operations, thus expanding 'no deforestation' commitment to its entire supply chain.

In 2015, GAR launched an updated and enhanced sustainability policy. The GAR Social and Environmental Policy (GSEP) integrates and builds on its earlier sustainability policies, which applies to its entire operations, subsidiaries and suppliers. By end-2015, GAR completed a major initiative in mapping its supply chains to the mills.

5

WILMAR INTERNATIONAL

Wilmar, one of the largest companies listed on the SGX, shares interesting similarities and differences with GAR. Both companies were founded by immigrant Chinese entrepreneurs in Indonesia and are dominant players in the global oil palm industry. Wilmar distinguishes itself from GAR on account of its more diversified business model that includes sugar, fertilizer and consumer food businesses. It would also be interesting to observe how these companies counter the current low commodity price environment and evolve in the future, which is discussed in the concluding sections of this chapter.

Genesis

The founders of Wilmar are Kuok Khoon Hong and Martua Sitorus. The Kuoks were a Chinese immigrant family who started with a rice and flour shop. The current patriarch Robert Kuok rose to be one of the world's top sugar traders. Robert's nephew, and Wilmar's current chairman and CEO, Kuok Khoon Hong founded Wilmar with a partner in 1991. As of 31 December 2014, the Kuok Group and Kuok Khoon Hong own 32% and 12% stakes in Wilmar respectively, the American food processing and commodities trading company — Archer Daniels Midland holds a 17% stake, the Executive Deputy

Chairman — Martua Sitorus holds a 9% stake and the balance of 30% is free floating stock.

Wilmar entered the agri-business as an oil palm trading company. The company simultaneously acquired a land bank of 7,100 hectares in Western Sumatra, Indonesia and established its first oil palm plantation in this land bank. In 1991, Wilmar also started merchandising oil palm, acquired two crushing plants each with a capacity of approximately 50 MT per day, acquired a refinery with a capacity of approximately 100 MT per day and started construction of a 700 MT capacity refinery in Indonesia.

Evolution

Wilmar, in its quest to become an integrated agri-business operator , rapidly set up downstream oil palm facilities, started developing, branding and marketing its own oil palm based products, established fertilizer plants and diversified into sugar milling and processing.

Please refer to Table 2 in Appendix 1 for the key milestones in Wilmar's evolution.

Business & Financial Review

Wilmar, a company that has grown organically and inorganically during the nine year period 2006 to 2015, has also diversified its businesses to include sugar and branded downstream products (Figure 1).

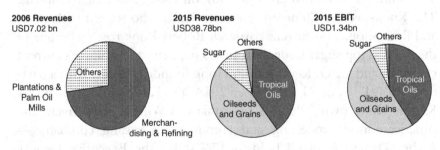

Figure 1

Source: Wilmar Financial Statements, World Bank Commodity Pink Sheet and authors' calculations.

Total Assets

(USD 'MT)

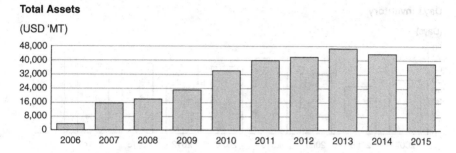

Figure 2

Source: Wilmar Financial Statements, World Bank Commodity Pink Sheet and authors' calculations.

Revenues & EBITDA Margin

(USD 'MT)　　　　　　　　　　　　　　　　　　　　　　　(%)

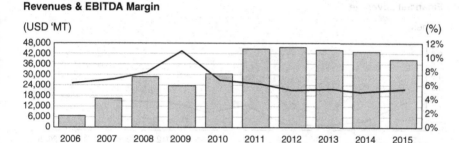

Figure 3

Source: Wilmar Financial Statements, World Bank Commodity Pink Sheet and authors' calculations.

The company registered an impressive average annual growth (AAG) in total assets of 45% during the decade ended December 31 2015 (Figure 2).

Revenue AAG has been slower than asset growth at 28% due to falling commodity prices. The trend in revenue growth compared to the World Bank's Agricultural Commodity Price Index is discussed in the chapter "Investing In Agri-Business Companies: Takeaways". Characteristic of commodity companies that expand into downstream operations and supply chain management, Wilmar's EBITDA margin has progressively declined to 5.4% in 2015 from 6.4% in 2006 (Figure 3).

Days Inventory

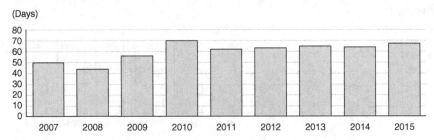

Figure 4

Source: Wilmar Financial Statements, World Bank Commodity Pink Sheet and authors' calculations.

Financial Leverage

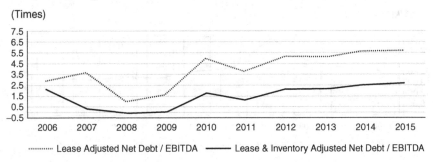

Figure 5

Source: Wilmar Financial Statements, World Bank Commodity Pink Sheet and authors' calculations.

Inventory days have increased to 68 days in 2015 from 29 days in 2006 (Figure 4).

Lease and inventory adjusted financial leverage has been rising since 2012 due to the declining trend in agricultural commodity prices (Figure 5). The company is exposed to a moderate level of financial risk.

Wilmar's evolution to one of the largest companies listed on the SGX is not without controversy. The US weekly news magazine, Newsweek, ranked Wilmar as the least environment friendly company (500th company in the list of 500 companies surveyed) in its 2012

Green Rankings. In 2013, Norway's sovereign wealth fund (SWF) — Government Pension Fund Global — disclosed that it had sold its holdings in 23 oil palm companies including Wilmar citing environmentally harmful industry practices.

Bloomberg in its 13 March 2015 article stated:

> *"Greenpeace videos, alleging that consumer industry oil palm buyers including Unilever Plc contributed to deforestation, had amassed millions of YouTube hits. Environmentalists confronted the Chief Executive Officer of Kellogg Co. about oil palm purchases from Wilmar on investor calls."*

This spurred Wilmar and 30 other firms including Unilever and McDonald's Corporation to pledge to purchase oil palm sourced from sustainable sources by year-end-2015. Kuok Khoon Hong, after interacting with NGOs like Catapult and Forest Trust, assumed the challenging responsibility of *"getting outside suppliers — including the more than 800 mills that send CPO to Wilmar's refineries and the thousands of farmers who sell its agents fruit"* to adopt sustainable oil palm practices.

Challenges

The challenges Wilmar faces in its current businesses are quite similar to GAR's challenges — ensuring environmentally friendly cultivation practices over a large scale operation and weathering low commodity prices. Wilmar's EBITDA in USD terms has been declining since 2012.

Another challenge Wilmar faces is the integration risks associated with its joint venture with First Pacific to acquire Goodman Fielder (GF). GF, which has been an Australia centric consumer food company thus far, has stated that its mission is to build a *"leading Asia Pacific consumer foods business"* post acquisition by Wilmar — First Pacific JV. Whether Wilmar will be able to replicate its success with the agri-business industry and its existing consumer foods business which it operates in many countries including China, Indonesia and India in the GF joint venture remains to be seen.

In conclusion, what distinguishes GAR and Wilmar is that while GAR is mostly an integrated oil palm operator, Wilmar has a more diversified business model. Also based on recent developments in both companies at the current juncture, it appears that while GAR is poised to further expand its presence in the oil palm industry, Wilmar may evolve into a conglomerate if the GF acquisition is a precursor of things to come.

If Wilmar is able to implement this diversification strategy successfully, it would benefit on two counts. First, operating and financial performance would tend to be less cyclical given the defensive nature of the mass market consumer food business. EBITDA margin and leverage metrics would improve as consumer food companies with established brands tend to generate better EBITDA margins and have lower financial leverage than agri-business companies. Second, the company is less likely to become a target of short sellers/independent research firms like Olam and the Noble Group.

6

OLAM INTERNATIONAL

Of the three agri-business companies covered in this book, Olam International distinguishes itself from Golden Agri Resources (GAR) and Wilmar International (Wilmar) in that it is engaged in the 'seed to shelf' supply chain management of multiple agricultural and industrial raw materials, as opposed to GAR's and Wilmar's core business of cultivating, processing and marketing agricultural commodities. Hence, the risks Olam is exposed to, its earnings drivers and balance sheet structure are quite different from GAR's and Wilmar's.

This chapter explains in non-technical terms, the evolution and performance of Olam's business and its prospects. It also analyses the key conclusions of the controversial Muddy Waters (MW) research report published in November 2012, which led to Olam filing a suit against MW and subsequently withdrawing it.

Olam in ancient Hebrew means 'Transcending Boundaries'. The name is apt for in 2015, Olam's silver jubilee year of operations; the company with business operations in 65 countries is engaged in the supply chain management of over 20 commodities employing 23,000 people to service 13,800 customers. Olam's two major shareholders who together hold over 70% stake in the company are Temasek Holdings and Mitsubishi Corporation. Temasek Holdings has a 51.4% stake in Olam. Mitisubishi Corporation acquired a 20% stake for SGD915 million in September 2015.

Genesis

In 1989, Olam began its business in Nigeria as a single product, single employee company exporting cashews from Nigeria to India, by the Kewalram Chanrai Group with a seed capital of USD100,000 in a bid to earn foreign exchange, especially US Dollars. By 1991, the company had expanded its product suite to include cotton and shea nuts exports and moved its headquarters to London. Olam continued on its path of growth, sourcing agricultural commodities from more countries, predominantly African nations, and adding more commodities to its portfolio. Its clients included multinational food and beverage giants like Nestle, Mars and Kraft.

Evolution

It was at this juncture that the Singapore Trade Development Board, now called International Enterprises Singapore (IE Singapore) invited Olam to move its headquarters to Singapore from London. Olam recognised the twin benefits of this invitation i.e., an opportunity to gain a foothold into resource rich Asia and operating out of Singapore, a less expensive global financial centre, that offered benefits of a conducive legal and regulatory environment to conduct a multinational business, a low tax regime, being strategically located amidst the resource rich geographies of Asia, Australia and Africa and a high quality talent pool.

Olam continued to grow organically until 2009, when its CEO Sunny Verghese spearheaded a change in strategy to accelerate growth through greenfield projects. These acquisitions served to strengthen Olam's commodity processing/downstream capabilities, thereby strengthening its market position in the global agricultural and industrial supply chain market.

Please refer to Table 3 in Appendix 1 for the key milestones in Olam's evolution.

Sunny Verghese said in an interview with African Business Magazine[1] in 2013 that the three guiding principles of Olam's businesses are identifying adjacencies, migrating to adjacent businesses and differentiating before scaling. These guiding principles are best enunciated in Sunny Verghese's words:

"We were exporting raw cashews from Nigeria to India where most of the processing of those cashews took place. From that, we moved into other adjacencies. We migrated into neighbouring geographical adjacencies and then eventually to value-chain adjacencies. So, from first sourcing, originating and exporting raw cashews, the value chain migration meant that we went into processing those cashews ourselves, first in India, then in Vietnam, then in Brazil and then in Africa. Today we have processing facilities in Nigeria, Mozambique and in Tanzania. We are the largest African-origin processors of cashews today — in addition to processing in India and in Vietnam and other places as well. Our strategy for pursuing profitable growth has always anchored around finding these near adjacencies. We define an adjacent opportunity, or possibility, where there is customer sharing or supplier-sharing or cost-sharing or capability-sharing with our existing businesses.

We moved from cashews and edible nuts, then to peanuts and from peanuts we moved into almonds and from almonds we moved into hazelnuts....Today, we manage a supply chain for all of these four edible nuts and in the future, we will get into walnuts, macadamias, into pistachios because we don't have to go and find new customers. The same set of customers who buy cashews and salt and roast them, also salt and roast mixed nuts. The basic processing and blanching of various edible nuts has many similarities and there is significant customer sharing for many of the edible nuts. Because of all of that, the risk of execution of migrating from the cashew business to the peanut business and then to the almond business and then to the hazelnut business is greatly reduced. The whole growth has been modelled around finding these adjacent businesses and migrating into them....

The third rule is that we have to first differentiate before we scale. We will not allow any of our businesses to grow unless they have

---

[1] Source: Africa Business Magazine dated 13 August 2013 "Olam's Blueprint for Success"

established some differentiation, some new angle, and then they can grow very fast. First, we are differentiated at the sourcing-organisation end because we procure our raw materials as close to the farm gate as possible. Most of our competitors will source at the port city.... The second point of differentiation is at the customer end.... We offer them organic certification, factory produce certification, Rainforest Alliance certification if that is what they want.... The third point of differentiation is that we are selectively integrated in the supply chain. Unlike our competitors, we are involved upstream with plantations and farming...."

Olam's Businesses & Financials

In 2005, the year when Olam floated a SGD245 million IPO and was listed on the SGX, it had 14 agricultural products in four business segments — confectionery & beverage ingredients; edible nuts, spices & beans; fibre & wood products; and food staples & packaged foods. Over a relatively short period of ten years, Olam's product portfolio expanded to encompass 44 agricultural commodities across 16 business units in five business segments (Table 1).

Financial Review

Aided by an expansion of product portfolio and an increase in the volumes traded, Olam's sales volume grew by over eight times to 19,518 metric tonnes (MT) by FY2015[2] from 2,052 MT in FY2004 (Figure 1). The edible nuts, spices and beans and food staples is the primary EBITDA driver accounting for 33% of EBITDA, followed by followed by the confectionery & beverage ingredients division (29%), food staples and packaged foods division (22%) packaged foods and the industrial raw materials division (16%) (Figure 2). The

---

[2] In 2015, Olam changed its financial year to 31 December from 30 June. So the data presented in this chapter for FY15 encompasses the 18-month period 1 July 2014 to 31 December 2015. For all previous years, data presented is for a 12-month period.

Table 1:   Olam's Five Business Segments

Segment	Products
Edible Nuts, Spices & Vegetable Ingredients (formerly known as **Edible nuts, spices and beans**)	• Edible Nuts (cashew, peanuts, almonds, hazelnuts and sesame) • Spices & Vegetable Ingredients (including onion, garlic, and tomato)
Confectionery & beverage ingredients	• Coffee • Cocoa
Industrial raw materials	• Natural Fibres (cotton) • Wood Products • Rubber • Fertiliser • Special Economic Zone (SEZ)
Food staples & packaged foods	• Rice • Sugar and Natural Sweeteners • Grains (including wheat, corn and barley) • Palm • Dairy • Packaged Foods
Commodity financial services	Market making, risk management solutions & commodity funds management

Source: www.olamgroup.com.

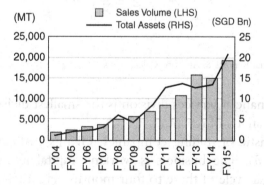

Figure 1

Source: Olam Annual Reports & Authors' Calculations.

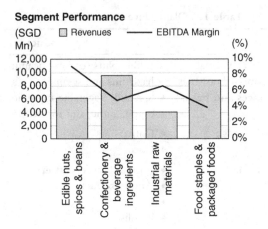

Figure 2

Source: Olam Annual Reports & Authors' Calculations.

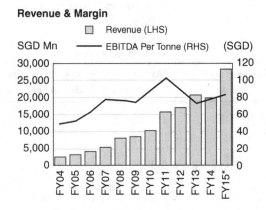

Figure 3

Source: Olam Annual Reports & Authors' Calculations.

commodity financial services division is the smallest division accounting for less than 1% of revenues.

Characteristic of trading companies, Olam's EBITDA margin is thin (Figure 3). The business is working capital intensive, with a working capital cycle of three to four months (Figure 4).

Olam's business is not capital intensive per se when compared to infrastructure and telecom players. But as the company is in its

Working Capital Cycle

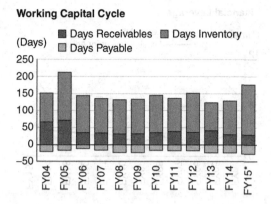

Figure 4

Source: Olam Annual Reports & Authors' Calculations.

Capital Expenditure

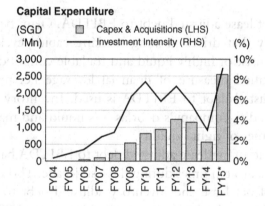

Figure 5

Source: Olam Annual Reports & Authors' Calculations.

growth phase, its capital intensity (Capital expenditure + Acquisitions/ Revenue) progressively increased from less than 1% in FY2004 and ranged from 7% to 10% during the period FY2009 to FY2015 (Figure 5). The spike in 2015 investments was due to the SGD1.62 billion acquisition of Archer Daniel Midlands' cocoa business in October 2015.

Financial leverage is a key indicator of financial risk a company is exposed to and a generally accepted measure of financial leverage is

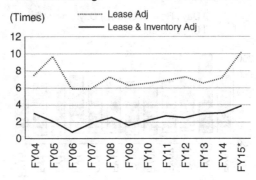

Figure 6

Source: Olam Annual Reports & Authors' Calculations.

the ratio of net lease adjusted debt to EBITDA. Olam typically holds high inventory that drives its long working capital cycle and these inventories consist of highly liquid and tradable commodities. So for Olam, a modified measure of financial leverage i.e. net lease and inventory adjusted debt to EBITDA is used. Inventory is deducted from a commodity company's debt as it is liquid and may be readily sold during times of tight liquidity.

Olam's ratio of net lease adjusted debt to EBITDA has been high, ranging from six to ten times during the last decade. Though the company's ratio of net lease and inventory adjusted debt to EBITDA is lower, this ratio has also been steadily climbing since FY09 (Figure 6).

The Muddy Waters Episode

Olam was cruising along smoothly, swiftly expanding its business and strengthening its capitalisation, leveraging on its status as a TPC. Temasek Holdings held a 16.32% stake in Olam as of 30 June 2011. In November 2012[3], MW Research published a research report in

---

[3] Source: http://www.muddywatersresearch.com/research/olam/initiating-coverage-olam/

which it categorised Olam as a "Strong Sell". This report drew parallels between Enron and Olam and its key conclusions of this report were:

1. *"Olam's Aggressive Accounting Masks its Poor Performance and Incentivises it to Spend Increasingly Precious Cash"*

   The MW research reports pointed out that Non Cash Accounting Gains (NCAG) like negative goodwill and biological gains boosted Olam's profit after tax (PAT) by 37.9% from FY2010 to FY2012.

2. *"Olam's Looming Solvency Crisis"*

   Olam *"seems to have had only three weeks of operating cash. The Company reported S$1.1 billion in cash, but that number is misleading. S$602.1 million of the cash balance appears to come from Olam withdrawing significant margin from its brokerage accounts."*

3. *"Olam's Trading Business appears to be a Failing Business Model."*

   ....Much of Olam's trading profit appears dependent on export incentives that Olam receives from governments. These programs are politically sensitive, and this type of income seems unsustainable...."

4. *"Olam is a Black Box"*

   "Our analysis of various analysts' financial models makes clear that they have no idea how Olam's financial statements work, based on widely varying estimates for virtually every model input. The Company publicly admits that its business is difficult to understand. Good things seldom come of investing in something one does not understand — particularly when there is a high degree of leverage."

5. *"Is Olam's Accounting Credible?"*

6. *"Olam's CapEx is Off the Rails"*

   Olam's snowballing CapEx appears to be destroying significant investor value and pushing the company toward collapse..."

Impact & Outcome

Olam's closing share price on 16 November 2012, the last working day before the MW report was published was SGD1.75. In the following three weeks, the share price declined by 21% to SGD1.39, a level which was last touched in March 2009. Olam sued MW for defamation on 21 November 2012 and subsequently withdrew the suit.

Olam, in its press release dated 5 April 2013 stated:

> "*While Olam has been able to serve notice on MW, it has been unsuccessful in serving Carson Block[4] despite its best efforts. In addition, after several months of investigation, no assets of consequence have been identified for either party against which claims can be made. After considering feedback received from several of its shareholders, Olam has decided it should now move forward and focus resources and management attention to deliver value for its continuing shareholders and other stakeholders.*"

MW, in its website states "*On November 30, 2012 MW made a bona fide offer to pay for Olam's debt rating. The company has refused to accept the offer of otherwise obtain a debt rating*".

On 3 December 2012, Olam announced a renounceable underwritten rights issue of US$750 million in principal amount of 6.75% bonds due 2018, with 387365,079 free detachable warrants ("Warrants"), each Warrant carrying the right to subscribe for one new ordinary share in the company. Temasek Holdings was the underwriter. The company received valid acceptances for about 110% of the principal amount and net proceeds from the issue amounted to SGD860.7 5million.

Looking back at the Muddy Waters Research

- *Aggressive Accounting:* Financial analysts would agree that profit after tax (PAT), also referred to as net income, is more a reflection of accounting profits than cash profits. Accounting policy requires and sometimes permits companies to report non-cash accounting gains and losses in their income statements. The reporting of NCAGs is not unique to Olam. Other NCAGs include fair value

---

[4] Carson Block is the founder of Muddy Waters Research.

gains/losses on investment properties reported by REITs and fair value gains/losses on derivatives reported by companies that have derivative exposures.

It must also be noted that the treatment of non cash items is symmetric i.e., should there be a decline in the valuation of biological assets, fair value losses in property and derivative losses, these would depress PAT. There is also a fundamental disconnect between the time of recognition of accounting profits/losses and actual cash inflows/outflows.

On account of these reasons, EBITDA and operating cash flows are considered more reliable measures of a company's profitability than PAT. As stated previously in this chapter, Olam has been consistently generating a positive EBITDA since FY2004. While Olam has consistently generated positive operating cash flows before working capital, interest expense and taxes, the trend of operating cash flows after taking into account the three aforementioned items has been volatile (Figure 7). This is only to be expected given the long working capital cycle and the sizable investments it makes.

- *Solvency*: While it is true that Olam's cash outstanding amounted to about 29 days of cost of goods sold in FY2012, it is line with the industry trend. GAR's and Wilmar's cash is equivalent to 23 days and 22 days respectively. Also, operating cash has been used to fund the purchase of the highly liquid inventory. The ratio of Olam's sum of cash and inventory to cost of goods sold was higher at 145 days (almost five months) by year-end 2012.

MW's statement that of the SGD1.11 billion cash outstanding as of 30 June 2012, SGD602.10 million came from withdrawal from

SGD 'Mn	FY2008	FY2009	FY2010	FY2011	FY2012	FY2013	FY2014	FY2015*
Gross Operating Cash Flow	371.52	346.05	461.33	811.09	894.17	1,073.78	1,175.48	1,705.89
Working Capital	133.84	266.65	(1,099.33)	(2,094.87)	(306.93)	(339.47)	(944.52)	(1,392.48)
Net Interest & Tax Paid	(1,216.87)	(1,024.69)	(215.58)	(339.35)	(399.78)	(484.13)	(529.64)	(832.16)
Operating Cash Flow	(711.52)	(412.00)	(853.58)	(1,623.12)	187.46	250.17	(298.68)	(518.75)

Figure 7 Annual Operating Cash Flows

Source: Olam Annual Reports.

brokerage accounts is incorrect. As stated by Olam in its response
dated 28 November 2014 to MW:

> "...*Margin account movements are mainly correlated with the net posi-
> tion on the hedges with brokers and commodity price changes on the under-
> lying. Draw down from broker accounts can be done only when excess cash
> is available in our accounts with brokers....*"

The declining trend in margin deposits observed in Figure 8 mir-
rors the trend in the prices of agricultural commodities (Figure 9).

Margin Accounts

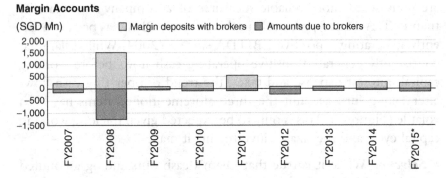

Figure 8   Margin Accounts
Source: Olam Annual Reports.

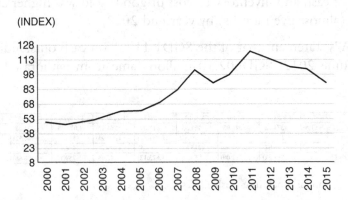

Figure 9
Source: http://www.worldbank.org/en/research/commodity-markets.

- *Sustainability of Olam's Business Model*: Olam is a diversified business operating across 16 platforms in 65 countries. So in the absence of an extraordinary event/situation, it is unlikely that all its businesses would fail simultaneously. Two years after the publication of the MW research report, Olam continues to generate a EBITDA and gross operating cash flows (Figures 3 & 6).
- *Olam is a black box*: Trading commodities, which are an inherently cyclical asset class, with significant exposure to derivatives to manage the resultant risks does make Olam and for that matter any company engaged in the supply chain management of commodities difficult to understand. The mark to market value of Olam's derivative exposures has fluctuated in line with commodity prices. But as per the company's audited financials these derivatives are predominantly used for hedging as opposed to speculating and the mark to market value of derivative liabilities is not excessive in relation to the scale of Olam's business (Figures 10 and 11).

Moreover, companies operating in complex industries such as agricultural trading, real estate, mining and financial services perform vital functions in the global economy. Mitigants to their complex business models include a track record of stable operating and financial performance, ownership by shareholders with strong financial

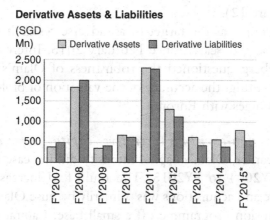

Figure 10

Source: Olam Annual Reports.

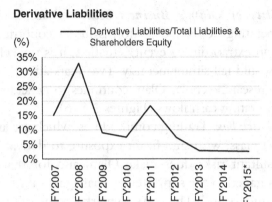

Figure 11
Source: Olam Annual Reports.

profiles and robust corporate governance track record, professional management and adequate and timely disclosures.

One way of gaining clarity is to benchmark Olam's performance with that of its peers. A peer comparison is conspicuous by its absence in the MW report. A comparison of Olam with its peers Bunge Limited and Noble Group is provided below. Olam is smaller in size than Bunge and Noble and has a much longer working capital cycle, which translates into a higher lease and inventory adjusted financial leverage (Figure 12).

Noble Group was the target of an adverse research report published by Iceberg Research since February 2015. Interestingly, both MW and Iceberg questioned the robustness of Olam's and Noble Group's accounting, the accuracy of the valuation of biological assets and drew analogies with Enron.

- *High and non-earnings accretive capital expenditures*: As explained earlier, Olam's capital intensity did increase significantly between FY2004 to FY2015. The multi-fold increase in capital expenditure and acquisitions was primarily because Olam embarked on its expansion programme off a small base. Capital expenditure and acquisitions were funded through a combination of debt,

	Olam International			Bunge Limited		Noble Group	
	FY13	FY14	FY15*	FY14	FY15	FY14	FY15
Revenues (USD 'Mn)	16,654	15,549	22,601	57,161	43,455	85,816	66,712
EBITDA Margin (%)	5.63%	6.02%	5.76%	3.17%	4.08%	1.23%	−0.48%
Total Assets (USF 'Mn)	10	11	17	21,432	17,922	20,090	17,074
Working Capital Cycle (Days)	99	106	148	27	30	2	3
Lease Adjsuted Net Debt/ EBITDA (Times)	6.57	7.09	10.02	1.93	2.28	4.00	Not measurable
Lease & Inventory Adjsuted Net Debt/EBITDA (Times)	3.02	3.08	3.84	(0.55)	0.77	(0.03)	Not measurable

* As Olam changed its financial year ending to 31 Dec in 2015, FY15 is an 18 month period Fy12 and FY13 are 12 month periods.

Figure 12 Peer Comparison

Source: Olam, Bunge & Noble Financial Statements.

equity and perpetual capital securities, thereby moderating the financial risk the company and the projects were exposed to.

With the benefit of hindsight, we can observe that Olam's expansion projects have been mostly successful, resulting in year on year increase in revenues and EBITDA during a period of declining agricultural prices (Figure 9) though the net lease and inventory adjusted financial leverage is elevated.

7

INVESTING
IN AGRI BUSINESS
COMPANIES: TAKEAWAYS

Investors proposing to invest in agri-business companies need to be aware of the type of agri-business companies they propose to invest in, the risks each category of company is exposed to and if they have the appetite — both monetary and psychological, to withstand these risks.

The businesses of integrated agri-business companies and supply chain operators are more complex than plantation operators as the former two categories of companies are exposed to a greater degree of FX, interest rate and derivative-related risks than plantation operators.

Investors need to be cognisant of a company's evolving business model. GAR started off as a large plantation operator and has evolved into an integrated producer of processed oil palm and allied products and has diversified into supply chain management through its joint ventures with Stena Weco and Stena Bulk. This change in business model has been accompanied by a significant increase in financial leverage. Hence it is essential for investors to continually assess if their investments are consistent with their risk appetite.

Agri-business companies are also particularly susceptible to attacks by short sellers and environmental groups. Short sellers tend to highlight these companies' high financial leverage, reliance on short term debt for inventory financing and the subjectivity involved in evaluating biological assets as risk factors in a bid to drive down share prices and profit from such declines.

It is a fact that Asian agri-business companies are more highly leveraged than their western counterparts and tend to finance their high inventory holdings using short term debt. The use of short term debt in Asia is because relationship banking is more prevalent in Asia, where banks extending committed lines are not the norm. Banks tend to renew the short-term debt of companies with a sound operating and financial performance and professional management with a sound corporate governance track record during normal times. But the risk of cancelling lines during times of cyclical downturn and tight liquidity does exist.

Environmentalists accuse companies engaged in oil palm cultivation and processing of land grabbing, destroying rain forests and wild life habitats, being responsible for declining bio-diversity and being among the largest emitters of carbon dioxide. The oil palm industry is attempting to sustain large scale oil palm cultivation without endangering the environment by securing the RSPO certification for the downstream applications of oil palm relating to food and beverage and the ISCC[1] certification. The International Sustainability and Carbon Certification System (ISCC System) is a system for certifying the biomass and bio energy industries, oriented towards the reduction of greenhouse gas emissions, sustainable use of land, protection of natural biospheres, and social sustainability. Nevertheless, 'ethical investors' are wary of investing in oil palm companies due to their environmental and social impacts.

Investors in these companies need to understand the complexity of agri-business models and the necessity of modifying standard

---

[1] International Sustainability and Carbon Certification.

corporate analytical tools and ratios to better reflect the underlying business and financial risks. Also, investors ought to be conscious of the 'caveat emtor' or investor beware principle in this instance. Only those investors who fully understand the inherent risks and mitigants and have an appetite for such stocks should invest in such companies. Others would be better off investing in index tracking funds.

8

THE BANKING TROIKA

"Look here, the financial world begins in Zurich. Zurich banks open at 9 o'clock in the morning, later Frankfurt, later London. In the meantime, New York is open. So London hands over financial money traffic to New York. In the afternoon New York closes; they had already handed over to San Francisco. When San Francisco closes in the afternoon, the world is covered with a veil. Nothing happens until next day, 9:00 A.M. Swiss time, then the Swiss banks open. If we put Singapore in between, before San Francisco closes, Singapore would have taken over. And when Singapore closes, it would have handed over to Zurich. Then, for the first time since creation, we will have a 24-hour round-the-world service in money and banking."

Extract of Dr. Albert Winsemius[1]' conversation with Van Oenen of Bank of America in 1968 from Lee Kwan Yew's "From Third World To First"

Thus was born the then seemingly improbable idea to leverage on the recently independent and struggling city state of Singapore's location and transform it into one of the leading global financial centres within a decade. By 2014, finance and insurance together

---

[1] Dr. Winsemius was a Dutch economist who led the United Nations Industrial Survey Mission to Singapore and was Singapore's economic adviser from 1961 to 1984.

57

accounted for 11.80% of Singapore's SGD390 billion GDP. Financial inclusion achieved by Singapore is among the highest in the world with 98% of the population having a bank account with a formal financial institution.

Singapore's central bank, the Monetary Authority of Singapore (MAS) has designated five banks as domestic banking units — Bank of Singapore Limited, DBS Bank Ltd (DBS), Far Eastern Bank Ltd (FEB), Oversea-Chinese Banking Corporation Limited (OCBC) and United Overseas Bank Limited (UOB). Of these Bank Of Singapore is a wholly-owned private banking arm of OCBC and UOB has a majority 79% stake in FEB and the latter's accounts are consolidated with UOB. Hence, there are effectively three domestic banking groups operating in Singapore — DBS, UOB and OCBC.

The reason for discussing the evolution, performance and prospects of the three Singapore banks in a single, albeit long, chapter is that globally banking is a cyclical industry with the performance of the banks being closely correlated with the economies in which they operate. Banks operating in a geography tend to follow a trend and variation in individual banks' performance occurs on account of scale, ownership, business strategy, risk management practices, capital structure or dividend policy.

Banks mobilise and invest household savings, cater to mortgage and other loan requirements of households, extend loan financing and banking services to the corporate sector and also cater to the government's banking requirements. Hence, banks are subject to closer regulatory oversight than non-strategic manufacturing and service firms due to their systemic importance to the economy.

Genesis

The Development Bank of Singapore (DBS) was incorporated on 16 July 1968 and started operations on 1 September of the same year. The bank's main functions were to support Singapore's economic development and industrialization.

The idea of creating an economic body and a development bank to accelerate Singapore's industrialisation was mooted in a report by the United Nations Industrial Survey Mission. The economic body was to only proactively attract foreign investments into Singapore, provide industrial financing and manage industrial estates. The financing responsibility of the economic body was to be eventually transferred to the development bank.

The economic body that was established was the Economic Development Board (EDB), which was formed on 1 August 1961 to plan, co-ordinate and direct the industrialisation of Singapore. By 1967, the increasing need for industrial capital resulted in the formation of the DBS to take over the financial functions of the EDB. DBS' president and first chairman was Hon Sui Sen, who was concurrently the chairman of the EDB.

DBS, within a relatively short period of 47 years, has grown to be the largest bank in South East Asia by assets with 280 branches spanning across 18 markets. Temasek Holdings has an effective 28.94% stake in DBS as of 24 February 2015 and remaining shares are held by a host of asset management companies and retail investors.

The Oversea-Chinese Banking Corporation (OCBC) was incorporated on 31 October 1932 through the merger of three Hokkien banks — the Chinese Commercial Bank Ltd. (established in 1912), Ho Hong Bank Ltd. (1917) and Oversea-Chinese Bank Ltd. (1919) — during the Great Depression.

When OCBC began operations officially in January 1933, it was already one of the strongest local banks in the Straits Settlements. The bank survived the challenging period of the Japanese Occupation (1942 to 1945). During this period, the bank's head office was transferred to Bombay[2], India, before being re-registered in Singapore after the war. During the 1950s, OCBC was one of the few foreign banks to have branches operating in China.

OCBC's growth has been both organic and through acquisitions. Key acquisitions include: the Four Seas Communication Bank in 1972, then the oldest surviving bank in Singapore, Keppel Capital Holdings in 2001, Indonesia-based Bank NISP in 2005, an 87% stake

---

[2] Present day Mumbai.

in the insurance company Great Eastern Holdings in 2006, a 67% stake in Malaysia-based financial services provider PacificMas Berhad in 2008, ING Asia Private Bank in 2010, and a 97.52% stake in Hong Kong-based Wing Hang bank in 2014. OCBC also acquired minority stakes of 10% in Vietnam's VP Bank and 12.2% in China's Ningbo Commercial Bank in 2006.

As of year-end 2015, OCBC operations spanned across 18 markets with over 630 overseas branches and offices. As per OCBC's 2015 Annual Report, the Lee Foundation Group, associated with the founding Lee[3] family has a stake of 19.77% stake in the bank and remaining shares are held by institutional and retail investors.

United Overseas Bank (UOB) was founded as United Chinese Bank (UCB) by Datuk Wee Kheng Chiang. After the Great Depression, affluent Chinese businessmen from Sarawak and Penang, who had built their fortunes from trading in commodities such as rubber and pepper as well as shipping, pooled their resources to establish the UCB in Singapore. The Hokkien merchant network between Singapore, the Malayan peninsula and Sarawak provided a steady stream of customers for the bank. With a paid-up capital of one million dollars, the bank opened for business on 1 October 1935. It was the last bank to be set-up in Singapore during the pre-war years.

Despite being a family-controlled bank, it was run predominantly by a professional management team who had prior experience in managing older Chinese banks, particularly OCBC and the Ho Hong Bank. The bank's expansion was led by its then managing director, Wee Cho Yaw, who was the son of Wee Kheng Chiang, one of the founding pioneers of the bank. In 1965, the UCB changed its name to the United Overseas Bank (UOB) and opened its first overseas branch in Hong Kong. The bank was renamed to avoid a clash of names with an existing bank in Hong Kong.

Like OCBC, UOB's growth occurred organically and through acquisitions. Key acquisitions included: Chung Khiaw Bank in 1971, FEB in 1984, Industrial & Commercial Bank Limited in 1987,

---

[3] Lee Kong Chian founded OCBC.

	DBS	**UOB**	**OCBC**
Fitch	AA-/Stable	AA-/Stable	AA-/Stable
Moody's	Aa1/Negative	Aa1/Negative	Aa1/Negative
Standard & Poor's	AA-/Stable	AA-/Stable	AA-/Stable

Figure 1.   Credit Ratings & Outlooks as of 30 May 2016
Source: DBS, OCBC & UOB.

Philippines-based Westmont Bank and Thailand-based Radanasin Bank in 1999, Overseas Union Bank in 2001, Thailand-based Bank of Asia in 2004 and Indonesia-based PT Bank Buana in 2004-05. UOB also acquired minority stakes of 10% in Vietnam-based Southern Commercial Joint Stock Bank in 2007 and 15% in China-based Evergrowing Bank in 2010.

As of year-end 2015, the UOB Group has a network of more than 500 offices in 19 countries, predominantly in Asia Pacific with some presence in Western Europe and North America. Key shareholders include the founding Wee family who hold a 18% stake in UOB and the estate of Lien Ying Chow[4] and related entities with a 10.24% stake.

In 2014, Global Finance ranked the three Singapore banks — DBS, OCBC and UOB 12th, 13th and 14th respectively in terms of safety. Global credit rating agencies have assigned high investment grade ratings in the AA category, which underscores Global Finance's safety rankings (Figure 1).

Regulatory Oversight

A key reason for the evolution of Singapore as a global banking hub is the optimal supervision exercised by Singapore's central bank and banking regulator — the Monetary Authority of Singapore (MAS). The MAS' prudent regulations for the Singapore banks are in line with and in certain instances more rigorous than Basel III guidelines. A synopsis of the Basel III and MAS guidelines is provided in Appendix 2.

---

[4] Lien Ying Chow is the founder of Overseas Union Bank (OUB), which merged with UOB in 2001.

Singapore Banks Performance in Pictures

As mentioned earlier in this chapter, banking is a cyclical industry, whose performance is closely correlated with the macroeconomic performance of the geographies in which they operate. Two watershed events in the evolution of Singapore banks are the Asian Financial Crisis (AFC) of 1997–98 and the Global Financial Crisis (GFC) of 2007–08.

The economies most impacted by the AFC were Thailand, Indonesia, South Korea, Malaysia and The Philippines. The ratio of Singapore's banks non-performing loans (NPLs) to these five countries to the loans to these countries was sizable at 23.3% by December 1998, especially when viewed against the backdrop of the ratio of NPLs to total loans of 11.3%. Loan loss reserves the banks had provided for against their NPLs was a modest 53%. However, Singapore banks were well capitalized with a total CAR of 18.3%.

Data on the three Singapore banks' websites is only available from 2000, so this section discusses the evolution of Singapore banks during the 15 year period from 2000–2015, which encompasses the banks' recovery phase from the AFC, the run up to the GFC and the aftermath of the GFC.

Growth: Scale coupled with prudent lending practices are hallmarks of a strong financial system as these two parameters endow banks with the capability to withstand cyclical fluctuations. The three Singapore banks have achieved robust growth rates of almost 10% in total assets (Figure 2) and deposits (Figure 3) and 12% in loans (Figure 4) reflecting the high growth Asia Pacific region these banks' businesses are focussed on.

Business Mix: Politically and economically stable, Singapore continues to account for almost half of the three Singapore banks' loans (Figure 5). Exposure to Greater China in SGD terms is the highest for DBS, followed by OCBC and UOB. In aggregate, the high growth Asia Pacific region accounts for about 90% of the Singapore banks' loans. This regional concentration, focus on traditional banking products with relatively lesser exposure than the US and Europe-based banks to the riskier securitised loans and derivative businesses and improving

Total Assets

SGD 'Bn

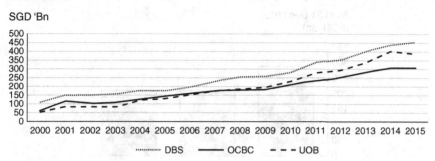

Figure 2

Source: DBS, OCBC and UOB Financial Statements.

Deposits

SGD 'Bn

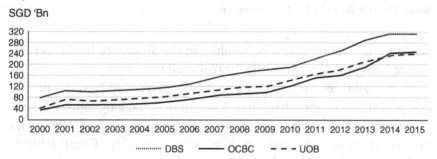

Figure 3

Source: DBS, OCBC and UOB Financial Statements.

Loans

SGD 'Bn

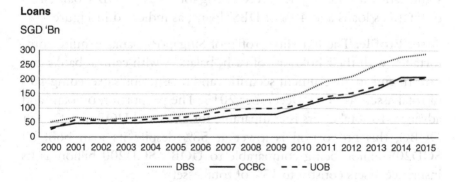

Figure 4

Source: DBS, OCBC and UOB Financial Statements.

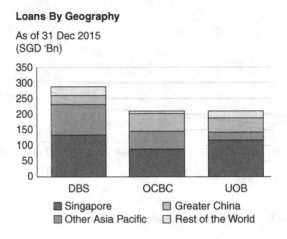

Loans By Geography

As of 31 Dec 2015
(SGD 'Bn)

Figure 5

Source: DBS, OCBC and UOB Financial Statements.

prudence in lending practices, resulted in the Singapore banks' performance being shielded from the 2007–08 GFC.

While all three Singapore banks have a diversified business profile comprising consumer banking, institutional banking and treasury operations, OCBC's business is even more diversified as 19% of its income is earned through its insurance subsidiary, Great Eastern Holdings in which it holds an 87% stake (Figure 6).

Though Singapore banks have diversified their loans across industries, their loan exposure to housing, building and construction is significant with this segment accounting for 49% of UOB's loans, 43% of OCBC's loans and 40% of DBS' loans, as indicated in Figure 7.

Asset Profile: The liquidity profile of Singapore banks is quite comfortable, with their holdings of cash, balances with central banks and investments in government securities and treasury bills exceeding 10% of total assets as of 31 December 2015. The proportion of loans and advances to total assets is comparable for DBS and UOB at 62%. For OCBC, this proportion is lower at 53% despite its loan book of SGD208 billion being comparable to UOB's SGD200 billion as its insurance assets constitute 15% of total assets.

Key strengths of the Singapore banks' asset profiles include a liquid balance sheet, a high proportion (over 70%) of assets being

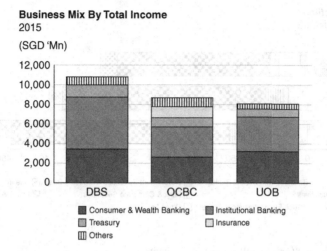

Figure 6

Source: DBS, OCBC and UOB Financial Statements.

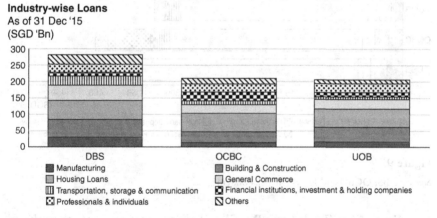

Figure 7

Source: DBS, OCBC and UOB Financial Statements.

deployed in the core and remunerative business of banking (Figure 8) and a very small proportion of business being run through associates and joint ventures, which constitute less than 1% of total assets. This implies that Singapore banks exercise management control over practically all their businesses

Asset Profile
As of 31 Dec '15

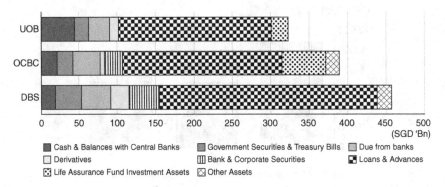

Figure 8

Source: DBS, OCBC and UOB Financial Statements.

Funding Mix
As of 31 Dec '15

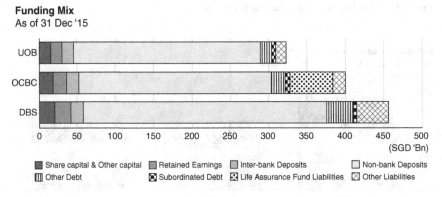

Figure 9

Source: DBS, OCBC and UOB Financial Statements.

Funding Mix/Liability Profile: Salient features of the three Singapore banks' funding mix are that they are well capitalised with shareholders' equity and retained earnings together accounting for around 7% to 10% of total funding, and non-bank deposits continue to be the major source of funding. Non-bank deposits, as a proportion of total deposits, for DBS and UOB stood at 70% and 76% respectively as of 31 December 2015. For UOB this figure is lower at 61%, with insurance liabilities at 14% of total liabilities adding an element of diversity to UOB's funding (Figure 9).

A key risk banks across the globe are exposed to is tenor mismatch i.e., they extend loans of varying tenors funded by deposits, which are predominantly short to medium term deposits. Should there be an unforeseen decline in the deposit renewal rate, banks would face a liquidity crunch and in extreme cases, a run on their deposits.

The Singapore banks have a comfortable deposit profile with current and savings bank accounts, which technically are the operating accounts of institutions and individuals and have no contractual expiry rate, accounting for 58% of DBS' total deposits including interbank deposits, 47% of OCBC's deposits and 42% of UOB's deposits (Figure 10). DBS has the most favourable deposit profile among the three domestic banks.

Loan to Deposit Ratio: Another measure of the tenor mismatch of banks is the loan to deposit ratio. A lower ratio indicates that a bank, under normal circumstances, is exposed to lesser degree of tenor mismatch. The three Singapore banks' loan to deposit ratio are at acceptable levels and have converged at around 85% since 2011 (Figure 11).

Income Trends: A bank's total income comprises of net interest income and non-interest income. Net interest income (NII) is the difference between the interest income a bank earns on its assets and the interest expense a bank pays on its liabilities. Non-interest income is the fee-based income a bank earns and includes fees earned from

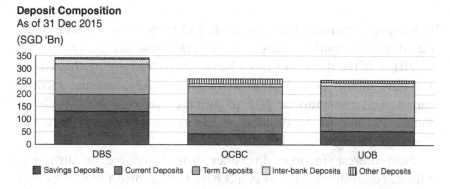

Deposit Composition
As of 31 Dec 2015
(SGD 'Bn)

DBS   OCBC   UOB

■ Savings Deposits   ■ Current Deposits   ■ Term Deposits   ☐ Inter-bank Deposits   ▥ Other Deposits

Figure 10

Source: DBS, OCBC and UOB Financial Statements.

Loan to Deposit Ratio

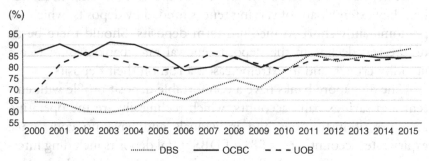

Figure 11

Source: DBS, OCBC and UOB Financial Statements.

Net Interest Income

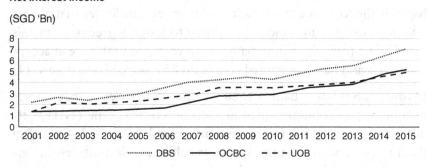

Figure 12

Source: DBS, OCBC and UOB Financial Statements.

brokerage, investment banking, trade and transaction services, loan-related, cards, wealth management and trading securities.

NII in of the three Singapore banks has trebled during the sixteen year nine month period 2000–2015 (Figure 12), but net income margin, i.e., the ratio of NII to average earning assets, declined (Figure 13) due to the declining trend in interest rates (Figure 14) witnessed during this period.

Non-interest income diversifies banks' income streams and enhances customer loyalty as banks have transformed themselves into a one-stop shop for a multitude of financial services. The share of

Net Interest Margin

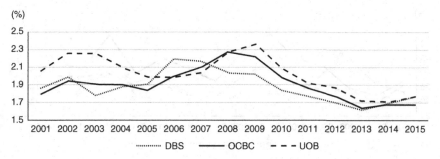

Figure 13
Source: DBS, OCBC and UOB Financial Statements.

Singapore Domestic 12-Month Interbank Interest Rate

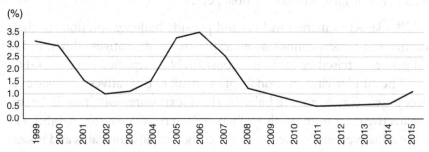

Figure 14
Source: Monetary Authority of Singapore & Association of Banks in Singapore (ABS).

Singapore banks' non-interest income in total income is significant, ranging from 35% to 45% of total income (Figure 15). OCBC's share of non-interest income has traditionally been the highest due to its sizable insurance operation through its subsidiary, Great Eastern Holdings.

Derivative Exposure: Warren Buffet famously said, "*Derivatives are financial weapons of mass destruction*". Derivatives, if used appropriately, may be used to hedge interest rate, foreign exchange, credit and commodity risks. However, exposure to derivatives with high embedded leverage has caused the collapse of several financial institutions

Non-interest Income/Total Income

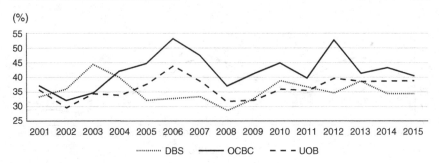

Figure 15

Source: DBS, OCBC and UOB Financial Statements.

including Lehman Brothers, AIG, Bear Stearns, Fannie Mae, Freddie Mac, Washington Mutual, Ambac, etc.

Banks act as market makers and provide hedging solutions to their clients and hence, cannot avoid exposure to derivatives. But the due diligence exercised by banks has considerably intensified since the GFC.

The underlying notional of a bank's derivatives exposure is accounted for as an off balance sheet exposure. But this is by no means the maximum liability of a bank's derivative-related liabilities as the derivatives' embedded leverage could amplify the gains and losses. The maximum derivative-related liabilities is dynamic and a function of the notional underlying amount, embedded leverage, the level of interest rate/exchange rate/commodity prices/credit, spreads at the settlement date and the availability of collateral, if any.

The three Singapore banks have tended to focus on their core banking businesses rather than providing derivative solutions to their clients, especially since the 2007–08 GFC. DBS has the highest derivative related exposure among the three banks in terms of the underlying notional. But DBS' ratio of derivative-related underlying notional to total assets has considerably declined since the GFC (Figure 16). The relatively more simple interest rate and FX related derivatives form bulk of the underlying notional (Figure 17) and the derivative-related mark-to-market asset and liabilities (Figure 18) is modest in relation to all three banks' size and liquidity.

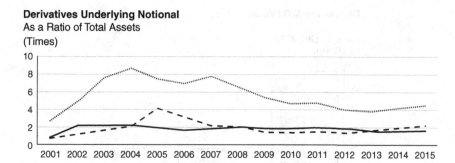

Figure 16

Source: DBS, OCBC and UOB Financial Statements.

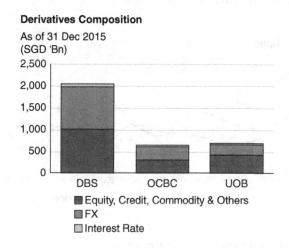

Figure 17

Source: DBS, OCBC and UOB Financial Statements.

Cost efficiency: Singapore banks have been cost efficient with their cost to income ratios, on an average, ranging from 40% to 45% (Figure 19). DBS has had the highest cost structure. OCBC has had the most efficient cost structure due to the higher proportion on its non-interest income arising from its higher margin insurance business.

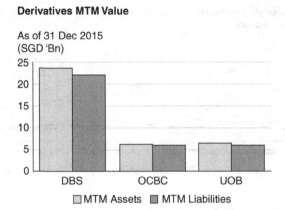

Figure 18

Source: DBS, OCBC and UOB Financial Statements.

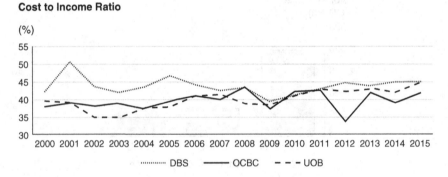

Figure 19

Source: DBS, OCBC and UOB Financial Statements.

Asset Quality: A quick measure of a bank's asset quality is the ratio of non-performing loans (NPLs) to risk weighted assets. After the AFC, the Singapore banks tightened their lending norms. This and the Singapore banks focusing on traditional banking as opposed to trading in collateralised debt and loan obligations, resulted in a declining trend of non-performing loans (NPLs), as a percentage of risk weighted assets to about 1% in 2015 from over 5% in 2001 (Figure 20).

NPL Ratio

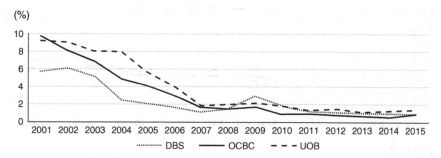

Figure 20

Source: DBS, OCBC and UOB Financial Statements.

NPL By Industry
As of 31 Dec '15
(SGD 'Mn)

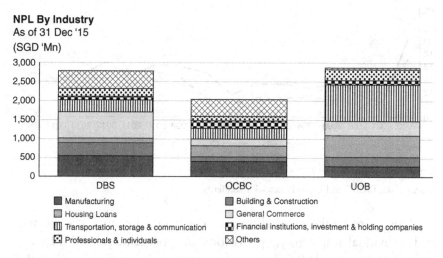

Figure 21

Source: DBS, OCBC and UOB Financial Statements.

An examination of industry-wise NPLs indicates that the ratio of industry-specific NPLs to loans extended is quite low ranging from 0.2% to 3.5% for all three banks across the eight industries (Figure 21). The sole exception is UOB's transportation, storage and communication NPLs, which account for a sizable 9.75% of UOB's loans extended to this industry.

Loan Allowance Cover

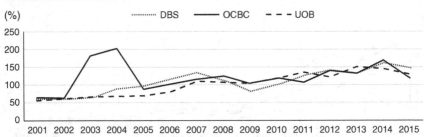

Figure 22

Source: DBS, OCBC and UOB Financial Statements.

Tier 1 Capital Adequacy Ratio

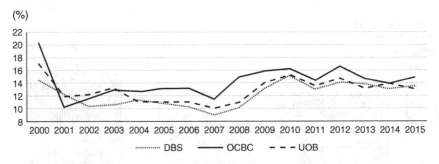

Figure 23

Source: DBS, OCBC and UOB Financial Statements.

Singapore banks' loan allowance cover i.e. the sum of collective and individual impairment provisions as a percentage of NPLs has improved to over 100% during the last decade, indicating that the Singapore banks have created adequate buffer to anticipated defaults in their loan portfolio (Figure 22).

Capital Adequacy Ratio (CAR): The three Singapore banks have traditionally been well-capitalised with their Tier 1 (Figure 23) and Total CARs (Figure 24) well above the MAS stipulated regulatory minimum of 9%.

Dividend Payout: Dividend payout; cash dividends paid as a percentage of net income, has declined over the last fifteen years, thereby enabling the banks to strengthen their capitalisation. The dividend

Total Capital Adequacy Ratio

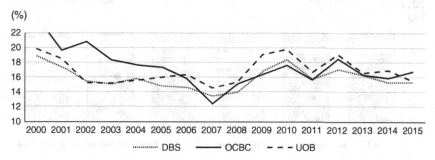

Figure 24

Source: DBS, OCBC and UOB Financial Statements.

Dividend Payout Ratio

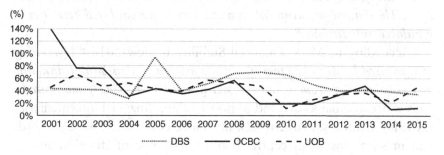

Figure 25

Source: DBS, OCBC and UOB Financial Statements.

payout for DBS, a Temasek Portfolio Company, has traditionally been the highest (Figure 25) among the three banks. Temasek, as Singapore government's investment arm, makes annual contributions to the nation's budget and hence steady dividend payouts from investee companies are crucial.

Shadow Banking

Investopedia defines a shadow banking system[5] as *"financial interme-diaries involved in facilitating the creation of credit across the global*

---

[5] Source: http://www.investopedia.com/terms/s/shadow-banking-system.asp

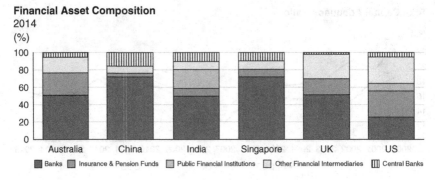

Financial Asset Composition
2014
(%)

Figure 26

Source: Global Shadow Banking Monitoring Report 2015.

financial system, but whose members are not subject to regulatory over-sight. The shadow banking system also refers to unregulated activities by regulated institutions."

According to MAS' Financial Stability Review 2014 *"Tightening of regulated lending has facilitated the growth in non-bank financing, but risks arising from shadow banking need to be closely monitored"*. This is because banks do lend to non-banking financial intermediaries (NBFIs) including hedge funds, insurance companies, pension funds and in some instances central banks. A significant deterioration in NBFIs' asset quality would in turn result in NBFIs defaulting on their loan repayments to banks.

According to the Global Shadow Banking Monitoring Report 2014, Singapore banks accounted for 72% of the nation's financial assets (Figure 26), among the highest in the world. The shadow banking sector in Singapore is smaller than most major economies, underpinning the robustness of the country's financial system.

Challenges

The key challenges facing the Singapore banks are sustaining growth and sustaining their strong market position in South East Asia while simultaneously maintaining their asset quality. The banking industry faces several headwinds at the current juncture.

Firstly the US Federal Reserve Rate hiked its benchmark interest rate by 0.25% to between 0.25% to 0.50% in December 2015. The US Federal Reserve has held its rate close to zero since the 2008 GFC. The US Federal Reserve effecting rate hikes could result in corresponding increases in Singapore's domestic interest rates.

According to the MAS' 2015 Financial Stability Report, the ratio of corporate debt to GDP has steadily increased from about 50% in the second quarter of 2008 to close to 150% in the second quarter of 2015. A rise in interest rates would lead to an increase in interest expense for companies, which would depress their profits and reduce their ability to repay principal.

Secondly, the price of crude oil plummeted to multi-year low at USD29.78/bbl by January 2016 before recovering to around USD50/bbl by end-2016. This bodes well for companies which consume energy as low oil price results in lower input costs and improved profitability. But oil and gas exploration and production companies and suppliers to these companies will witness a deterioration in profitability. Singapore banks have significant exposures in South East Asian corporates. Refined petroleum and petroleum gas together account for about a fifth of Malaysia's exports, while crude petroleum and petroleum gas account for about 15% of Indonesia's exports and almost all of Brunei's exports. Hence, Singapore banks may witness an increase in their special mention loans and NPLs, should the current trend of low crude oil price be sustained over a protracted period of time.

Thirdly, Singapore banks are likely to witness slippages in asset quality due to the slowing GDP growth in China and the performance of Singapore's real estate sector. Exposure to Greater China accounted for a quarter of the three Singapore banks' loans in 2015, with DBS' share being the highest. The share of building and construction loans and mortgage loans in total loans for the three Singapore banks was almost 45% by end-December 2015. The continued enforcement of cooling measures amid the tightened credit environment, a mounting supply of new homes, a weak leasing market and the impending rise in interest rates indicates that the property market is unlikely to turn around in the near future.

Finally, the emergence of 'fintech' is a challenge not just for the Sinagapore banking sector but for the global banking industry itself. In simple terms, fintech comprises three main developments: (1) the application of distributed ledger (blockchain technology) in finance; (2) automation in the provision of financial advice (robo-advisers); and (3) loan-based or capital raising platforms that directly connect issuers and investors (disintermediating the traditional role of banks) including crowd funding platforms and peer-to-peer (marketplace) lending.

The rapidly developing fintech industry will have long term implications on banks' business models, revenues, margins and their significance in the global market place. To counter this challenge, banks are promoting their own fintech arms, investing in fintech start-ups and engaging in 'creative disruption'.

It would be interesting to observe how fintech and banking evolve in the future. Will these two industries grow hand-in-hand, will fintech become a 'vendor' to banking, or will banking — one of the oldest industries in the world whose evolution can be traced to the emergence of barter — become an ancillary industry to fintech? Only time will tell.

Takeaways

Do these challenges imply that investing in Singapore banks is an unattractive proposition? No. Investors need to view the risks the Singapore banks are exposed to against the backdrop of their strong liquidity, robust capital adequacy and the current minimal level of NPLs that have been more than adequately provided for. In other words, banking is a cyclical industry and the Singapore banks are well-positioned to weather the risks of a potential rise in interest rates, sustained low crude oil prices, macroeconomic slowdown in China and a sluggish real estate market.

The inherent strength of Singapore banks becomes apparent, when their performance is benchmarked against the largest banks in the region (Figure 27).

SGD Million	DBS	OCBC	UOB	ICBC	Maybank	Bangkok Bank
Credit Ratings						
Fitch	AA-/Stable	AA-/Stable	AA-/Stable	A/Stable	A-/Negative	BBB+/Stable
Moody's	Aa1/Negative	Aa1/Negative	Aa1/Negative	A2/Negative	A3/Stable	Baa1/Stable
Standard & Poors	AA-/Stable	AA-/Stable	AA-/Stable	A/Stable	A-/Stable	BBB+/Stable
Financials						
Net Interest Income	7,100	5,189	4,926	110,697	4,958	2,259
Non-interest Income	3,687	3,533	3,122	35,238	3,283	1,776
Total Income	10,787	8,722	8,048	145,935	8,421	4,036
Net Interest Margin (%)	1.77	1.67	1.77	2.47	2.4	2.16
Non-interest Income/Total Income (%)	34	41	39	24	40	44
Cost to Income Ratio (%)	45	42	45	27	48	44
Dividend Payout Ratio (%)	34	11	45	33	76	37
Total Assets	457,834	390,190	316,011	4,840,936	233,300	111,410
Total Loans	283,289	208,218	203,611	2,601,068	149,362	73,422
Total Deposits	320,134	246,277	240,524	3,548,879	157,483	82,146
Loan to Deposit Ratio (%)	88.49	84.55	84.65	73.29	94.84	89.38
NPL Ratio (%)	0.9	0.9	1.4	1.5	1.43	2.75
Loan Allowance Cover (%)	148.00	119.60	130.50	156.34	72.00	185.30
Tier 1 CAR (%)	13.5	14.8	13.00	13.48	14.47	15.78
Total CAR (%)	15.4	16.8	15.60	15.22	17.74	17.87
Equity Market data						
Market Capitalization *(SGD million)	37,903	34,780	28,834	18,918	27,169	11,555
Current P/E*	8.61	9.24	9.30	4.14	11.77	8.88
Forward Looking P/E*	8.79	9.61	9.40	4.32	12.41	8.34

* As of May 20, 2016
Source: Banks' Annual Reports, Thomson Reuters

Figure 27. Peer Comparison

Source: Banks' Financial Statements, Bloomberg, www.oanda.com and authors' calculations.

The three banks compare favourably with regional peers in terms of scale, the relatively high contribution of non-interest income, cost effectiveness, asset quality, capitalisation and liquidity.

Cyclical fluctuations may result in share price volatility. But long term investors would find investing in Singapore banks an attractive proposition due to their fundamentally robust business and sound corporate governance practices.

9

THE SINGAPORE EXCHANGE

The Singapore Exchange (SGX) is an interesting example of a city state starting its stock exchange from the scratch and transforming it into a leading regional player by developing its product and service capabilities and offering an efficient and transparent operating environment. But the SGX is currently at a crossroads. In the absence of a large domestic economy providing it with trading volumes, other regional exchanges like the Hong Kong Exchange, the Shanghai and Shenzhen Exchanges in China and the Bombay and National Stock Exchanges in India have grown into much larger entities than the SGX in terms of market capitalisation.

But the SGX's prospects, though challenging, are not bleak. Singapore continues to rank high on the ease of conducting business index and offers a gateway to invest in the high-growth ASEAN region. Hence companies in China and India with global expansion aspirations are likely to view Singapore as a viable listing option. This chapter traces the SGX's evolution and its strengths, and limitations and opportunities that will shape its position in the global market place.

Genesis

The founding of the SGX, or more specifically its predecessor, the Stock Exchange of Singapore (SES), was as abrupt as the founding of the city state of Singapore. In May 1973, the Malaysian government had decided to discontinue the interchangeability of currency between Malaysia and Singapore.

> *"This decision affected the Stock Exchange of Malaysia and Singapore, which had a unique arrangement of having one stock exchange to serve the two countries. Starting from 9 May that year, authorised depositories, banks, stock brokers and solicitors in Singapore could no longer sign the declaration form for the registration of shares of Malaysian companies by Singapore residents.*
>
> *A three-man pro-tem committee was formed on 12 May 1973 to start conceiving a plan for the establishment of the Stock Exchange of Singapore at the earliest possible date. The committee was headed by Ng Soo Peng, who was then the chairman of the Stock Exchange of Malaysia and Singapore. The Second Reading of the Securities Industry Bill was brought into force on 23 May 1973. With the enactment of the Securities Industry Act 1973, the Stock Exchange of Singapore Ltd was incorporated on 24 May 1973."*

The Singapore Exchange (SGX), as we know today, was formed in 1999 through the merger of three companies — SES, Singapore International Monetary Exchange (Simex) and Securities Clearing and Computer Services Pte Ltd (SCCS). The SGX's largest shareholder is SEL Holdings Pte Ltd, a special purpose company set up under Section 11(2)(b) of the Exchanges (Demutualisation & Merger) Act 1999, to hold the SGX shares for the benefit of the Financial Sector Development Fund. SEL does not exercise or control the exercise of the votes attached to the SGX shares. Owing to the restriction in the exercise of the votes attached to the shares, SEL is not regarded as a substantial shareholder of SGX. SEL holds a 23.37% stake in the SGX.

Evolution

The SGX was listed in 2000 and its market capitalisation impressively more than tripled to USD640 billion as of 31 December 2015 from USD148.50 billion as of 31 December 2003.

The SGX operates the only integrated securities and derivatives exchange in Singapore along with related clearing houses. The SGX plays a key role in the positioning of Singapore as an international financing centre with about 45% of its listed companies based outside Singapore.

Please refer to Table 4 in Appendix 1 for the key milestones in SGX's evolution

In the decade and a half since its IPO, the SGX has evolved into the tenth largest stock exchange in Asia Pacific (APAC) accounting for around 3% of APAC's market capitalisation. The exchange is the premier stock exchange in APAC for the listing of maritime companies, mineral, oil and gas companies, integrated real estate companies and REITs and is one of the most international stock exchanges, with companies incorporated overseas accounting for 45% of its market capitalisation as of 31 December 2015. Figures 1 to 6 reflect those stock exchanges that are members of the World Federation of Exchanges (WFE) with the London Stock Exchange Group (LSEG) being a notable exclusion.

Financial Performance

The SGX's revenues have more than tripled to SGD779 million in FY2015 from SGD217 million in FY2001. The exchange has

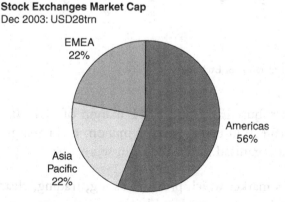

Stock Exchanges Market Cap
Dec 2003: USD28trn

Figure 1

Source: World Federation of Exchanges.

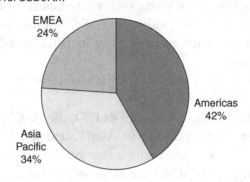

Stock Exchanges Market Cap
Dec 2015: USD67trn

Figure 2

Source: World Federation of Exchanges.

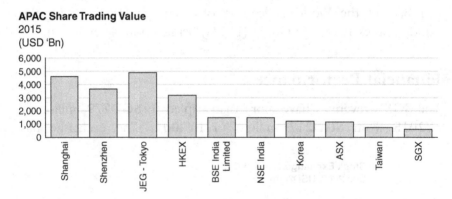

APAC Share Trading Value
2015
(USD 'Bn)

Figure 3

Source: World Federation of Exchanges.

sustained a robust EBIT and EBIT margin of SGD402 million and 52% in FY15 (2000 EBIT: SGD72 million, EBIT margin: 53%). The exchange is organised into three main segments:

- Securities market which provides listing, trading, clearing, depository, market data, and member services, connectivity, collateral management and issuer services. This is the key contributor to profits accounting for almost 56% of SGX's FY2015 EBIT.

SGX Market Cap

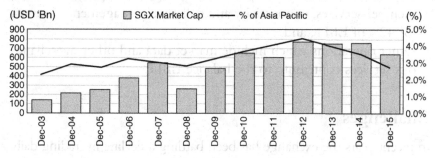

Figure 4

Source: World Federation of Exchanges.

Listed Companies: Number

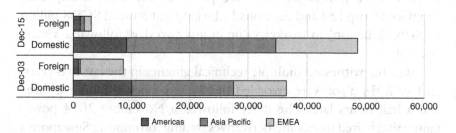

Figure 5

Source: World Federation of Exchanges.

Foreign Companies on SGX: Number

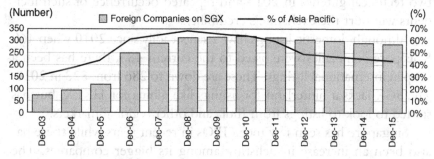

Figure 6

Source: World Federation of Exchanges.

- Derivatives market which provides trading, clearing, market data, member services, connectivity and collateral management accounts for 42% of EBIT, and
- Other operations which include market data and other miscellaneous services contribute to the balance EBIT.

Challenges

In recent years the exchange has been battling a decline in trading daily volumes, slowdown in IPOs and low volatility in the post-financial crisis era. Singapore is the world's third-largest foreign-exchange trading centre behind London and New York but stock trading value trails far behind regional giants like Shanghai, Shenzhen, Hong Kong and Tokyo.

Trading volumes dropped sharply after the penny-stock crash of 2013 when a plunge in the share prices of Blumont Group Ltd, LionGold Corp Ltd and Asiasons Ltd wiped out around SGD8 billion (USD6.35 billion) in market value in just two days following a massive rally.

SGX has witnessed multiple technical glitches in the last two years. In Dec 2014 a software error led the SGX to open the bourse three and a half hours late. The delay followed a November 2014 power failure that halted stocks and derivatives trading, prompting Singapore's central bank, the Monetary Authority of Singapore (MAS) to brand the lapse *"unacceptable"*. More recently, the securities market of SGX shut down since noon on July 14 2016, which caused much confusion among the market operators. The MAS has reprimanded SGX for the two technical glitches in 2014 and repeated occurrence of such incidents will hurt the exchange's credibility.

Although domestic listings have risen steadily since 2010 when 460 Singapore companies were listed to the current 483, there has been a drop in international listings. These are down to 286 from 323 in 2010. The SGX lacks a hinterland for listings like China for HKEX, but has started to look to listings from India and other regional markets.

Singapore has seen few mega IPOs in recent years while there has also been an increase in delisting among its bigger companies. The number of listed equity securities has shown a drop with the aggregate falling to 769 in 2015 from 783 in 2010. The software glitches, along with low volatility could exert downward pressure on the average daily trading volumes and revenue momentum.

The exchange has announced several plans to try and improve volumes, including a reduction in clearing fees and incentives for brokers who become market makers, though participants say those moves are yet to make a noticeable impact on liquidity. But most of the recent recovery in volumes is attributable to reduced board lot sizes which is helping lift retail participation and help reduce impact costs. That in turn could improve institutional participation and add momentum to the improving daily turnover from the recent lows. It would also give retail investors easier access to blue chips, moving them away from speculative stocks that were at the centre of the penny-stock crash.

But for now, the exchange is relying increasingly on its derivatives business, which recorded a 42% revenue growth in 2015. That was helped by the growth in trading volumes for its China index futures business.

The fixed income segment is also providing reason for cheer and the number of debt securities listed on the exchange has risen to 1,930 at the end-2015 from 1,742 in 2014 and 1,028 in 2010. In an effort to grant retail investors more access to bonds listed on the exchange, the SGX has amended its rules to allow issuers to offer new debt to such investors who can also buy these bonds six months after listing in smaller lots.

The decline in trading activity has forced stock exchanges to look elsewhere for growth with mergers and acquisitions between exchanges on the decline. In 2010, the SGX made an unsuccessful AUD8.40 billion bid for ASX Ltd, the Australian bourse.

The diversification campaign received fresh impetus with SGX acquiring the London-based Baltic Exchange in November 2016. The Baltic Exchange owns benchmark indices for global shipping rates and provides a trading platform for the multi-billion dollar freight derivatives market.

Takeaways

Despite the challenging operating environment, the outlook for the SGX holds promise. As a monopoly operator in Singapore with strong barriers to entry present in the form of regulation, expertise and clientele built over the years, the SGX has evolved into an entity with a dominant business position and a strong financial profile. While the SGX is smaller than its global peers that benefit from being domiciled in large economies or are more acquisitive, its net cash position[1] and a consistent and high dividend paying track record make it an attractive investment proposition for investors seeking recurring returns.

Peer Comparison

USD'Mn, FY2015	SGX	ASX	HKeX	JEG(1)	LSEG(2)	ICE(3)
	FYE Jun 30	FYE Jun 30	FYE 31 Dec	FYE 31 Mar	FYE 31 Dec	FYE 31 Dec
Revenue	578	647	1,578	1,039	3,510	4,682
EBITDA	341	403	1,301	589	1,046	2,124
EBITDA Margin (%)	59%	62%	82%	57%	30%	45%
Net Income	259	300	1,023	401	526	1,295
Net Income Margin (%)	45%	46%	65%	39%	15%	28%
Cash Dividends Paid	223	263	389	244	181	358
Divident Payout Ratio	86%	87%	38%	61%	34%	28%
Debt	—	—	440	289	2,371	7.308
Unrestricted Cash	470	1,482	14,308	591	1,362	627
Net Debt/EBITDA (Times)	Net Cash	Net Cash	Net Cash	Net Cash	0.97	3.15
Market Capitalization*	6,227	5,752	30,863	6,775	14,086	30,495
Current P/E*	23.82	23.74	28.44	16.87	28.05	21.65
Forward Looking P/E*	23.24	22.40	34.79	19.10	23.98	18.95

Market capitalisation as on year end
PE As of 15 July 2016
(1) Japan Exchange Group, Inc.
(2) London Stock Exchange Group plc
(3) Intercontinental Exchange, Inc

Source: Financial Statements of respective stock exchanges and authors' calculations

---

[1] Net cash position implies that a company's unrestricted cash balance exceeds its total debt

The launch of the landmark Stock Connect trading platform between Hong Kong and Shanghai has triggered hopes similar connections could emerge between other regional bourses. A link between stock broking houses in Singapore, Malaysia and Thailand, known as the Association of Southeast Asian Nations (ASEAN) Trading Link, is expected to evolve into a formal connection between the region's exchanges. The SGX has inked a partnership with the Taiwan Stock Exchange in January 2016. Such direct connections between exchanges replace mergers and acquisitions as the industry's growth engines.

There are expectations the exchange could further reduce board lot size and this will continue to support the rebound in daily traded volumes.

Still, growth will hinge on the derivatives business as interest rates normalise and volatility picks up. The exchange is clearly taking advantage of Singapore's premium positioning as a trading centre for energy derivatives, rubber products and iron ore. Singapore accounts for 60% of Asia's commodity derivatives volumes, over half of its credit derivatives trade, 43% of its foreign exchange derivatives volumes and about a third of its interest rate and equity derivatives volume.

10

KEPPEL CORPORATION

Keppel Corporation is a household name in Singapore with strong market positions in three core businesses — offshore and marine, infrastructure and property that employ about 30,000 people from close to 30 countries. But the genesis of Keppel Corporation occurred more than a century before the Port of Singapore Authority corporatised its Dockyard Department to form Keppel Shipyard (Pte) Ltd.

Since the discovery of the harbour in 1819 that ultimately led to the incorporation of the present day Keppel Corporation, the company has been restructured several times and has entered and exited businesses, notably banking. But it has over the years become a global leader in its core business of ship repair and conversion, specialised shipbuilding and offshore rig design, construction and repair. Over the years, Keppel Corporation diversified into infrastructure, property and banking (which it divested) and has built an investment portfolio valued at SGD9.14 billion as of 31 December 2015.

Fraser & Neave (F&N) and Keppel Corporation offer an interesting study in contrasts. Two home grown conglomerates that have professional and competent managements, built strong market positions in their core businesses, generated profits consistently and whose stock generated robust returns have evolved very differently. While F&N's businesses were purchased by overseas companies, Keppel Corporation continues to operate as a Singapore headquartered multinational conglomerate. This chapter and the next explore the reasons for the divergent growth paths of these iconic companies.

Genesis

In 1819, William Farquhar, the first Resident of Singapore reportedly discovered a *"new harbour"* to the west of the settlement which was growing around the Singapore River. In 1848 Captain Henry Keppel who sailed to Singapore aboard the Meander too discovered the sheltered deep-water harbour. He wrote in his diary[1]:

> *"In pulling about in my gig among the numerous prettily wooded islands on the westward entrance to the Singapore river, I was astonished to find deep water close to the shore, with a safe passage through for ships larger than the Meander. Now that steam is likely to come into use this ready-made harbour as a depot for coals would be invaluable. I had the position surveyed, and sent in with my report to the Board of Admiralty; as it was, the forge was landed, and artificers employed under commodious sheds, all under the eyes of the officers on board."*

The Admiralty did not take Captain Henry Keppel's advice but the harbour was eventually developed for shipping and came to be known as The New Harbour. The name remained until 1900, when Keppel now a 92 year old Admiral was on a visit to Singapore. The Acting Governor, Sir Alexander Swettenham, renamed the harbour Keppel to honour him. The road leading to the harbour was named Keppel Road 15 years earlier.

The development of the harbour, triggered by the opening of the Suez Canal in 1869 and the increased use of steam ships since their first appearance in the early 1840s, was the most significant event in mid-19th century Singapore. It fuelled the island's prosperity.

---

[1] "Tough Men Bold Visions: The Story of Keppel" by Richard Lim, downloaded on 5 February 2015 from http://www.kepcorp.com/en/content.aspx?sid=59

Since the founding of Singapore, all commercial activity had been carried out at the Singapore River. Hence there was considerable vessel traffic at the mouth of the river. This situation was exacerbated by the opening of the Suez Canal and the increased use of steam ships, which needed coal. Coal had to be carried to Singapore by sailing vessels, brought ashore in lighters, stored, and then taken out again in lighters when needed. There was no space along the crowded river for a coal depot.

The development of the New Harbour to the south west of the river mouth became inevitable. The deep water close to shore made it easy for the steamers to load and unload their coal and cargoes. Shipping companies, beginning with P&O, moved in to build wharves at New Harbour. As the ship traffic at Singapore increased, the construction of docking facilities was a natural corollary. The two major players in the docking market were the New Harbour Dock Company and the Tanjong Pagar Dock Company. Tanjong Pagar Dock Company gradually acquired all its competitors i.e. the docks and wharves along New Harbour. By the time it merged with the New Harbour Dock Company in July 1899 the Tanjong Pagar Dock Company owned the entire wharf frontage except the P&O wharf.

Evolution

By 1903 the Tanjong Pagar Dock Company monopolised Singapore's port and shipping business and was the seventh largest in the world in terms of shipping tonnage. But the facilities, which had not been developed since 1885, were grossly inadequate; the company's four graving docks could only service small ships, which had to queue for repairs; it lacked modern equipment; and there was no railway to service the docks. The company drew up a SGD12 million modernisation plan, which was rejected by the London-based board. As shipping was of economic importance and a key employment generator in Singapore, the government expropriated the Tanjong Pagar Dock Company in 1905 and transformed it into the publicly owned Tanjong Pagar Dock Board.

The modernisation programme was implemented during the next few years. By 1913, when the board was reconstituted into a corporate statutory body, the Singapore Harbour Board, the upgrading was almost completed. King's Dock, the second largest in the world, was opened later that year, and the Empire Dock was finished in 1917. The peninsular railway linking Johor to Prai was completed in 1909, and the Singapore railway was extended from the harbour to Kranji, opposite Johor Bahru. The port's modernisation coincided with the rapid opening up of Malaya and the world demand for tin and rubber.

The Singapore Harbour Board was one of Singapore's largest employers; its workforce doubled to 7,000 workers in 1939 from 3,500 in 1914. After the end of World War II, another extensive modernisation programme was carried out in 1946. In 1956 the Queen's Dock was inaugurated. With independence, the Port of Singapore Authority (PSA) was set-up to take over the port. The cargo handling and ship repair facilities were separated. The Singapore Drydocks and Engineering Company was formed in August 1968 to take over the Dockyard Department of PSA and was subsequently renamed Keppel Shipyard (Private) Limited.

Please refer to Table 5 in Appendix 1 for the key milestones in Keppel Corporation's evolution.

Business Review

By year-end 2015, Keppel Corporation had grown to a SGD28.92 billion asset conglomerate that generated SGD1.51 billion operating profits. The company manages four businesses — offshore and marine, infrastructure, property and investments. Geographically, 67% of Keppel Corporation's 2015 revenues were generated in Singapore followed by Far East & other ASEAN countries (17%), Brazil (10%), and the rest of the world (6%).

Offshore & Marine (O&M)

The marine and offshore industry is of critical importance to Singapore's economy. Singapore has a 70% market share in the global market for jackup rigs and conversion of Floating Production Storage and Offloading (FPSO) units. This industry employed 75,000 workers in 2011. Output and gross value added stood at SGD12.9 billion and SGD 4.5 billion respectively.

Keppel Offshore & Marine (O&M) is a global leader in offshore rig design, construction and repair, ship repair and conversion, and specialised shipbuilding operating across 20 yards worldwide. The O&M division comprises three unlisted operating entities:

- Keppel FELS is a leading designer and builder of high-performance mobile offshore rigs,
- Keppel Shipyard has a long track record in the repair, conversion and upgrading of a diverse range of vessels. Keppel Shipyard is a leader in the conversion of FPSO, Floating Storage and Offloading and Floating Storage and Re-gasification Units, and
- Keppel Singmarine operates the specialised shipbuilding division and focuses on new buildings of diverse types of ships.

Infrastructure

Keppel Infrastructure (KI) drives the Group's strategy to invest in, own and operate competitive energy and infrastructure solutions and services. In Gas to Power, KI has a track record of developing, owning and operating power plants in Brazil, China, the Philippines and Nicaragua. In Singapore, it operates a 1,300 MW gas fired combined cycle power plant on Jurong Island. Through its subsidiary, Keppel Seghers, its advanced technology solutions addresses a wide spectrum of environmental issues such as solid waste, wastewater, drinking and process water, biosolids and sludge.

Keppel DHCS, a KI subsidiary, is the largest district cooling service provider in Singapore, providing cooling services though the development and operation of such systems at major business parks.

Keppel Infrastructure Trust (KIT) is a listed business trust that provides investors with an opportunity to invest in energy and environmental infrastructure assets. KIT currently owns Senoko

Waste-to-Energy Plant, Keppel Seghers Tuas Waste-to-Energy Plant and Keppel Seghers Ulu Pandan NEWater Plant.

Keppel Telecommunications & Transportation (Keppel T&T) is a leading service provider in the Asia-Pacific region and Europe with businesses in Logistics and Data Centres.

Keppel DC REIT is the first data centre real estate investment trust (DC REIT) to be listed in Asia. It invests in a diversified portfolio of income-producing real estate assets used primarily for data centre purposes, with an initial focus on Asia-Pacific and Europe.

Property

Keppel Land, the property arm of the Keppel Group, is one of the largest[2] full service property companies listed on the Singapore Exchange. It is engaged in the development of residential and office properties and has sponsored two fund management vehicles — Keppel REIT, a pan Asian commercial REIT and Alpha Investment Partners, Keppel Land's wholly owned fund management arm. Keppel Land is a leading prime office developer in Singapore whose landmark developments include Marina Bay Financial Centre, Ocean Financial Centre and One Raffles Quay.

Delisting of Keppel Land

On 23 January 2015, Keppel Corporation launched a voluntary unconditional cash offer to purchase all outstanding shares of Keppel Land, in which it has a 54.6% stake. Keppel Corporation has adopted a two tier price approach to privatize Keppel Land, as detailed below:

- A base offer price of SGD4.38 per share of Keppel Land, and
- A higher offer price of SGD4.60 per Keppel Land share to be paid when Keppel Corporation acquires Keppel Land shares or receives acceptances that will entitle it to exercise its rights of compulsory acquisition under the Companies Act.

---

[2] By total assets

The higher offer price values Keppel Land at SGD7.10 billion and Keppel Corporation's would have to pay investors a maximum sum of SGD3.22 billon to assume full ownership of Keppel Land. Keppel Corporation's consolidated cash balance as of 31 December 2014 was SGD5.74 billion is adequate to fund this purchase. However, the company has funded this acquisition through a combination of cash and debt.

As of 31 March 2015, Keppel Corp acquired a 95.1% stake in Keppel Land. Trading of Keppel Land shares were suspended on 30 March 2015 and Keppel Corp has announced its intention to take Keppel Land private. The remaining shareholders may opt not to sell their shares to Keppel Corp but they would have practically no say in the management of Keppel Land going forward.

The rationale for this acquisition, in the words of Mr. Loh Chin Hua, Chief Executive Officer of Keppel Corporation is:

> *"Through this offer, we will unlock value for Kepcorp shareholders who will see a strong and immediate accretion to Earnings Per Share and Return on Equity. It will also allow Kepcorp to further develop and achieve greater scale for the property business leveraging on the Keppel Group's financial and organisational strengths."*

Secondly, taking Keppel Land private would reduce its exposure to the oil and gas sector, the outlook for which is not very favourable for the next 12 to 18 months and correspondingly increase its exposure to the property business.

Thirdly, the share price of Keppel Land was trading at SGD3.65 per share on 20 January 2015 (on the eve of the announcement), a discount of 62% to its all-time peak price of SGD9.60 per share as of 2 April 2007. Given the government's cooling measures in place and the likelihood of interest rates rising, there is limited upside to Keppel Land's share price in the next 18 to 24 months. Keppel Corporation may be purchasing Keppel Land's shares at a lower price, thereby retaining its option of booking extraordinary gains when the market turns around and the valuation of property stocks improve.

Investments

Keppel Corporation has also built a strategic investment portfolio, which was valued at SGD9.14 billion as of 31 December 2015. Key constituents of this investment portfolio are k1 Ventures, KrisEnergy and M1 Limited (through Keppel T&T). k1 Ventures is a diversified investment company with stakes in companies across key diverse sectors of transportation leasing, education, oil and gas exploration, and automotive retail. KrisEnergy is an independent upstream company focused on the exploration for, and the development and production of oil and gas in Southeast Asia. KrisEnergy has 15 licences in Cambodia, Indonesia, Thailand and Vietnam covering a gross acreage of approximately 56,400 sq km and operates seven of the contract areas.

M1 is an integrated communications service provider in Singapore, with more than 1.7 million customers. It provides a full range of voice and data communications services over its 2G/3G/3.5G network, as well as fixed and mobile broadband. M1 also provides international call services to both mobile and fixed line customers. It has partnered operators globally to provide its customers coverage and roaming services in over 230 countries and territories. In a major restructuring exercise, Keppel Corporation plans to consolidate its interests in business trust management, REIT management and fund management businesses under a wholly-owned unit Keppel Capital. This is expected to increase contribution from this business as it creates a capital recycling platform, allowing it to invest without solely depending on its balance sheet.

Financial Review

During the ten year period 2006 to 2015, Keppel's revenues grew by 35% to SGD10.3 billion in 2015 from SGD7.60 billion in 2006. As seen in Figure 1, Keppel's O&M division continues to be the key revenue driver accounting for over 60% of Keppel's consolidated revenues. Also, while Keppel Corporation continues to be Singapore centric, with Singapore accounting for 67% of consolidated revenues, Far East & ASEAN and Brazil have emerged as the significant revenue generators accounting for 17% and 10% of Keppel's consolidated revenues in 2015 (Figure 1).

Business Wise Revenues

Geographic Composition of Revenues

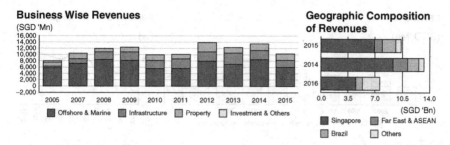

Figure 1

Source: Keppel Corporation's 2006 to 2015 Annual Reports and authors' calculations.

Operating Profit Composition

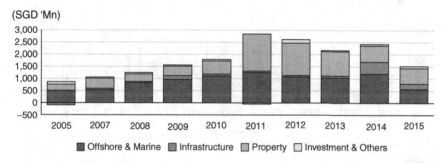

Figure 2

Source: Keppel Corporation's 2006 to 2015 Annual Reports and authors' calculations.

As seen in Figure 2, property accounted for 42% of operating profits, followed by offshore and marine (39%), infrastructure (15%) and investments (4%). The offshore and marine division traditionally used to be the largest contributor to operating profits. In 2015, Keppel's property division emerged as the largest contributor to operating profits both on account of the cyclical downturn in the O&M industry and Keppel Corporation purchasing the 45.4% stake in Keppel Land and delisting Keppel Land. Prior to the delisting, Keppel Corporation held a 54.6% stake in Keppel Land.

Keppel's EBITDA has increased, both in SGD terms and as a percentage of its revenues during the last decade. Notwithstanding the decline in revenues and EBITDA in 2015, Keppel's adjusted EBITDA margin (the sum of EBITDA and dividends as a percentage of revenues) remained healthy at 20% (Figure 3).

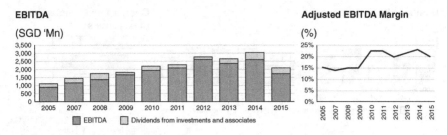

Figure 3

Source: Keppel Corporation's 2006 to 2015 Annual Reports and authors' calculations.

Investments

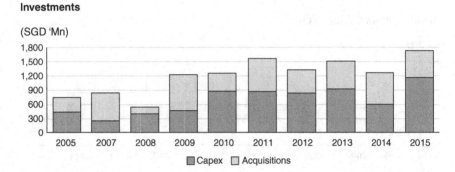

Figure 4

Source: Keppel Corporation's 2006 to 2015 Annual Reports and authors' calculations.

Keppel's businesses are capital intensive in nature and the group since 2009 has incurred over SGD1 billion per annum of capital expenditure and acquisitions (Figure 4).

While Keppel has progressively reduced its dividend payout over the years from a peak of 99% in 2007 to 40% in 2015 (Figure 5), dividend payout continues to be substantial. Investment intensity (the sum of capex and acquisitions as a percentage of revenues) has ranged from 10% to 17% since 2006.

Despite the capital intensive nature of business and sizable dividend payout, Keppel's financial leverage was low, mostly at less than 1.0x till end-2014. The SGD3.0 billion spent on delisting Keppel Land private resulted in cash balance declining to SGD1.89 billion as of end- 2015 from SGD5.74 billion as of end-2014 and a sharp increase in financial leverage to 3.44x as of end-2015 (Figure 6).

Dividend Payout & Investment Intensity

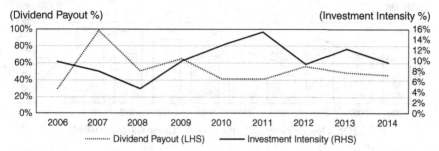

Figure 5

Source: Keppel Corporation's 2006 to 2015 Annual Reports and authors' calculations.

Net Lease Adjusted Debt To EBITDA

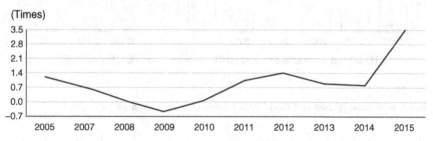

Figure 6

Source: Keppel Corporation's 2006 to 2015 Annual Reports and authors' calculations.

Challenges

The key challenges Keppel Corporation faces are the improving but still low oil prices, the Singapore government's cooling measures targeted at the real estate industry, the likelihood of interest rates rising and the outcome of allegations of paying kickbacks to the Brazilian state-run oil company Petrobras and rig builder Sete Brasil.

The performance of Keppel Corporation's O&M business is closely correlated to crude oil prices. It is only when crude oil prices are at a level that makes crude oil exploration worthwhile does Keppel Corporation secure a robust inflow of contracts. The crude oil supply

O&M Net O&M Order Book & Crude Oil Prices

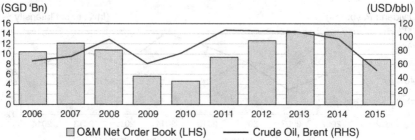

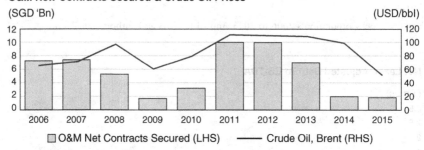

Figure 7

Source: www.kepcorp.com and World Bank Commodity Pink Sheet.

glut coupled with the OPEC maintaining its production has led to a steady and sharp decline in the average annual price of crude oil (Brent) from USD108.86/bbl in 2013 to USD98.94/bbl in 2014 and further to USD52.37/bbl in 2015. This has resulted in a decline in Keppel's net O & M order book and new contracts secured (Figure 7).

The Singapore government's measures cooling measures targeted at reining in the price increase in the property sector coupled with new property launches has resulted in an accumulation of Keppel Land's properties held for sale to SGD6.66 billion by end-December 2015 from SGD1.98 billion as of end-December 2010. It would take some time for this property stock to be liquidated especially since the US Fed's tapering measures would result in a rise in interest rates from the second half of 2016. High interest rates would translate into increased interest expense and lower profits for Keppel Corporation.

In one of Keppel's largest markets outside Singapore i.e. Brazil, a parliamentary commission has ordered enquiry into ten companies including a Keppel FELS Brasil unit for allegations of kickbacks paid to Petrobras and Sete Brasil. Another Singapore corporate, Sembcorp Marine, was also accused of paying bribes to Petrobras. Both Keppel and Sembcorp have denied all charges of corruption. These charges, if proved, would constitute a franchise risk to Keppel.

The first three above-mentioned challenges Keppel Corporation currently faces are a fallout of the inescapable phenomenon of business cycles, several of which the company has weathered. The Group's strong market position in its core businesses, a strong balance sheet, professional management and the advantage of being a Temasek-linked company would enable the company overcome the challenging business environment. Taking a step back and observing the evolution of this century old company offers interesting insights.

Takeaways

Keppel Corporation operates in industries that are of strategic importance to Singapore i.e., offshore & marine and infrastructure and also in property, which is a key driver of Singapore's economy. Hence Temasek Holdings, Keppel Corporation's founding shareholder has treated its stake in the company as a strategic shareholding. Temasek has been Keppel Corporation's single largest shareholder, with a stake consistently in excess of 20% since 2006.

This is in contrast to Temasek's investment in Fraser & Neave, which operated in consumer focused industries such as food& beverage and breweries, in addition to property. F&N was a financial investment which Temasek made when F&N's share price was low in 2008 during the global financial crisis and sold a couple of years later by which time the share price had appreciated considerably.

Another difference between Keppel Corporation and F&N is that F&N built its largest business i.e., brewery, as a joint venture with Heineken. The differences that arose in the joint venture partners' strategies paved the way for Heineken ultimately acquiring F&N's brewery arm, Asia Pacific Breweries (APB). Keppel Corporation, on the other hand, chose to build its flagship business i.e., offshore & marine, in a predominantly organic manner and its acquisitions and joint ventures were not significant enough to acquire Keppel Corporation itself.

A third difference between the two entities, whether by design or accident, is that while F&N's peers in other geographies like Kirin, ThaiBev and Heineken held stakes in F&N/APB at various points of time, Keppel Corporation's key shareholders besides its strategic investor Temasek have been financial investors like asset management companies and high net worth individuals. This contributed to Keppel Corporation's stable ownership structure and facilitated the company in growing a business which was of key importance to Singapore.

11

FRASER & NEAVE

The venerable 133 year old Fraser & Neave (F&N), one of Singapore's oldest companies, is no longer a Straits Times Index (STI) constituent; Hutchison Port Holdings Trust replaced F&N in April 2013. Nevertheless, the evolution of F&N from a single business company selling beverages to Singapore's clubs, hotels and residences to a home grown conglomerate with interests in food & beverage, breweries, real estate and publishing and printing and finally to two distinct entities, that overseas companies own, highlights a few interesting issues.

Firstly, what was the rationale for a successful conglomerate to break up into entities running distinct businesses? Secondly, why did Heineken and TCC choose to purchase the brewery and other businesses of F&N respectively? Thirdly, is F&N's acquisition by foreign companies indicative of Singapore's attractiveness as an investment destination and if so, why?

Genesis

Two Englishmen, John Fraser and David Chalmers Neave, who were partners in a printing business, formed the Singapore and Straits

Aerated Water Company in 1883. The company devoted the next two years to market research before employing a staff of 20 people and embarking on the production and distribution of 'soda water, seltzer water, potassium water, lemonade, tonic and ginger ale' from a factory at Battery Road, Singapore.

The founders were desirous of retiring about fifteen years after starting their aerated water business. In 1898, they formed a new public company christened Fraser & Neave with a capital of SGD350,000 comprising SGD225,000 equity shares and SGD125,000 debentures. The printing and aerated water businesses were sold to F&N for SGD290,000 in cash and shares. F&N issued 2,000 shares, of which 1,500 were offered to the public. F&N's IPO was oversubscribed two and a half times.

Evolution

What began as a single company in 1883 evolved into a large conglomerate with interests in food and beverage, breweries, real estate and publishing by the beginning of the 21st Century. F&N had successfully forged a joint venture (JV) with Holland-based Heineken N.V. to launch its breweries business, secured the Coca-Cola bottling franchise for Singapore and Malaysia, assumed control of the retail chain Cold Storage Holdings jointly with Goodman Felders Watties, acquired stakes in Times Publishing Group and the property company, Centrepoint Limited and launched real estate investment trusts (REITs). F&N had grown so eminent that Lee Hsien Yang, who also served as the Chairman of the Civil Aviation Authority of Singapore, Board Member of the Singapore Exchange, Independent Director of the DBS subsidiary Islamic Bank of Asia and Member of the Governing Board of the Australia and New Zealand Banking Group and is the brother of Singapore's Prime Minister Lee Hsien Loong, was its Non-Executive Director and Chairman from 2007 to 2013.

Please refer to Table 6 in Appendix 1 for the key milestones in F&N's evolution.

By 2008, F&N's shareholders were among the largest banks and financial institutions in ASEAN. OCBC was F&N's largest shareholder with a 20.37% stake as of 30 September 2008.[1] Temasek Holdings acquired a 14.79% stake for SGD900 million, thereby becoming F&N's second largest shareholder. Institutional shareholders held 80.52% of F&N's total outstanding shares, of which the key shareholders besides OCBC and Temasek were the Great Eastern Group and Aberdeen Asset Management.

F&N's businesses were managed by professionals; hence the company's performance continued to improve year on year unaffected by the changes in its shareholding. F&N's market capitalisation as of 30 September 2010 was SGD9.13 billion; a 112% increase over the SGD4.31 billion trough as of 30 September 2008 which reflected the then ongoing global financial crisis. In 2010, Temasek Holdings sold its stake to the Japanese beverage manufacturer, Kirin Holdings for SGD1.33 billion, raking in capital gains of 48% in two years.

The disintegration of the conglomerate F&N occurred in 2012 which was the last year it operated as a conglomerate. F&N's market capitalisation had soared to SGD13.36 billion by 30 September 2012, a growth of 4600% since its IPO 131 years ago. The company deployed assets of SGD14.65 billion, on which it generated revenues and net income of SGD5.57 billion and SGD1.01 billion respectively. Breweries was F&N's largest business accounting for 43.4% of the FY2012 PBIT followed by property development & investment (38.4%), food and non-alcoholic beverage (13.1%) and publishing and printing (5.1%).

It was at this juncture that the Thai billionaire Charoen Sirivadhanabhakdi tried to acquire F&N's stake in Asia Pacific Breweries (APB) in July 2012 but lost out to F&N's joint venture partner, the Dutch brewing major, Heineken NV which purchased F&N's stake in APB for SGD5.6bn in September 2012. By 2012 APB and Heineken had been partners for 81 years. F&N and Heineken had 39.7% and 42% stakes in the SGX listed APB respectively.

---

[1] F&N has a 30 September year ending

The Brewery Business

APB, one of the largest brewers in Asia Pacific with a footprint in 14 markets, had built its business driven mainly by its popular brand 'Tiger Beer'. Heineken, a global brewer that owned the iconic brand 'Heineken' and marketed several brands like Tiger, Anchor, Cristal and Kingfisher, was seeking to capitalise on the high growth Asian markets.

However, APB's and Heineken's strategies were fundamentally different. APB, which was incorporated as Malayan Breweries, had become the market leader in the Singapore and Malaysia beer markets by the end of the 1980s. In 1989, the company embarked on a new international growth strategy under the leadership of General Manager, later CEO, Koh Poh Tiong. Koh compared the company's new strategy to a boxing competition:

> "*Tiger was an amateur fighter. So we thought: forget about countries like Japan and the USA with their heavyweight brands. Let's forget about Europe, but focus on Asia Pacific, a very large area. Let's grow in our own front yard and backyard. Markets like Vietnam, China and Thailand — those fit in our strategy perfectly*".

Heineken operated as a globally integrated company with a presence in all beer sub-markets. According to its 2012 annual report, it was "*the world's most international brewer*", as underscored by this quote:

> "*Wherever you are in the world, you are able to enjoy one of our brands. Our principal global brand is Heineken, the world's most valuable international premium beer brand. In our global portfolio Heineken sits alongside a number of international premium, regional, local and specialty beers and ciders*".

While the relationship between APB and Heineken was mostly positive, there was inherent tension regarding the promotion of the Heineken brand in each of the markets versus Tiger or other local brands. This tension became apparent in the 2006 law suit both companies were engaged in over the appointment of a CEO for their China arm, Heineken-APB China Pte. Ltd (HAPBC). Despite this lawsuit, the partnership between APB and Heineken continued till 2012.

HAPBC had created an extensive sales network in China, which however did not generate much growth or profits. The company went through another reorganisation in 2011, this time focusing on the international premium beer segment. APB divested HAPBC's 49% stake in Jiangsu Dafuhao and ownership of the Shanghai-based brewery. By the end of 2011, Heineken-APB (China) Holdings (HAPBH) had a 100% stake in four breweries in China — Hainan Asia Pacific Brewery, Guangzhou Asia Pacific Brewery, Heineken Trading Shanghai and Heineken-APB Shanghai.

APB had been exporting Tiger Beer to India for almost a decade, which was distributed through premium outlets. In 2008, Asia Pacific Breweries Aurangabad Limited (APBAL) launched locally brewed Tiger Beer in Mumbai, India, after acquiring a stake in a brewery in Aurangabad, Maharashtra. Heineken entered the Indian market through an investment in United Breweries Limited (UBL), in which it bought a 37.5% stake of UBL following a global takeover of Scottish and Newcastle in January 2008. From the beginning, UBL viewed APB as a significant competitor and expressed discontent over the fact that Heineken had parallel market operations in India through APB while being a significant shareholder with UBL. In December 2009, Heineken acquired APBAL from F&N for USD37.14 million and transferred APBAL's operations to UBL.

In July 2012, Charoen's Thai Beverage PLC ("ThaiBev"), Thailand's largest beverage company producing alcoholic and non-alcoholic beverages, offered to buy a 22% stake in F&N, in an effort to expand its presence in the region's beer market. Simultaneously, Kindest Place Groups, owned by the son-in-law of ThaiBev's owner, agreed to take a combined 8.4% stake in APB. At that time, Heineken was already in the process of mapping out its growth strategies in Asia Pacific, and ThaiBev's offer came as potential threat to these ambitions. Heineken responded by bidding for a takeover of APB, offering USD4.07 billion (at USD40 per APB share) to buy F&N's direct and indirect interests in APB as well as USD130 million for

F&N's interest in the non-APB assets held by Asia Pacific Investment Private Limited (APILPL), a 50:50 joint venture between Heineken and F&N.

Shortly after Heineken's announcement, ThaiBev's offered to increase its stake for F&N by an additional 4.2%, taking its total holding to 26.2%. With this move, ThaiBev became the largest shareholder in F&N, threatening Heineken's plan to gain full control over the company. Within days, on August 17, 2012, Heineken raised its offer price to USD4.32 billion for F&N's entire (39.7%) stake in APB and USD130 million for F&N's interest in the non-APB assets held by APIPL. The companies signed a binding agreement to this effect. On September 19, 2012, Heineken acquired all APB shares held by Kindest Place Groups for a total price of USD941.6 million. APB became Heineken's wholly owned subsidiary and was delisted from the SGX in February.

Food & Beverage

Even after F&N's sale of its stake in the APB business, the food and beverage business owned a host of market leading brands including 100PLUS, Ice Mountain, Seasons, Fruit Tree, Magnolia, Daisy, FarmHouse, Nutrisoy, Nutritea and aLIVE. Charoen considered F&N attractive enough to pursue its acquisition. Two of Charoen's companies, TCC Assets Limited and ThaiBev were engaged in a bidding war with the Indonesian billionaire Stephen Riady's Overseas Union Enterprise Limited (OUE) to acquire F&N. The bidding war began when TCC Assets and ThaiBev announced a mandatory conditional cash offer for F&N of SGD8.88 per share, a 4% premium over F&N's 12 September 2012 closing price of SGD8.51; triggered by the combined holding of the two Thai companies reaching 30.36%.

OUE entered the fray on 15 November 2012, making a counter offer of SGD9.08 per share. On 18 January 2013 TCC Assets and Thai Beverage made a counter offer of SGD9.55 per share. OUE withdrew from the race on 21 January 2013, by which time TCC Assets and Thai Beverage controlled 90.28% of F&N. As of

30 September 2013, institutional shareholding (including TCC Assets, Thai Beverage and allied entities) was 94.99%, which reflects the total control the TCC Group has over F&N.

Real Estate

In 1990, F&N acquired SGX-listed Centrepoint Properties Limited, the owner and operator of a single mall on Orchard Road, Singapore — Centrepoint Shopping Centre. This entity was the launch pad for the construction and operation of retail malls, office and residential projects, business parks, serviced residences and REITs in Singapore, Australia, China, United Kingdom, The Philippines and Vietnam.

F&N had delisted Centrepoint Properties Limited from SGX in 2001. In 2006 the company was rebranded as Frasers Centrepoint Limited (FCL) and was relisted on the SGX in 2014. FCL launched its first REIT, Frasers Centrepoint Trust (FCT) which was listed on the SGX in 2006. FCT's principal activity is to invest in income producing retail properties located in Singapore and overseas.

In 2008, FCL acquired a 17.7% stake in Allco Commercial REIT and a 100% stake in Allco Commercial REIT's manager, and rebranded the REIT as Frasers Commercial Trust (FCOT), which was listed on the SGX-ST. FCOT's principal activity, is to invest in income producing commercial office properties located in Singapore and Australia. In October 2013, FCL wholly acquired the Australian property group, Australand Holding Limited (Australand) for AUD2.6 billion (SGD2.46 billion). As of 31 December 2013, FCL's and Australand's total assets stood at SGD11.47 billion and SGD3.39 billion (AUD3.81billion) respectively.

During the ten year period ending 30 September 2014, FCL's assets had more than tripled to SGD16.89 billion from SGD5.08 billion as of 30 September 2005. Its stock price (adjusted for dividends and stock splits) over a period of slightly more than seven years rose by 87% to SGD2.02 per share as of 23 January 2015 from SGD1.08 per share as of 6 November 2007, translating into an average annual return of 12.1%.

FCL's success story highlights the prerequisites for success in cyclical real estate industry i.e., strong in-house property development capabilities across key real estate sub-markets including residential, retail, office and hospitality, a geographically diversified and granular portfolio, execution of successful acquisitions and importantly the backing of financially sound controlling shareholders, initially F&N and subsequently TCC.

Publishing

F&N acquired its founders' printing issues at the time of its initial listing in 1898. It then acquired a 20.1% stake Times Publishing in 1995 and progressively increased it to a majority stake by 2000. Times Publishing was delisted from the SGX in 2001. The printing business has been consistently profitable, with its PBIT growing in absolute terms. But its share in F&N's PBIT stands at a miniscule 1.2% in FY2013 on account of the higher growth registered by the food & beverage and property businesses. The group initiated a sale process of its publishing arm after a strategic review in June 2008. But the plan was shelved after the collapse of Lehman Brothers soured market conditions.

The market capitalization[2] of Fraser & Neave Limited and Frasers Centrepoint Limited are SGD4.09 billion and SGD5.04 billion respectively aggregating SGD9.13 billion, which is 32% lower than the peak financial year-end market capitalization of SGD13.36 billion as of 30 September 2012. The reduction was also due to S$5.3 billion returned to shareholders in 2013 and 2014. F&N is now smaller than when it operated as a conglomerate but its development over the years offers food for thought.

Takeaways

A review of F&N's evolution from 1898 to date offers insights into why the conglomerate disintegrated. One possible reason could be

---

[2] As of 27 January 2015.

that the business model of its major business i.e. brewery was built with a JV partner, Heineken, whose global growth strategy was diametrically opposite to F&N's regional growth strategy.

A second reason could be the absence of a promoter family holding a controlling stake in the company, which had two consequences. One, the company's strategy was shaped and spearheaded by high calibre professionals and this translated into consistent growth and profits. Second, a history of key shareholders like Temasek and Kirin treating their stakes in F&N as a portfolio investment as opposed to a strategic long term investment made it easier for TCC to fulfil its aspiration of becoming a regional food and beverage giant by acquiring a 94.99% stake in F&N.

Thirdly, foreign companies like Heineken, Kirin and TCC acquiring stakes in Singapore companies are becoming increasingly common. In July 2013 Swiss chocolate makes Barry Callebaut acquired Singapore-based Petra Foods for SGD1.09mn (USD860mn). The Asian Legal Insider dated 11 January 2015 states that foreign acquisitions of Singapore companies tripled from 2011 to SGD27.2 billion in 2014.

According to Ng Wai King, partner at Wong Partnership, sound governance and management practices, clear and predictable rules, regulations and legislation and less likelihood of fraud drive overseas interest in Singapore companies. Ng also stated:

"Another aspect is that Singapore companies have the benefit of taking advantage of the incentives and tax framework that companies here enjoy. So what it means is that a lot of companies are bought up in Singapore with the plan to have operating subsidiaries overseas. So when you're buying a Singapore company, you're not just buying a Singapore business, you're buying a business across the region."

12

SEMBCORP INDUSTRIES

The STI's constituents include four engineering companies — Sembcorp Industries ("Sembcorp"), its 61% subsidiary Sembcorp Marine, SIA Engineering and ST Engineering. Sembcorp is involved in utilities, developing, owning and operating energy and water assets; and urban development. Sembcorp Marine is a leading global marine and offshore engineering group, focussed on four key capabilities: rigs & floaters; repairs & upgrades; offshore platforms and specialised shipbuilding.

SIA Engineering is an aircraft maintenance, repair and overhaul (MRO) company providing total maintenance solutions to international airlines. ST Engineering provides aerospace, electronics, land systems and marine solutions and services to government, commercial, industrial and in particular defence customers.

Sembcorp attractiveness to a potential investor stems from not just its strong business and financial position but also the fact that its handsome stocks return generated in the last ten years. The company differentiates itself from other companies in which Temasek has a majority stake in that its dividend payout has been mostly moderate during the period 2005 to 2015, ranging from 30% to 40%.

Genesis and Evolution

Sembcorp Industries was incorporated in 1998. Currently, Temasek owns a 49.5% stake in Sembcorp with the latest filing showing that about 80% of the company's issued share capital was owned by institutional investors. It has today become an established provider of essential energy and water solutions to both industrial and municipal clients. Some also consider the company a world leader in marine and offshore engineering and a well-recognised name in urban development (consisting of industrial parks as well as business, commercial and residential space) in Vietnam, China and Indonesia.

Please refer to Table 7 in Appendix 1 for the key milestones in Sembcorp's evolution.

Business Review

Utilities

Sembcorp's wholly owned subsidiary Sembcorp Utilities operates in energy, water and on-site logistics and solid waste management segments of utilities services. It has a presence in 50 locations across the world.

Energy: Ever since Sembcorp set-up Singapore's first privately-developed independent power in 2001, it has grown to control power capacity of over 10,000 megawatts in 9 countries across Asia driven by both conventional and renewable sources. It has a presence in the 50 locations across the world. Over the next three years a total of 3,700 MW of power generating capacity will be commissioned in both thermal and renewable energy units in China, India, Singapore, Myanmar, United Kingdom and Bangladesh. The renewable energy units are based on wind power and energy-from-waste.

Water: Sembcorp possesses management capacity of close to nine million cubic meters per day and serves locations in five continents with a range of services from supply of potable and industrial water to specialised industrial wastewater treatment, water reclamation and desalination.

On-site logistics and solid waste management: The Company has built on its energy and water expertise to offer add-on services in a bundled offering to clients in energy intensive industrial segments like petrochemical and chemical hubs. The services include service corridor, asset protection and hazardous waste incineration services.

Marine

This business is conducted through its 61% subsidiary Sembcorp Marine Ltd which offers integrated marine and offshore engineering that includes services such as ship repair, shipbuilding, ship conversion, rig building & repair to offshore engineering & construction. It has strategically located shipyards in Singapore, India, Indonesia, the United Kingdom and Brazil. Broadly the company's turnover is driven by rig building, offshore & conversion/fixed platform, repairs and other services. The biggest revenue contributor is the rigs and floaters business, which has been consistently accounting for two-thirds of revenue, with offshore business being the second highest revenue contributor. The order book position of SGD10.4 billion stretching out to 2020.

Urban Development

The company has a track record over 20 years in master planning, land preparation and infrastructure development to transform raw land into urban developments. This has translated into urban developments like industrial parks and other business, commercial and residential properties in Vietnam, China and Indonesia. This unit plays a vital role in supporting the industrialisation and urbanisation of some of the fastest growing economies in the region, since it is key to attracting local and international investments. To that extent accessibility to ports and airports and plug-and-play concept has been critical for the success of Sembcorp's projects.

Financial Review

During the eleven year period (2005 to 2015), Sembcorp' revenues have grown by 28% to SGD9.55 billion in 2015 (Figure 1), with the utilities and marine businesses contributing to 96% of total revenues.

Revenue Composition

(SGD 'Mn)

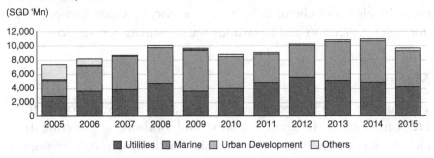

Figure 1

Source: Sembcorp Financial Statements and authors' calculations.

Segment-wise Profit From Operations

(SGD 'Mn)

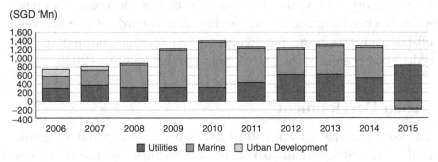

Figure 2

Source: Sembcorp Financial Statements and authors' calculations.

Sembcorp's urban development business is small in relation to its utilities and marine businesses, accounting for less than 1% of revenues. Revenues peaked to SGD10.89 billion in 2014 before declining by 12% in 2015 due to the cyclical downturn in the marine industry.

The marine and utilities divisions historically accounted for almost all of Sembcorp's profit from operations, which has stagnated since FY11 mirroring the stagnation in revenues (Figure 2). In 2015 the marine division reported SGD342 million operating losses. This resulted in a halving of consolidated profit from operation to SGD631 million in 2015 from SGD1.30 billion in 2014.

EBITDA

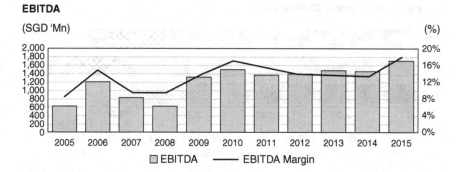

Figure 3
Source: Sembcorp Financial Statements and authors' calculations.

Marine Orderbook

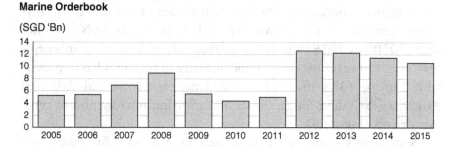

Figure 4
Source: Sembcorp Financial Statements and authors' calculations.

EBITDA margin however improved to 18% in 2015 from 13% in 2014 due to the SGD370 million under significant items such as gain reported on sale of subsidiaries including its 40% stake in SembSita Pacific, Sembcorp Bournemouth Water Investment and 51% stake in Zhumadian China Water Company Limited (Figure 3).

Global macroeconomic uncertainty coupled with major oil and gas companies announcing reductions in their capital expenditures and crude oil prices declining since the second half of 2014 have resulted in a year-on-year decline in Sembcorp's marine order book position since 2013 (Figure 4).

Geographic Composition Of Revenues

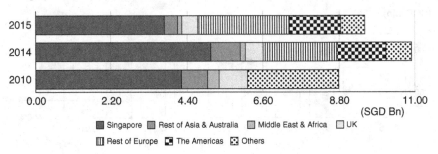

Figure 5

Source: Sembcorp Financial Statements and authors' calculations.

Singapore continues to be Sembcorp's largest contributor to revenues, accounting for approximately half of Sembcorp's revenues since 2010. In 2015, Singapore accounted for 39% of Sembcorp's revenues. However the geographic diversity of revenues has improved with Europe (33% in 2015), The Americas (16%) and Asia and Australia (excluding Singapore at 4%) evolving into significant revenue drivers (Figure 5).

Sembcorp's investments have risen by around 3.5x since 2005 (Figure 6). Investment intensity i.e. the sum of capital expenditures and equity investments expressed as a percentage of revenues, increased to 22% in 2015 from 6% in 2005. The company maintained a moderate dividend payout so that borrowings raised to fund debt are kept under control (Figure 7).

Hence, financial leverage, as defined by the ratio of net debt to EBITDA and net lease adjusted debt[1] to EBITDA, has been consistently low at less than 1.0x till year-end 2013. In certain years Sembcorp

---

[1] Net debt is total borrowings less cash. Net lease adjusted debt is the sum of net debt and the debt equivalent of leases. The debt equivalent of leases is computed by multiplying lease rentals by a factor of eight, a standard industry practice. In Sembcorp's case, the values of net debt and net lease adjusted debt are quite close as the company tends to purchase assets i.e. incur capital expenditure rather than lease them.

Investments

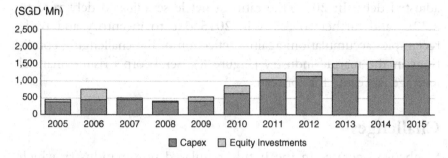

Figure 6

Source: Sembcorp Financial Statements and authors' calculations.

Dividend Payout & Capex & Equity Investment Intensity

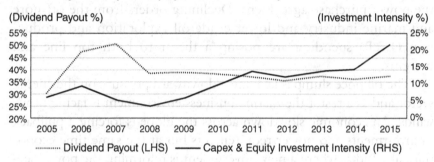

Figure 7

Source: Sembcorp Financial Statements and authors' calculations.

Financial Leverage

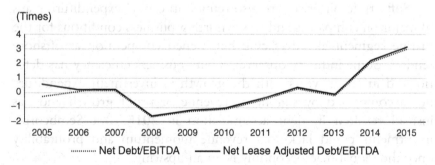

Figure 8

Source: Sembcorp Financial Statements and authors' calculations.

has been in a net cash position i.e., its cash balance exceeded its lease adjusted debt. In 2014, the ratio of net lease adjusted debt rose to 2.32x and further to 3.22x in 2015 due to inventory and trade receivables accumulation; again a reflection of the challenging conditions in the marine industry (Figure 8). Sembcorp's rising financial leverage is a cause for concern.

Challenges

Sembcorp operates in the highly regulated power industry which depends on the regulatory environment in most countries of operations. In jurisdictions like India, where significant capacities are to go on stream, there are concerns such as supply of coal and around the power purchase agreement. Declining orders from the offshore and marine industry and lower crude oil exploration and production (E&P) spending are posing a threat to both top line and margins.

The oil price slump is keeping a downward pressure on the energy sector and as a result the marine business environment is facing headwinds. An economic slowdown across the globe is forcing a pullback in investments and power requirements but at the same time economies like India, where a new government is reforming the power sector, and China, where environmental protection and market forces are being prioritised, will present opportunities. These difficult conditions are already reflected in margin strains.

Soft crude oil prices are also reining in capital expenditure plans of major oil companies and this is hurting business conditions for the marine segment already facing heightened competition at offshore tenders. Some industry observers opine business efficiency has deteriorated in recent years with the growth in investment expenditure not accompanied by significant revenue or profit growth and has instead resulted in debt accumulation in 2015. But Sembcorp's investments could kick-start revenue momentum and profitability once the global macroeconomy is on an upswing.

Takeaways

Sembcorp has major capacities going on-stream till 2018 which will see the addition of 3,700 MW to the power generating capacity and 1.3 million cubic metres per day to the water and waste water treatment capacity.

A key factor to watch is the shift in the utilities dynamics, as the non-Singapore power generation capacities exceed those at home giving greater stability to margins in that business. However, greater revenue contributions from new jurisdictions like India (power) and Brazil (rig-building) could lead to some margin variations.

The weakness in the offshore and marine industry and soft oil prices are posing near term challenges for the marine segment but the order book despite the decline is sizable offering visibility to revenues till 2020. Sembcorp's geographic and business prospects support its long term business growth. Overall emerging market's oil demand is estimated to double in the next 10 years, which would boost capital expenditure on oil exploration benefitting players like Sembcorp.

Sembcorp's utilities business continues to build on its developer, owner and operator model to execute large-scale greenfield energy and water projects, growing its presence in emerging markets and water-stressed regions. Its marine business has diversified its product mix, extending its services to segments such as drillships and semi-submersible crane vessels, while staying abreast of new technology solutions. As the company positions itself for the long haul, its efforts are seen bearing fruit in the years to come and thus may not be attractive for traders who hope to make quick profits, especially in this environment.

13

SINGAPORE TECHNOLOGIES ENGINEERING LIMITED

Singapore Technologies Engineering Limited ("ST Engineering") is an integrated engineering company specialising in solutions and services for the aerospace, electronics, land systems and marine sectors. The company has grown to become one of Asia's largest defence and engineering groups. Asia continues to be ST Engineering's largest market accounting for 58% of 2014 revenues, followed by USA (23%), Europe (5%) and other countries (14%). ST Engineering's commercial customers contribute to 64% of its revenues while defence customers make up the balance 36%.

ST Engineering's stock has long been considered a defensive stock i.e. product demand does not fluctuate significantly across business cycles given the essential nature of solutions and services it offers to its customers, particularly its defence customers. This is evident from ST Engineering's order book that has been growing for most part of the last 11 years (2005 to 2015). However characteristic of defensive companies, the stock returns are also lower than companies whose performance is highly correlated to business cycles.

This chapter analyses the company's growth during the past decade and explores how the industry developments are likely to impact its performance going forward.

Genesis

This Singapore-based company was founded on 27 January 1967 as Chartered Industries of Singapore (CIS), to manufacture 5.56 millimetre ammunition rounds for the M-16 rifles the Singapore Armed Forces (SAF) were to use. Its factory at Jalan Boon Lay was inaugurated on 27 April 1968. CIS and a number of defence-related companies created during the 1970s were grouped under holding company Sheng-Li in 1974. Sheng-Li was renamed Singapore Technologies in 1990 and was acquired by Temasek Holdings in 1994.

Temasek Holdings is ST Engineering's single largest shareholder, with a stake of about 50% at year-end 2014. Excluding Temasek Holdings, other institutional investors held about 30% of the Group's shares, with retail investors holding the rest.

Please refer to Table 8 in Appendix 1 for the key milestones in ST Electronics' evolution.

Business Review

Since its modest beginning 48 years ago, the company has grown into a SGD8.17 billion conglomerate with a global network of 100 subsidiaries and associated companies in 46 cities across 24 countries. Its sprawling network is manned by an army of around 23,000 employees with operations in Americas, Europe, Asia and Oceania. By geography, Asia accounted for 74% of group revenue, the US businesses contributed 24% and the share of Europe remained low at 1% in the 2014.

The company's businesses include solutions and services in the Aerospace, Electronics, Land Systems and Marine sectors.

Aerospace

The aerospace sector of ST Engineering operates a global MRO network with facilities and affiliates in the Americas, Asia Pacific and Europe. It is the world's largest commercial airframe MRO provider with a global customer base that includes leading airlines, airfreight and military operators. The integrated service provider offers a spectrum of maintenance and engineering services that include airframe, engine and component maintenance, repair and overhaul; engineering design and technical services; and aviation materials and asset management services, including Total Aviation Support.

Electronics

The Electronics sector specialises in the design, development and integration of advanced electronics and communications systems. Its capabilities are in Rail & Intelligent Transportation; Satellite & Broadband Communications; Info Comm Technologies; Command & Control operations, Training & Simulation; Intelligent Building & Security Systems and Cybersecurity.

With extensive experience and global track record, its Smart Solutions have helped many cities in their "Smart" journey in several key verticals, namely: Community, Environment, Mobility, Safety & Security and Connectivity. Given rapid urbanisation globally, there will be much opportunity and demand by the government and commercial sectors for greater Smart Solutions to create even more Smart Cities worldwide.

Land Systems

The land systems sector delivers integrated land systems, specialty vehicles and their related through life support for defence, homeland security and commercial applications. Marine segment provides turnkey building, repair and conversion services for a wide spectrum of naval and commercial vessels. In the defence area it focuses on markets like Brazil and Singapore while pursuing contracts globally. In the construction equipment business it is putting greater emphasis on expanding international sales in emerging markets in the African continent, Latin America and Asia. ST Engineering is banking on the development in the Western and Central parts of China which is expected to herald the next wave of large-scale construction and development activity in the country.

Orderbook

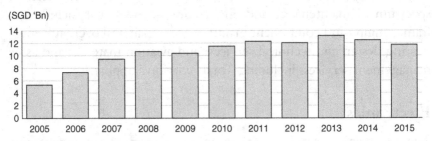

Figure 1

Source: ST Engineering Annual Reports and authors' calculations.

Marine

The marine sector provides turnkey building, repair and conversion services for a wide spectrum of naval and commercial vessels. In shipbuilding, it has the proven capabilities to provide turnkey solutions from concept definition to detailed design, construction, on-board system installation and integration, testing, commissioning to through-life support. It has also established a track record in providing high engineering content shiprepair and ship conversion services for a worldwide clientele. ST Marine also provides a suite of sustainable environmental engineering solutions via its environmental engineering subsidiaries led by STSE Engineering Services Pte Ltd (STSE).

As mentioned in the introductory section, ST Engineering's thus far defensive business underpinned the rapid growth of its order book until year-end 2013. But a challenging business environment in Europe and the weakness in the specialty vehicles business in China resulted in a two consecutive years of shrinkage in the order book to SGD11.70 billion, as indicated in Figure 1. ST Engineering's order book shrunk by 11% since 2013.

Financial Review

ST Engineering's revenues almost doubled to SGD6.34 billion during the eleven year period 2005 to 2015 (Figure 2). However, revenues

Revenue Composition

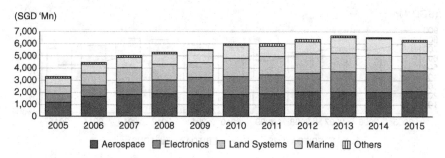

Figure 2

Source: ST Engineering Annual Reports and authors' calculations.

Composition Of Profit From Operations

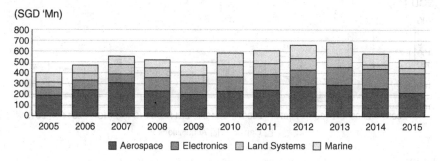

Figure 3

Source: ST Engineering Annual Reports and authors' calculations.

have been declining, albeit marginally, since 2013 reflecting the lower order book. The company's business is diversified with the aerospace division accounting for 33% of consolidated revenues in 2015, followed by electronics (28%), land systems (22%) and marine (16%).

But the aerospace division drives the company's profitability, accounting for 44% of the 2015 profit from operations (Figure 3), followed by electronics (35%), marine (14%) and land system and others (7%).

ST Engineering's EBITDA margin has been on a downward trend both in SGD terms and as a percentage of revenues. EBITDA

EBITDA

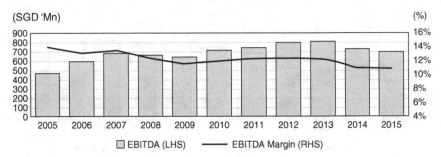

Figure 4
Source: ST Engineering Annual Reports and authors' calculations.

Investments

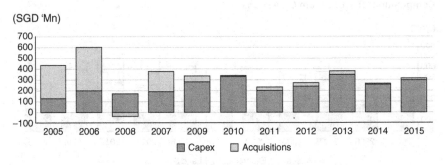

Figure 5
Source: ST Engineering Annual Reports and authors' calculations.

margin declined from a peak of 14% in 2007 to 11% in 2015 (Figure 4), which is a cause for concern.

ST Engineering's investments i.e. the sum of capital expenditure and acquisitions, has shrunk in monetary terms over the years (Figure 5).

Investment intensity i.e. investments expressed as a percentage of revenues has also declined from a peak of 13% in 2005 to a mere 5% in 2015. The company's dividend payout continues to be high, though it has declined to about 88% in 2015 from a peak of almost 100% in 2005 (Figure 6).

The decline in investment intensity and dividend payout, coupled with the non-deployment of the SGD716.65 million bond proceeds

Dividend Payout & Investment Intensity

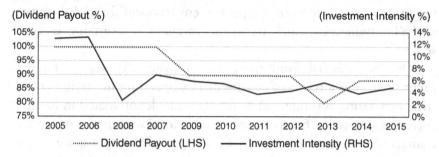

Figure 6

Source: ST Engineering Annual Reports and authors' calculations.

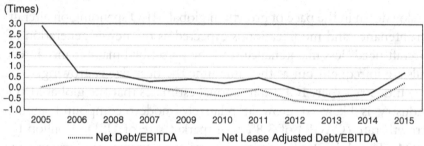

Figure 7

Source: ST Engineering Annual Reports and authors' calculations.

it raised in 2009, has enabled the company to reduce its financial leverage i.e. the ratio of its net lease adjusted debt to EBITDA. ST Engineering, whose financial leverage was moderate at 2.88x in 2005 was in a net cash position i.e. its cash exceeded its debt, in 2014 (Figure 7). In 2015 financial leverage was low but rose to 0.78x due to higher working capital consumption.

Challenges

The global defence market remains difficult with shrinking budgets, and the budget sequestration in the US will only further add surplus capacity. In such conditions many governments are looking to domestic producers, intensifying the competitive environment for global players like ST Engineering, 36% of whose revenues is from the defence sector.

On the financial front the Group remains exposed to foreign exchange risk as a result of its subsidiaries operating in foreign countries, generating revenue and incurring costs denominated in foreign currencies, as well as from operations of its local subsidiaries which are transacted in foreign currencies. Challenges to the Aerospace sector are issues relating to aviation safety, geopolitical risks, health scares and economic growth prospects in China and Europe.

Takeaways

A slowdown in the pace of growth in global MRO spending on aircraft maintenance and modification is expected as the newer generation of aircraft needs less maintenance, and the prescribed maintenance intervals are infrequent but at the same time the fleet size is growing.

Industry expert ICF International estimates that the global MRO industry is likely to grow at relatively modest compound annual growth rate (CAGR) of 3.8% to a market size of USD90 billion by 2024. The Asia Pacific region is projected to fuel this growth by expanding to USD29.2 billion in the next decade.

Growing urbanisation presents opportunities for intelligent transportation for its electronics sector. The sector's Rail Electronics, Intelligent Transportation Systems, fleet management solutions enable cities to move people around efficiently and safely. Emerging countries like China would be building more metro lines to cope with their increasing urban population. Developed countries like the USA, would be looking to upgrade their existing metro systems. In Singapore, the government is continuing to expand MRT capacity. More maintenance/ upgrade is likely to happen.

ST Engineering is well-poised to capitalise on the growth opportunities Asia offers. But it remains to be seen whether the industry environment will support the company's continued expansion.

14

SIA ENGINEERING COMPANY

SIA Engineering Company ("SIA Engineering"), the smallest of the three engineering companies that constitute the STI, provides aircraft maintenance, repair and overhaul (MRO), and is a good example of how the geographically central location of Singapore can be leveraged in the Asia Pacific region whose growth is set to accelerate and propel global growth in the coming years.

Investors who wish to gain an exposure to the aviation sector without the accompanying risks of fuel costs and passenger load factor would find SIA Engineering's stock attractive.

Genesis and Evolution

SIA Engineering Company (SIA Engineering) is a subsidiary of Singapore Airlines (SIA), which holds a 77.52% stake in the company. International funds like Matthews International Capital Management, Seafarer Capital Partners LLC, The Vanguard Group Inc. and Dimensional Fund Advisors LP are some of its other major shareholders owning less than 7% stake in aggregate, according to Thomson Reuters data.

The erstwhile engineering division of SIA was hived off as a separate company in 1992. It was listed on the Singapore Exchange in 2000 following an IPO with the stated purpose of allowing the company to be more independent and grow faster than if it had remained fully owned by SIA.

Please refer to Table 9 in Appendix 1 for the key milestones in SIA Engineering's evolution.

Business Review

SIA Engineering's services can be broadly divided into aircraft & component overhaul, fleet management and line maintenance services. The aircraft maintenance, repair, and overhaul industry was the result of airlines' strategy of committing technicians lying idle between in-house jobs, to performing third-party contracted repairs. The airlines were motivated by the prospect of drawing profits and productivity out of an underutilised resource.

The company offers maintenance, repair and overhaul of aircraft; engines and related components with services include airframe maintenance and overhaul, line maintenance and technical handling, component maintenance and overhaul, fleet management program, engine overhaul, passenger-to-freighter conversion, cabin modifications and training academy. The Singapore-headquartered company also has operations in Australia, China, Indonesia, Ireland, the Philippines, Taiwan, the US and Vietnam, with 25 joint ventures and subsidiaries. The SIAEC Group provides extensive maintenance, repair and overhaul (MRO) of aircraft to more than 80 international airlines worldwide. With certifications from more than 20 airworthiness authorities, SIAEC's six hangars and 22 in-house workshops in Singapore provide complete MRO services in airframe, component, engine, aircraft conversions and modifications to major airlines from four continents.

Revenues, EBITDA and EBITDA margin have been declining since FY2013[1] because the new generation aircraft need lesser maintenance but this is set to change in the long term. In the medium term, however, the sluggish trend is likely to be sustained as most

---

[1] SIA Engineering's year ending is on 31 March

major carriers in Asia, including Singapore Airlines, operate young aircraft fleets that moderate fuel expenses and maintenance costs.

"*Advancements in the newer generation engines have improved their reliability while the older generation engines are being phased out. These developments will continue to result in a reduction in engine shop visits in the next few years,*" the company stated during its 2014–2015 earnings release. Still the number of airplanes in the region is rapidly rising so the demand for maintenance will grow sharply in the long term.

Minimal maintenance costs thus means expanding intervals between checks and the current decline in workshop visit frequency is expected to continue in the near future. The company is using this opportunity to retrain its labour force to equip them with cross functional skills thereby improving workforce allocation efficiency.

The maintenance, repair and overhaul (MRO) industry is expected to see Asia Pacific displace North America as the biggest region in the world with a growth that is outpacing all the other markets. According to Frost & Sullivan, Asia Pacific is currently the third largest market (USD12.57 billion) after North America (USD18.55 billion) and Europe (USD13.53 billion) While the global MRO market is projected to grow at 3.9% CAGR in the next 7 years, the Asia Pacific is projected to grow at 5.7% CAGR during the same period to become the largest MRO region by value (USD23.14 billion) by 2022 (Figure 1).

SIA Engineering signed a joint venture with Boeing in 2015 to provide engineering, materials management and fleet support solutions for Boeing aircrafts. The joint venture company Boeing Asia Pacific Aviation Services, 49 percent owned by SIA Engineering, will help SIA Engineering expand its maintenance, repair, and operations business over the longer term.

Financial Review

Singapore Airlines is SIA Engineering's major customer accounting for 69% of the company's revenues and 44% of the subsidiaries

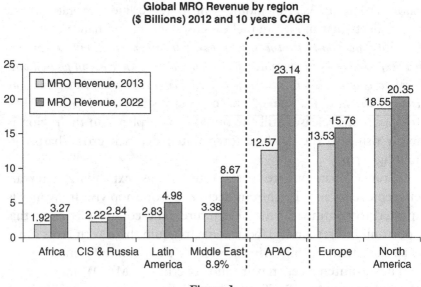

Figure 1

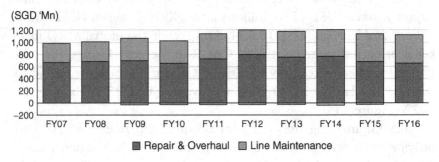

Figure 2

Source: SIA Engineering Annual Reports, Interim Financial Statements and authors' calculations.

revenues in FY16. However, Singapore Airlines accounted for just 21% of SIA Engineering's associates and joint ventures revenues.

SIA Engineering's revenue growth has been lower than Sembcorp Industries' and ST Engineering's revenue growth at just 16% over a 11-year period 1 April 2005 to 31 March 2016 (Figure 2). During the last decade the share of the repair and overhaul division's revenues

Revenue Composition

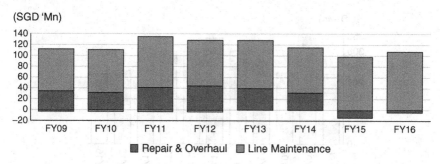

Figure 3

Source: SIA Engineering Annual Reports, Interim Financial Statements and authors' calculations.

in total revenues has declined from 68% in FY07 to 59% in FY16, while the share of the line maintenance division's revenues has correspondingly increased to 41% in FY15 from 32% in FY07.

But SIA Engineering's line maintenance business is its more profitable business, as indicated by the operating profits of the two divisions (Figure 3).

An interesting aspect of SIA Engineering's business is that in addition to the MRO business it owns, it also has stakes in 26 joint ventures in nine countries. So in addition to EBITDA, SIA Engineering earns a steady stream of dividends from its associates and joint ventures (Figure 4). Dividends grew by 1.65x to SGD157.55 million in FY14 from SGD59.16 million in FY06, before halving to SGD78.57 million in FY16 (Figure 4). Despite the decline, dividend income continue to be sizable and serve to augment SIA Engineering's cash flows and liquidity. Does this mark the transition of SIA Engineering from a MRO operator to holding company with investments in MRO across the globe? Only time will tell.

Figure 5 indicates the adjusted EBITDA margin, which is the sum of EBITDA and dividends expressed as a percentage of revenues, declining since FY14 on account of the newer and technologically advanced fleets that require lesser maintenance.

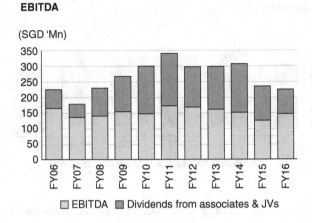

Figure 4

Source: SIA Engineering Annual Reports, Interim Financial Statements and authors' calculations.

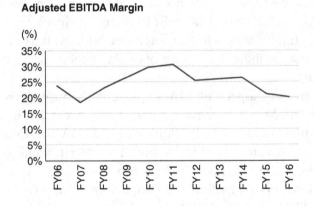

Figure 5

Source: SIA Engineering Annual Reports, Interim Financial Statements and authors' calculations.

SIA Engineering's investments, consisting of capital expenditure and acquisitions, have been modest in relation to its scale of operations (Figure 6).

The low investment intensity has enabled the company pay high dividends (Figure 7) and also accumulate sizable deposits, most of

Investments

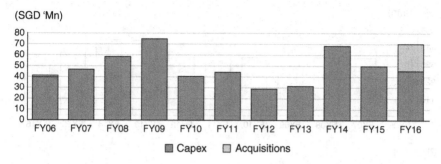

Figure 6

Source: SIA Engineering Annual Reports, Interim Financial Statements and authors' calculations.

Dividend Payout & Investment Intensity

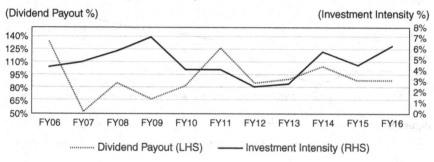

Figure 7

Source: SIA Engineering Annual Reports, Interim Financial Statements and authors' calculations.

which are placed with Singapore Airlines and are interest earning (Figure 8).

SIA Engineering's financial leverage is low though the company has transitioned to a net debt position (debt exceeds cash; excluding the deposits placed with SIA) from a net cash position (cash exceeding debt) since 2011. SIA started entering into large operating lease contracts since 2011 and this resulted in still low but rising financial leverage (Figure 9).

Deposits Placed With Singapore Airlines

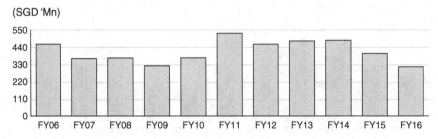

Figure 8

Source: SIA Engineering Annual Reports, Interim Financial Statements and authors' calculations.

Net Lease Adjusted Debt To EBITDA

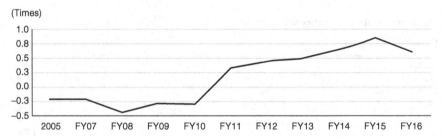

Figure 9

Source: SIA Engineering Annual Reports, Interim Financial Statements and authors' calculations.

Challenges

The operating environment is challenging in the near term as airlines extend maintenance cycles amidst financial difficulties and overcapacity in the region. The company has warned about reduced engine shop visits due to improved reliability of newer generation engines and the phase-out of older generation engines. Singapore's high labour costs and inflationary pressures will exert some stress on the company's profit margins.

Also depressing SIA Engineering's profitability is the negative carry on account of the sizable deposits earning returns (interest income) that are lower than the returns from its core business. The company must explore avenues to minimize the negative carry.

A few of the company's joint ventures are targeting older models for the engine repair business and their phase-out will impact SIA Engineering's business. The fact that the company has businesses in several countries laid out under various subsidiaries and joint ventures, raises the risk of currency mismatches since the revenues and expenses could be in different currencies. This is an important issue since associates and joint ventures comprise a third of its EBITDA. The sector is exposed to regulatory risk but given the strategic importance of the airline business, it is unlikely there could be any adverse regulations.

Takeaways

While the current operating environment is sluggish, this industry has high barriers to entry and the oligopolistic market structure provides firms have little incentive to engage in price wars. SIA Engineering is ideally positioned to capitalize on long term opportunities given its locational advantage. It is well positioned to benefit from its strong market position; it has the highest market share of capacity and traffic in Asia Pacific region, a region whose growth rate is expected to outpace global growth.

With increasing cost pressures, North American and European suppliers are shifting to lower-cost regions such as Asia Pacific, South America, and Eastern Europe. The fleet management joint venture with Boeing, and recent agreements with Airbus and Singapore Airlines are some of the initiatives that will enhance long term earnings.

SIA Engineering has been at the forefront of the industry because of its preparedness to handle Singapore Airlines' modern fleet. This gives it a head-start to independently pursue business opportunities outside the scope of the parent airline's carrier business.

15

THE GAMING DUOPOLY

"The gambling known as business looks with austere disfavour upon the business known as gambling."

Ambrose Bierce (1842 to circa 1914)

American literary personality, Ambrose Bierce, would have been a very happy man had he witnessed the Singapore Government herald organised and remunerative gaming on the island while simultaneously curbing its adverse socio-economic effects.

As a city state with a strong location advantage but with minimal natural resources and the absence of an expansive and scenic country side, Singapore has always adopted a forward looking view to retain and strengthen its relevance in the global business, cultural and tourist map. The city organises a host of annual and biennial events including ComunicAsia, FormulaOne Grand Prix, Women's Tennis Association Championships, the Singapore Airshow, Food & Hotel Asia and WasteMET Asia to sustain and accelerate its inbound visitor arrivals.

According to the World Tourism Organization (UNWTO), Asia Pacific attracted an estimated 263.3 million tourists (23.2% of the 1.13 billion of the global tourist traffic) in 2014 (Figure 1). Singapore spanning an area of 716 km² is the fourth largest tourist destination in Asia Pacific accounting for 6.2% of Asia Pacific's tourist arrivals

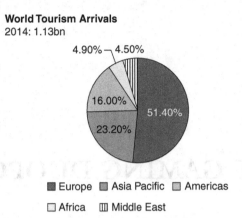

Figure 1

Source: World Tourism Organization, UNWTO Tourism Highlights 2015.

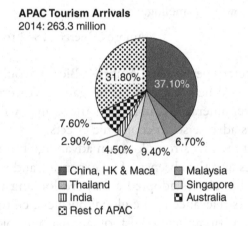

Figure 2

Source: World Tourism Organization, UNWTO Tourism Highlights 2015.

after China, Hong Kong and Macau combined, Malaysia and Thailand (Figure 2).

The ability of Singapore to attract more tourists than larger countries with more attractions like India and Australia not only reflects its foreigner friendly environment and suitability for short haul trips but also its entrepreneurial spirit that drives the country to successfully incubate new ventures that sustain its position as a preferred tourist destination.

One such venture was facilitating the establishment of the two IRs — Resorts World Sentosa (RWS) and Marina Bay Sands (MBS). But the legalisation of gaming and approving the building of IRs in Singapore was a sensitive issue. Concerns regarding the social repercussions of gaming addiction, excessive accumulation of household debt to finance gaming addiction and losses, providing 'legal' channels for money laundering and the potential rise of organised crime prevailed.

Lee Kuan Yew's statement effectively summarises the inevitable legalisation of gaming in Singapore and associated concerns:

> "When I was a student in England, the only casino in Europe was in Monaco. The younger ministers have said look, we must have a casino. Otherwise, we are out of the circuit of this fast set that goes around the world, with F1 and so on. And it will increase the tourist trade because the casino will pay for all the shows. Otherwise, the shows are too expensive. So I've been resisting it and I've told the Prime Minister, I said no, no, don't do that, you'll bring mafias here and money laundering and all kinds of crime.
>
> Then I see the British having casinos and Switzerland having casinos. I said God, the world has changed. If I don't change, we'll be out of business. So alright, we'll put up two casinos, so obviously they are not going to target Singaporeans because there are not enough numbers for two casinos. So they got to bring them in from China, India and elsewhere and we have passed legislation to say that any family can ask for a ban on … It is useless to resist when it is everywhere."

The Ministry of Trade and Industry carried out a study on the economic, tourism and social aspects of having a casino within an IR, while the Feedback Unit (now REACH) held dialogue sessions with public groups including those from the religious, grassroots and business communities.

While the government wanted to reap the benefits of enhancing Singapore's attraction as a tourist destination, generate employment opportunities and create entertainment options for the entire family, it also wanted to ensure the opening up of the gaming industry in Singapore did not create adverse socio-economic consequences. So an entry fee of either SGD100 per visit or SGD2,000 for unlimited access for 12 months to any one of the IRs was levied on Singapore citizens and permanent residents.

The casino component of the IRs was debated in Parliament in January 2005 and by March; consortiums from the United States, South Africa, Singapore, Australia and Hong Kong had submitted concept proposals for the Marina Bay IR, with the highest bid coming in at SGD5.8 billion.

Calling for the Bids

On 18 April 2005 the Singapore Government announced its decision to invite proposals to develop two IRs with casinos at Marina Bayfront and Sentosa. A gaming regulatory body — the Casino Regulatory Division (CRD) was constituted under the Ministry of Home Affairs on 27 June 2005. The Government set prices for both the sites instead of calling for a tender and through the Singapore Tourism Board invited concept proposals. This allowed the bidders to compete on the strength of their concept proposals. The government also announced the judging criteria for the bids: tourism appeal (40%), architectural concept and design (30%), development investment (20%) and track record of the operator (10%).

The Government, CRD (presently known as CRA — Casino Regulatory Authority) and the two licensed operators Genting Singapore Plc. and Las Vegas Sands worked together to inaugurate RWS in January 2010 and MBS in June 2010.

The 2008 Global Financial Crisis

The construction phase of the two IRs coincided with the 2008 global financial crisis, which affected MBS more than RWS. LVS, which was amidst a financial crisis, found it difficult to raise funds for its multiple projects. Its share price plummeted by more than 90% and there were rumours of LVS being on the brink of bankruptcy.

Table 1 Project-related Specifics for the Two Projects

	Marina Bayfront	Sentosa
Land Value	SGD1.20billion (then about USD755million)	SGD625million
Bidders	1. Las Vegas Sands Corp. (LVS) & City Developments Limited (CDL) consortium, 2. Harrah's Entertainment & Keppel Land consortium, 3. Genting International & Star Cruises consortium, and 4. MGM Mirage & CapitaLand consortium	1. Eighth Wonder, Publishing & Broadcasting Limited & Melco, International Development Limited, Isle of Capri and Casinos Inc consortium, 2. Genting International, Star Cruises & Universal Studios consortium, and 3. Kerzner International & CapitaLand consortium
Winning bid	LVS & CDL consortium	Genting International, Star Crusies & Universal Studios consortium
Investment committed by the winning bid	SGD3.85billion in addition to the land cost	SGD6.59billion in addition to the land cost
Other details	• The Singapore property developer, CDL later withdrew citing the invasiveness of probity checks. • LVS' strength in the meetings, incentives, conventions and exhibitions (MICE) sector as well as the distinctive design elements of its proposed architecture were cited as key factors in its winning bid. • Analysts had previously ranked LVS behind the other bidders, in part due to its lack of a local partner.	Despite winning the bid for the resort, CRD warned Genting International that it was still subject to scrutiny and a casino licence was not guaranteed due to concerns by the Singapore government over Stanley Ho's stake in Star Cruises. Genting International responded by buying over Star Cruises' 25 per cent stake in the IR for a cash consideration of SGD1.49billion. Genting committed to invest SGD6.59bn in the project.

Table 2   The key milestones in making the casinos operational

15 November 2005	Request for Proposals for Marina Bayfront launched
14 February 2006	Casino Control Bill passed in Parliament
1 March 2006	Casino Control Act was assented to by the President
28 April 2006	Request for Proposals for Sentosa launched
26 May 2006	Marina Bayfront IR project awarded to Las Vegas Sands Corporation
8 December 2006	The Sentosa Integrated Resort project awarded to Infinity@ The Bay Pte Ltd, a joint venture company between Genting International and Star Cruises
13 April 2007	During the International Association of Gaming Regulators (IAGR) mid-year Steering Committee Meeting held in Singapore, CRD and the Nevada Gaming Control Board (NGCD) sign a Statement of Co-operation.
11 June 2007	The official Letter of Acceptance (LOA) signing ceremony to award the tender for the milestone Casino Licensing Application System (CLAS) was held. CLAS is the first of its kind to be used by a casino regulator in Asia-Pacific.
2 April 2008	The CRA was formed as a new statutory board under the MHA to administer and enforce the Casino Control Act.
1 July 2008	Casino Control Act becomes fully operational
5 December 2008	CLAS operational
8 January 2009	The inaugural CRA Technology Forum held. Over 20 representatives from major manufacturers and independent test labs from around the world, the two casino operators, and guests from the Singapore Accreditation Council attended. The forum serves as an annual platform for discussion on matters regarding the regulation of gaming technology.
15 January 2009	Technical Standards for Electronic Gaming Machines and the Slot Management System finalised and published on the CRA website
20 January 2010	RWS inaugurated
23 June 2010	MBS officially inaugurated

In November 2008, LVS chairman and chief executive Sheldon Adelson flew to Singapore to meet government officials and reaffirm LVS' commitment to the MBS project. LVS then suspended development work on projects in Las Vegas and Macau and channelled its financial resources to MBS. The company also raised SGD3.2billion through a stock offering, with Adelson putting in more than USD1billion of his own money, and successfully requesting the government's approval to inaugurate MBS in stages.

The project continued to suffer construction delays due to high prices of concrete after an embargo on sand exports by regional countries and the bankruptcy of a number of sub-contractors. Heavy rainfall and labour shortages also contributed to the delays and resulted in a 100% escalation in project cost to SGD7.7 bn. In December 2009 LVS announced that MBS would open on a phased basis and commence operations in April 2010.

It was relatively smooth sailing for Genting International (which was renamed as Genting Singapore Plc. — "GENS" in 2009). GENS, a 51.9% subsidiary of Malaysia-based gaming major — Genting Berhad, accessed multiple funding sources even amidst the global financial crisis. This included two rounds of equity financing in 2007 and 2009 aggregating SGD3.80billion[1], a SGD866million convertible bond issue in 2007, SGD3.23billion debt raised during the period 2008–2010 and SGD643.86million raised from the sale of its UK casinos to a subsidiary of Genting Bhd. The SGD8.54billion raised during the four year period 2007–2010 funded the SGD7.22billion project cost (including the SGD625 million land cost) and the SGD1.49billion acquisition of Star Cruises' 25% stake in the Sentosa IR.

Casino Regulation

The CRA awarded both the IRs a 30-year concession period that included a 10-year exclusivity period. The Singapore corporate income tax (levied on all corporations) and casino tax are lower than in most other Asia Pacific gaming jurisdictions.

---

[1] Equity of SGD2.30bn and SGD1.50bn was issued in 2007 in 2009 respectively

Table 3　Corporate Income Tax Levies by Country

	Corporate Income Tax	Casino Tax (%)	Comments
Australia	30.0%	EGMs: 16.4%–31.6% VIPs: 9.0% to 10.0%	Casino tax varies across states
Macau	Nil	37.8%–39.0%	
Malaysia	25.0%	25.0%	
Singapore	17.0%	5.0%	For premium players
		15.0%	For other players
South Korea	24.2%	39.0%	For locals
		10.0%	For foreigners
The Philippines	30.0%	15.0% + 2.0% Heritage fee	For high rollers & junkets
		25.0% + 2.0% Heritage fee	For other players
Vietnam	25.0%	Nil	

While these measures enabled LVS and GENS to recover their investment and generate robust profits, the IRs and domestic patrons (Singapore citizens and permanent residents — SCPRs) were subject to stringent restrictions to control gaming-related socio-economic issues.

The maximum allotted gross gaming floor area was 15,000 square metres per IR. SCPRs are subject to a SGD100 daily levy and SGD2,000 annual levy. CRA's close regulatory scrutiny of both the casinos is evident from the fines levied by CRA doubling to almost SGD1.80 million during the financial year ended 2013 (FY2013) from SGD954,000 in FY2012. Average daily visits by SCPRs declined to 17,000 in FY13 from 20,000 in FY10.

The Juggernaut Rolls

Aided by insurmountable barriers to entry on one hand and constrained by restrictions on SCPR patronage on the other, RWS and MBS started operations in 2010 amid much fanfare. Theme parks, hotels, restaurants, convention centres and shopping malls formed an integral part of the IRs. This was not just to comply with the Singapore government's directive that the IRs need to be family-friendly leisure and entertainment destinations but also made immense sense from a business perspective.

Business & Financial Review

The IR model enabled MBS and RWS to attract both mass market and affluent patrons (Figure 3) to their casinos and the non-gaming component of their business (i.e., theme parks, hotels, restaurants, convention centres and shopping malls) built customer loyalty, added an element of diversity to their businesses and augmented profits. The two IRs started generating SGD7.5 billion gross gaming revenues (GGR) per annum (Figure 4) within a year of starting full scale operations. As of end- 2015, MBS had a lead over RWS in terms of market share. MBS's 60% market share is on account of its proximity to Singapore's Central Business District, its premium market positioning and the success of its Meetings, Incentives, Conferences and Exhibitions (MICE) facilities.

Singapore became the second largest player in the Asia Pacific gaming industry, with its market share rising to an estimated 11% in 2013 from nil in 2009 (Figure 5).

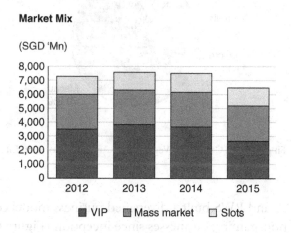

Market Mix

Figure 3

Source: Genting Singapore PLC and Las Vegas Sands Annual Reports & Interim Financial Statements.

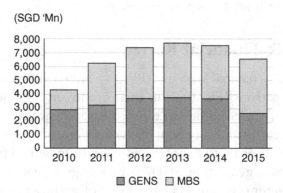

Figure 4

Source: Genting Singapore PLC and Las Vegas Sands Annual Reports & Interim Financial Statements.

Figure 5

Source: Genting Singapore PLC and Las Vegas Sands Annual Reports & Interim Financial Statements.

Both MBS and RWS built a diversified business model comprising gaming and non-gaming businesses since inception (Figure 6). MBS's and RWS's EBITDA margins (EBITDA/Revenues) are robust at over 35% (Figure 7) despite declining year on year since 2010 due to

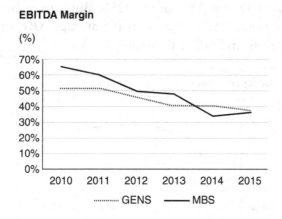

Revenue Composition

(SGD 'Mn)

Figure 6

Source: Genting Singapore PLC and Las Vegas Sands Annual Reports & Interim Financial Statements.

EBITDA Margin

(%)

Figure 7

Source: Genting Singapore PLC and Las Vegas Sands Annual Reports & Interim Financial Statements.

impairment of receivables from VIP customers and the challenging macroeconomic conditions. The EBITDA margin is primarily driven by the casino's win rate, which though loaded in favour of the casino varies from quarter to quarter. But MBS's higher win rates in its casino business and its luxury hotel commanding higher room rates that the RWS' hotels have resulted in MBS' higher EBITDA margin.

The extent of cash generated by the two IRs is evident from the reduction in their debt levels during the period 2010–2015. GENS' (the company which owns RWS) net cash position (i.e., GENS' cash balance exceeded its outstanding debt) improved to SGD1.01 billion as of end- 2015 from SGD176.88 million as of end- 2010[2]. MBS' parent, LVS did not report MBS' debt in 2010 and 2011. But, MBS' net financial leverage ratio (the ratio of debt less cash to EBITDA) has moderated and has improved to 1.80x by end-2015 from 2.80x as of end-2012.

The performance of the hotels at MBS and RWS underscores the success of the IR business model. The hotels at both the IRs consistently clocked occupancy rates in excess of 90% and average room rates (ARR) in excess of SGD400 per night (Figures 8 & 9). These ratios compare favourably with the Singapore hotels' average occupancy rate of 85% in 2015 and ARR of SGD258. But it must be noted that the Singapore hotels' ARR represents the average ARR of the entire gamut of hotels from budget to luxury.

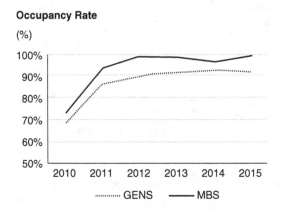

Figure 8

Source: Genting Singapore PLC and Las Vegas Sands Annual Reports & Interim Financial Statements.

---

[2] After adding the SGD2.30 billion perpetual capital securities issued in 2012 to debt

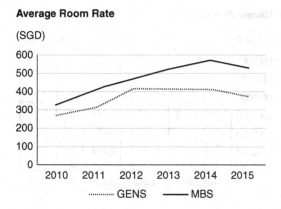

Figure 9

Source: Genting Singapore PLC and Las Vegas Sands Annual Reports & Interim Financial Statements.

Singapore was not the first country to build an IR. But the country was at the forefront in approving the operation of large scale casinos without exacerbating the risk-taking behaviour of the local population. The IR model and the Singapore casino regulations have become a blueprint, which many countries like The Philippines, South Korea, Vietnam, Cambodia and possibly Japan are trying to emulate. In a bid to expand its geographic footprint, GENS and a leading Anhui-based property developer — Landing International Development Limited, entered into a 50:50 joint venture in January 2014 to develop an USD2.2 billion IR at Jeju in South Korea.

Challenges

Despite the sterling performance of the two IRs, Singapore's gaming industry does face serious challenges. The primary challenge is the intensifying competition in the Asia Pacific region. The proliferation of IRs in low cost destinations like The Philippines, Vietnam and Cambodia have partially contributed to Singapore's GGR stagnating at SGD7.50 billion during the last three years. South Korea and possibly Japan setting up new IRs pose an additional threat.

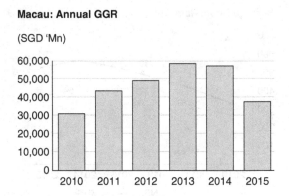

Figure 10
Source: Macau Statistics and Census Service.

The Chinese government's anti-corruption crackdown since the second quarter of 2014 has not only resulted in Macau's GGR declining since 2Q 2014 but has also affected Singapore's VIP gaming revenues (Figure 10). In 2015, Singapore's GGR declined by 14% while Macau's GGR declined by 35%.

Another risk is the high level of trade receivables MBS and RWS have accumulated, a trend which could depress profitability and liquidity especially during a cyclical downturn. Casinos have the option to solicit affluent (VIP) patrons by either extending credit directly to the patrons or paying international marketing agents (IMAs or junket operators) to source VIP patrons. The Singapore IRs have opted for the former route. Hence, the Singapore IRs' net trade receivables tend to be higher than their Asian counterparts (Figure 11). Impairment of trade receivables has adversely affected the EBITDA margin of both IRs, who have tightened their credit extension norms to tackle this issue going forward.

Takeaways

Notwithstanding these risks, the two IRs having the financial muscle to tide over a period of lower profits and the current significant tourist inflow should enable the country remains a force to be reckoned with in the global gaming industry.

Receivables Days

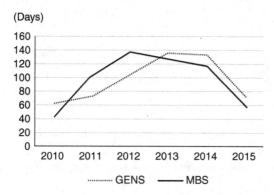

Figure 11

Source: Genting Singapore PLC and Las Vegas Sands Annual Reports and authors' calculations.

MBS is an unlisted entity. GENS has paid a dividend per share of just one cent per annum and for the last four years (2011 to 2015). GENS's share price has appreciated considerably since listing. This stock will suit those investors who are seeking long term returns but not those who require a recurring dividend income stream from their investments.

16

THE SINGAPORE PROPERTY SECTOR: AN OVERVIEW

The real estate sector is one of the pillars of the Singapore economy. Construction and ownership of dwellings accounted for 4.1% and 4.9% of the 2015 GDP at current prices, aggregating 9.2%. The share of these two sectors has progressively increased to 9.2% in 2015 from 8.3% in 2011. Home ownership rate of resident households has progressively peaked to 92% in 2000 from 58.8% in 1980 and has slightly moderated to 90.3% in 2014. Nevertheless, Singapore has among the highest home ownership rates in the world.

A significant proportion of Singapore's wealthiest have their fortunes tied to the real estate sector because of the city state's finite amount of land and rising property values. Newspaper readers cannot help but observe the preponderance of investment advisors advertising for seminars in which participants can learn to become wealthy by investing modest capital in real estate. But success in real estate investing may be achieved only if the investor is able and willing to remain invested through business cycles and understands the types of real estate investment and the risks and prospects of investing in this sector.

Investing in real estate can be broadly categorized into two types — active and passive. Active investing involves purchasing property, which would yield rental income and capital gains from sale of property. Capital gains or losses i.e. the difference between the sale price and purchase price of property of properties is amplified should investors use 'leverage' while purchasing properties. Leverage is an investment practice in which the property purchaser funds a fraction of the property price through own funds and the balance through borrowing. Should the property price appreciate the investor would repay the outstanding loan amount to the lender and get to retain his/her initial down payment plus the price appreciation. A decline in property prices to an extent that the (now) diminished market value of the property is lower than the outstanding loan would lead to widespread loan defaults, as was witnessed during the 2007–08 GFC. This is because the property purchaser would have to cough up his/her own funds in addition to the proceeds from property sale to repay the lender.

Passive investing in real estate involves investing in stocks and bonds issued by real estate companies. As in the case of agri-business companies, the investor needs to be aware that property companies are of several types with varying risks and returns associated with investing in each of the types.

Property companies may be broadly categorized into three types — property developers, property investment companies, and full service property companies. Property developers are companies that are engaged in the purchase of land, construction of properties and sale of completed properties to end-users. Property investment companies (PICs) own a portfolio of rental income generating properties. Their income is more stable than that of property developers, whose income from sale of completed properties is linked to the demand for property and property prices. Real estate investment trusts (REITs) are a special category of PICs. In Singapore, the MAS has stipulated that REITs ought to distribute at least 90% of their profits as unit distributions. Hence investors requiring recurring income tend to invest in REIT units. Full service property companies are engaged in property development, property investment and property fund management. Property fund management involves property companies engaging in active and passive property investment on behalf of the investors in their property fund business.

The following three chapters focus on a full service property company (CapitaLand), a company that is predominantly engaged in property development (CDL) and a property investment company (Global Logistic Properties).

The property market comprises five sub-markets — residential, office, retail, industrial and investment.

Residential: The Singapore residential market consists of a public housing market operated by the statutory board — Housing Development Board (HDB) and a private housing market. This section focusses on the private housing market. Figure 1 depicts the performance of the residential price and rental indices since January 2010.

Figure 1 indicates that after a period of steady appreciation in residential property prices and rents till end-2013, there has been a quarter on quarter decline in both property prices and rents. This is an outcome of the cooling measures implemented by the Singapore government coupled with an increasingly uncertain global macroeconomic environment.

Singapore Government's Cooling Measures: The government has been trying to cool the market with various measures since 2009, hurting volumes, bringing down rents and triggering pricing frictions between developers keen to offload bulging inventories.

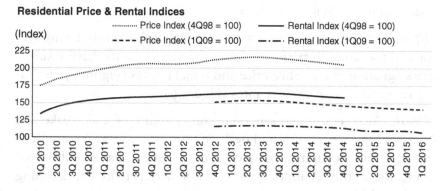

Residential Price & Rental Indices

Figure 1

Source: Urban Redevelopment Authority (URA).

Meanwhile, buyers have remained on the sidelines in anticipation of a possible relaxation of high transaction costs currently built into Additional Buyers' Stamp Duty and Sellers' Stamp Duty. Marginal buyers are also being kept out with the implementation of the Total Debt Service Ratio, which caps a household's total monthly debt repayment obligation to 60% of household income. Figure 2 provides the timeline of the property cooling measures implemented by the government of Singapore.

These cooling measures and the resultant decline in price levels have had a threefold impact on the private residential property market. First, developers have deferred property launches resulting in a 50% decline in the pipeline supply of residential units to 53,512 units as of March 31 2016 from a peak of 88,623 units as of March 31, 2013 during the period January 1, 2010 to March 31, 2016. Second, there has been a more pronounced 74% decline in take-up of property units to 1,419 units as of March 31, 2016 from a peak of 6,526 units as of March 31, 2012. Figure 3 depicts the pipeline and take-up trends in the private residential market since January 1, 2010.

The third impact of the property cooling measures has been the steady increase in private residential property vacancy rates to 7.5% as of March 31, 2016 from 4.6% as of March 31, 2010, as observed in Figure 4.

The performance of the other real estate sub-markets has mirrored the trends in the residential market during the last twenty five quarters ending March 31, 2016.

Office: The continued contraction in Singapore's manufacturing sector and the sluggish performance in the service sector have resulted in a stagnation in the office price and rental indices (Figure 5), declining supply and high vacancy rates (Figure 6).

Retail: Weak consumer sentiment on account of the weakening domestic macro economy and declining tourist arrivals on account of the uncertain global macroeconomic environment have resulted in a stagnation in the retail price and rental indices (Figure 7), declining supply and high vacancy rates (Figure 8).

Effective Date	Major Cooling Measures that Affect Residential Property Market
14 September, 2009	1. Interest absorption scheme (deferment of instalments until TOP) and interest-only housing loans (interest payment only until TOP) were scrapped for all private properties.
20 February, 2010	1. Introduction of SSD for residential property and land sold within one year of purchase.
	2. LTV lowered to 80% from 90% on all housing loans except HDB loans.
30 August, 2010	1. Holding period for imposition of SSD increased to three years from one.
	2. Minimum cash payments raised to 10% from 5% for buyers with one or more outstanding housing loans.
	3. LTV lowered to 70% from 80% for second properties.
14 January, 2011	1. Holding period for imposition of SSD increased to four years from three.
	2. SSD rates raised to 16%, 12%, 8% and 4% of consideration.
	3. LTV lowered to 60% from 70% for second property.
	4. LTV for non-individual residential purchasers capped at 50%.
8 December, 2011	1. ABSD introduced for further cooling measures:
	- Foreigners and non-individuals pay 10%, PRs buying second and subsequent property pay 3%, Singaporeans buying third and subsequent property pay 3%.
	2. Developers purchasing more than four residential units and following through on intention to develop residentialproperties for sale would be waived ABSD
	- To qualify, developers have to produce proof of development and sale within five years.
6 October, 2012	1. Mortgage tenures capped at a maximum of 35 years.
	2. For loans longer than 30 years or for loans that extend beyond retirement age of 65 years: LTV lowered to 60% for first mortgage and to 40% for second and subsequent mortgages.
	3. LTV for non-individuals lowered to 40%.
12 January, 2013	1. ABSD: Citizens pay 7/10% on second/third purchase (from 0/3%); Permanent Residents (PR) pay 5/10% for first/second purchase (from 0/3%); foreigners and non-individuals now pay 15%.
	2. LTV for second/third loan now 50/40% from 60%; non-individuals' LTV now 20% (from 40%).
	3. Mortgage Servicing Ratio (MSR) for HDB loans now capped at 35% of gross monthly income (from 40%); MSR for loans from financial institutions capped at 30%.
	4. PRs no longer allowed to rent out entire HDB flat.

Figure 2

Source: www.srx.com.sg, MAS, URA and HDB.

Effective Date	Major Cooling Measures that Affect Residential Property Market
29 June, 2013	1. TDSR: Financial institutions are required to consider borrowers' other outgoing debt obligations when granting property loans. His total monthly repayments of his debt obligations should not exceed 60 per cent of his gross monthly income.
	2. In particular, MAS requires:
	- borrowers named on a property loan to be the mortgagors of the residential property for which the loan is taken;
	- "guarantors" who are standing guarantee for borrowers otherwise assessed by the financial institutions at the point of application for the housing loan not to meet the TDSR threshold for a property loan to be brought in as co-borrowers; and
	- in the case of joint borrowers, that financial institutions use the income-weighted average age of borrowers when applying the rules on loan tenure.
27 August, 2013	1. Singapore Permanent Resident Households need to wait three years from the date of obtaining SPR status, before they can buy a resale HDB flat.
	2. Maximum tenure for HDB housing loans is reduced from 30 years to 25 years. The Mortgage Servicing Ratio (MSR) limit is reduced from 35% to 30% of the borrower's gross monthly income.
	3. Maximum tenure of new housing loans and re-financing facilities granted by financial institutions for the purchase of HDB flats (including DBSS flats) is reduced from 35 years to 30 years. New loans with tenure exceeding 25 years and up to 30 years will be subject to tighter LTV limits.
9 December, 2013	1. Reduction of Cancellation Fees From 20% to 5% for Executive Condominiums.
	2. Resale Levy for Second-Timer Applicants
	- Formerly second timers are not required to pay a levy. This is applicable to only new EC land sales which are launched on or after 9th December 2013.
	3. Revision of Mortgage Loan Terms
	- From a previous mortgage servicing ratio (MSR) level of 60% to now 30% of a borrower's gross monthly income. The MSR cap will apply to EC purchases from 10th December 2013 onwards.

Figure 2 (*Continued*)

Take Up & Pipeline Supply

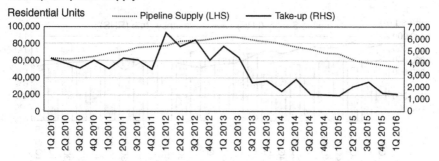

Figure 3

Source: URA.

Vacancy Rate

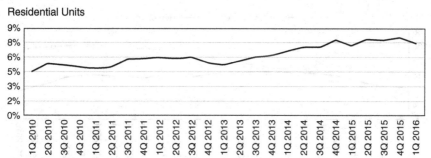

Figure 4

Source: URA.

Office: Price & Rental Indices

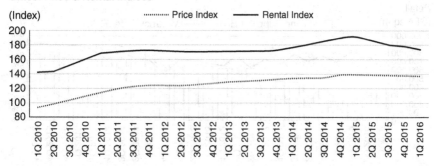

Figure 5

Source: URA.

Pipeline Supply & Vacancy Rate

Office

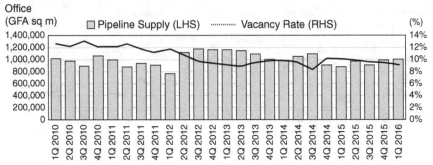

Figure 6

Source: URA.

Retail: Price & Rental Indices

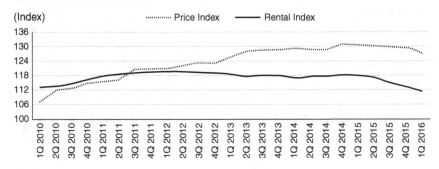

Figure 7

Source: URA.

Pipeline Supply & Vacancy Rate

Retail

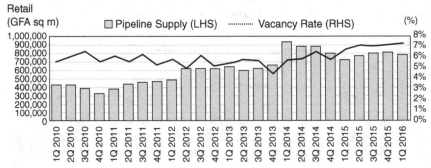

Figure 8

Source: URA.

Industrial Stock

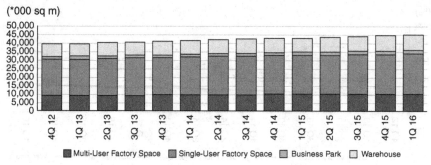

Figure 9

Source: Jurong Town Council.

Industrial Price & Rental Indices

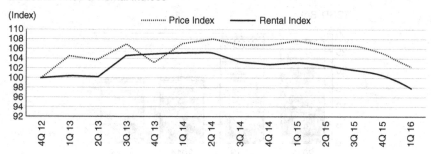

Figure 10

Source: Jurong Town Council (JTC).

Industrial: The stock of industrial space has risen by 14% during the period December 31 2012 to March 31 2016, as observed in Figure 9.

This, coupled with the sizable addition to the supply of industrial space scheduled in 2016, has resulted in a decline in industrial price and rental indices (Figure 10) and vacancy rates stagnating/climbing up (Figure 11). Vacancy rates in the more expensive and customized business park space continues to be high at over 15% as of March 31 2016.

Industrial Vacancy Rates

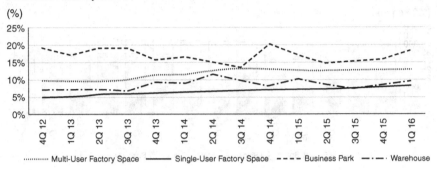

Figure 11

Source: JTC.

Investment Sales

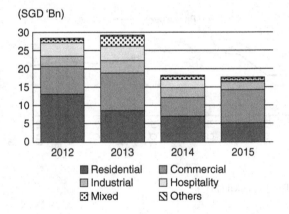

Figure 12

Source: Savills Research & Consultancy.

Investment sales are sales executed by property developers and PICs, property funds and retail investors, especially high net worth investors, not for owner occupation but as an investment to earn recurring rental income and capital gains on sale of such properties. Investment sales in 2015 was the lowest since the GFC, as depicted in Figure 12.

The reason, in addition to the challenging macroeconomic environment, according to the property research and consultancy firm Savills was *"unexpected negative developments pertaining to the Chinese currency which translated to increased volatility in the global financial markets"*.

However, Savills believes that the large deals in the pipeline including Asia Square Tower 1, CPF Building and a 50% stake of 78 Shenton Way, which if executed would result in a recovery of the investment sales market.

Outlook

The outlook for all sub-markets of the Singapore property market is muted due to domestic and global macroeconomic uncertainty, tightened lending norms implemented by banks and the risk of the US Federal Reserve hiking interest rates which might result in a corresponding increase in domestic interest rates. The above-mentioned risks are exacerbated by the sizable supply of residential, office, retail and industrial properties that are scheduled to enter the market in 2016, as shown in Figure 13.

The following three chapters focus on a full service property company (CapitaLand), two Real Estate Investment Trusts (CapitaLand Malls Trust and Ascendas REIT) and a property investment company (Global Logistic Properties). Each of these companies offer unique propositions to investors.

CapitaLand, after tasting success in its business ventures in Singapore and China, where it was one of the first overseas companies to set up shop, is now making its presence felt in Indonesia, Malaysia and Vietnam. The two REITs that are constituents of the STI — CapitaLand Malls Trust and Ascendas REIT, offer investors exposure to the retail and industrial property sectors respectively and recurring cash returns. Global Logistic Properties is unique in that it has no exposure in the Singapore market but instead is a market leader in three of the four markets it operates — Brazil, China & Japan. It is the third largest logistics player in the US.

Pipeline Private Residential Supply

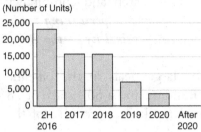

Pipeline Office Supply

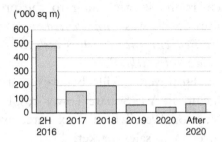

Pipeline Retail Supply

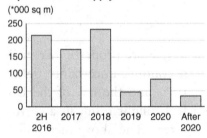

Pipeline Industrial Supply

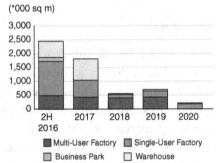

Figure 13

Source: URA and JTC.

17

CAPITALAND

CapitaLand Limited is Southeast Asia's largest listed property company and one of Asia's largest integrated and listed property companies and also one of the earliest foreign developers to tap China. The company is now leveraging its success in its core markets of China and Singapore and replicating the business model in Indonesia, Malaysia and Vietnam.

This chapter, when read in conjunction with the following chapters on City Developments Limited (CDL), CapitaLand Mall Trust (CMT), Ascendas REIT (A-REIT) and Global Logistic Properties (GLP), will enable readers to understand the different types of real estate companies, the varying degree of risks these companies are exposed to and the mitigating factors to these risks. Like banks, real estate companies' performance closely tracks business cycles i.e. they are cyclical stocks.

Factors such as the ability to purchase land and accumulate a land bank at competitive prices and execute projects in a timely and cost effective manner are company specific. Other factors such as demand for real estate properties, interest rates, the quantum of loan a property buyer may access to purchase the property (i.e., the loan to value ratio) and the tax regime (stamp duty and registration charges for buying a property and applicable capital gains tax while selling the property) are extraneous. These extraneous factors are beyond the

control of property companies and tend to affect all property companies operating in the same geography and sub-market (i.e., residential,
retail, office, industrial and hospitality) similarly.

Genesis and Evolution

CapitaLand was formed in 2000 following the merger of the Singapore
government-owned Pidemco Land and DBS Land, the real estate arm
of DBS Group. The company was listed on the SGX in November 2000.

CapitaLand is a pioneer in the Singapore real estate industry.
Recognising that growth options are limited if operations were to be
restricted to the city state of Singapore, the company quickly diversified geographically across several countries and across all real estate
sub-markets. CapitaLand began operations as a Singapore-centric
property developer and as of 31 December 2015 reported total assets
of SGD47 billion and post-tax profits of SGD1.50 billion. The company also sponsored Singapore's first REIT — CapitaLand Mall
Trust, which was listed on the SGX in July 2002.

The rationale for sponsoring and listing a REIT is to inject the
stable properties that generate recurring rental income into the REIT.
The sponsor generates sizeable profits by selling the recurring income
generating properties to the REIT, diversifies funding by reducing
reliance on debt and also by virtue of holding a sizeable stake in the
REIT earns recurring distributions. Investors requiring recurring
income stand to benefit as REITs are by regulation required to pay at
least 90% of their taxable income as unit distributions. This 'asset
recycling model' of developing high quality recurring income generating properties and injecting them into REITs was a financially savvy
business strategy soon replicated by other prominent Singapore-based
real estate operators.

Temasek is CapitaLand's principal shareholder with a 39.6% stake
with the balance shares held by institutional (39.1%) and retail
(21.3%) investors. The company's visibility globally is evident in the
geographical distribution of its shareholders. 52.6% of CapitaLand's
shareholders are in Singapore, followed by North America (12%),

Asia ex-Singapore (5.5%), UK (4.1%), Europe ex-UK (3.9%) and the rest of the world (22%).

Please refer to Table 10 in Appendix 1 for the key milestones in CapitaLand's evolution.

Business Review

As of 2015, CapitaLand operates four directly and fully owned business units — CapitaLand Singapore (CLS), CapitaLand China (CLC), CapitaLand Mall Asia Limited (CMA) and The Ascott Limited (Ascott). CLS and CLC concentrate on the residential, office and integrated developments in their respective core markets of Singapore and China; while CMA and Ascott continue to focus on shopping malls and serviced residences respectively.

CapitaLand Singapore owns and manages commercial properties and develops residential properties in Singapore and Malaysia for sale. In 2015, this division accounted for 26% of revenues and 21% of EBIT.

CapitaLand China is involved in residential, commercial and integrated property development in China, being one of the earliest foreign developers to enter China over 20 years ago. CapitaLand has a presence in the clusters of Shanghai/Hangzhou/Suzhou/Ningbo, Beijing/Tianjin, Guangzhou/Shenzhen, Chengdu/Chongqing and Wuhan.

CapitaLand Mall Asia is among Asia's largest shopping mall developers, owners and managers with portfolio in Singapore, China, India, Japan and Malaysia. At the end of last year it owned and managed 104 shopping malls across 54 cities across these countries with total property value of approximately SGD41.2 billion and a total gross floor area (GFA) of about 100 million square feet. Of these, 88 malls are operational and 16 are under development. Its malls in China especially are performing well, generating robust rental income. China's drive to make its economy consumption driven, shifting away from an export-driven model should benefit the retail sector and therefore this business unit.

Ascott is the largest international serviced residence owner-operator in the world; Ascott has operations in 95 cities in 27 countries. It is an international serviced residence owner-operator with operations in key cities of Americas, Asia Pacific, Europe and Middle East. It operates three brands, namely Ascott, Somerset and Citadines which own and manage over 43,000 units in 277 properties. Nearly a third of these properties are located in China. The pace of growth in key markets like China is expected to be stepped up in coming years as the company eyes its targeted goal of 80,000 units by 2020. Through the above-mentioned four entities, CapitaLand holds stakes in five sector focussed REITs (Table 1).

Business restructuring was underway in 2014 as is evident from the privatisation of CapitaLand Mall Asia Limited (CMA) which cost CapitaLand SGD3.06 billion, and in the divestment of Australand Property Group (ALZ). This streamlining of operations is helping improve operational efficiencies as it has increased focus on Singapore and China, while continuing to exit some businesses in United Kingdom and India (Figure 1).

CapitaLand's geographic diversity imparts an element of stability to its operations. For example, while Singapore residential sales declined sharply since 2013 due to the government implementing property cooling measures, there has been a pickup in China residential sales (Figure 2). CapitaLand has sustained the increase in residential sales in China up to 30 June 2016, despite China experiencing a macroeconomic slowdown.

Financial Review

CapitaLand, with its businesses predominantly domiciled in the Asia Pacific region, has witnessed high growth and improving disposable incomes, and has more than doubled its assets during the eleven years ending 31 December 2015, achieving a CARG of 10%. The company's assets even during the 2007–08 global financial crisis did not shrink (Figure 3).

Two striking features of CapitaLand's growth are that the company chose to focus more on businesses that generate stable,

Table 1 CapitaLand's Five Sector Focussed REITs

REIT	Focus	CapitaLand Stake (%, a)	Market Capitalization (SGD Million, b)	Market Value of CapitaLand's stake (SGD Million)
Ascott Residence Trust	Serviced residences, rental housing properties and other hospitality assests	46.20	1,864.00	861.17
CapitaLand Commercial Trust	Ten prime commercial properties in Singapore and an 18% stake in Malaysia-based commercial REIT, Quill Capita Trust	31.90	4,538.00	1,447.62
CapitaLand Mall Trust, Singapore's largest REIT by market capitalization and an independent constituent of the STI	Retail properties	29.30	7,722.00	2,262.55
CapitaLand Malaysia Malls Trust	Retail properties in Malaysia	36.50	1,054.22	384.79
CapitaLand Retail China Trust	Retail properties in China	27.70	1,283.00	355.39
Total Value of CapitaLand's Holding				5,311.52

a: Shareholding as per the 2015 Annual Report
b: As of 11 July 2016
Source: Bloomberg, Reuters and CapitaLand disclosures.

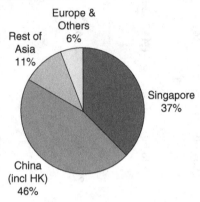

Assets By Geography
31 Dec 2015: SGD47.1 bn

Figure 1

Source: CapitaLand Annual Reports and authors' calculations.

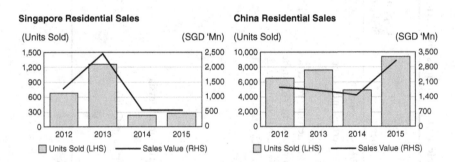

Figure 2

Source: CapitaLand Annual Reports and authors' calculations.

recurring cash flows and ensured that it maintained ample liquidity during the high growth phase.

Investment properties (2005–15 CARG: 11%) that generate rental income and associates and joint ventures (CARG: 13%) that generate dividend income grew at a faster pace than CapitaLand's property development business (7%) during the last eleven years.

CapitaLand has also maintained a comfortable liquidity position to ensure the timely completion of its projects in its capital intensive

Asset Composition

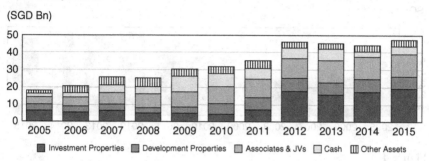

Figure 3

Source: CapitaLand Annual Reports and authors' calculations.

business. Consolidated cash tripled to SGD6.31 billion as of 31 December 2013 from SGD2.11 billion as of 31 December 2005. Its cash balance declined by SGD3.56 billion in 2014 to SGD2.75 billion primarily due to CapitaLand's SGD3.06 billion voluntary conditional cash offer to increase its stake in CapitaLand Mall Asia to 100% from 65.4% in 2013. CapitaLand Mall Asia was delisted in 2014. This move underscores CapitaLand's two pronged strategy of running a profitable but cyclical property development business while simultaneously focussing on businesses that generate recurring cash flows to impart stability to its business and cash flow profile.

Key risks real estate companies are exposed to are an accumulation of development properties and the resultant increase in financial leverage.

The growth in CapitaLand's development properties has been commensurate with its business expansion, with the accumulation of development properties being more pronounced in SGD terms, coinciding with the Singapore government implementing cooling measures since 2010 and the slowdown in the Chinese property market since 2014 (Figure 4).

In tandem with business growth, CapitaLand's financial leverage has increased from a trough of 18% in 2009 to 45% in 2015. Financial leverage is measured by the net loan to value ratio. Net loan is defined as total debt less cash. Value is the sum of a real estate operator's investment and development properties. If the reported value of

Development Properties

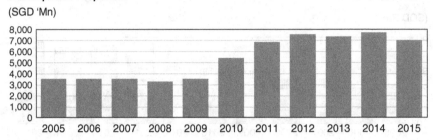

Figure 4

Source: CapitaLand Annual Reports and authors' calculations.

Net Loan to Value Ratio

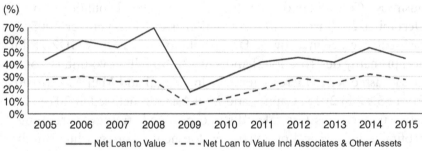

Figure 5

Source: CapitaLand Annual Reports and authors' calculations.

CapitaLand's associates, joint ventures (in which CapitaLand has less than 50% stake) and other assets are added to investment and development properties, the net loan to value ratio is lower at 7% in 2009 and 28% in 2015. However CapitaLand's financial leverage, while still lower than the peak since 2005, is increasing (Figure 5).

While integrated property companies borrow to fund both property development and businesses that generate recurring income, companies that generate significant recurring incomes that meet interest expenses tend to have more stable financial profiles. In addition to cyclical property development income, CapitaLand earns

Recurring Income Interest Cover

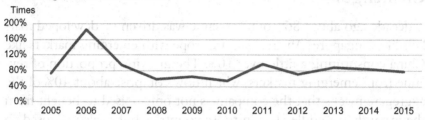

Figure 6

Source: CapitaLand Annual Reports and authors' calculations.

Dividend Payout

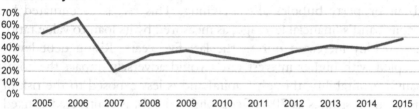

Figure 7

Source: CapitaLand Annual Reports and authors' calculations.

recurring income comprising rentals, fees, dividends from associates and joint ventures and interest from its cash balances. The coverage of these recurring income streams to borrowing costs has consistently improved to almost 3.0× in 2015 from 1.7× in 2005, which is a testimony to CapitaLand's financial strength (Figure 6).

CapitaLand's dividend payout is moderate at 49% in 2015, though it has steadily increased from the 2007 trough of 20% (Figure 7).

The company also possesses ample financial flexibility to tide over the macroeconomic uncertainty prevailing in the two major geographies it operates — Singapore and China. As of 31 December 2015, CapitaLand's total debt was SGD16.06 billion. The company's SGD4.17 billion consolidated cash balance, SGD5.55 billion bank lines of credit and its holdings in the five REITs it has sponsored, whose market value is SGD5.31 billion as of 11 July 2016, together offer a coverage of 94% to total debt.

Challenges

A decade ago about 86% of its revenue was driven by developed markets like Singapore, Australia, and Europe with emerging markets like China constituting a little over 10%. The growing proportion of revenue from emerging markets, which now comprise about 40% of the aggregate means that the company is not only poised to benefit from the expanding middle class in those countries but is also exposed to the associated economic risks.

The company has benefited from the low interest rate environment since the global financial crisis and as interest rates normalise, demand could be impacted with monetary authorities' concerns about property bubbles also weighing. This risk is accentuated by CapitaLand's financial leverage, as measured by its loan to value ratio, has steadily increased during the last five years. Rising debt levels coupled with higher interest rates would adversely impact the company's profitability, though CapitaLand is less exposed to the risk of rising interest rates as 70% of consolidated debt is contracted at fixed interest rate.

Takeaways

CapitaLand is well positioned to leverage on China's rapid urbanisation drive. Chinese leaders have pledged to loosen their grip on residence registration, or *hukou*, to try to remove obstacles to the urbanisation drive. It is targeting migration of some 100 million rural workers into cities by 2020. China aims to boost domestic consumption by increasing the proportion of urban residents among its population of almost 1.4 billion to 60% by 2020, up from 53.7% now.

China's highly fragmented property sector has about 80,000 developers and it comprises 15% of GDP. But with the industry maturing and REITs assuming a greater role in purchasing completed properties, a consolidation wave is likely to emerge. Stanchart expects consolidation to result in the top 16 listed developers' market share to rise to 31% by 2023 from 16% in 2013.

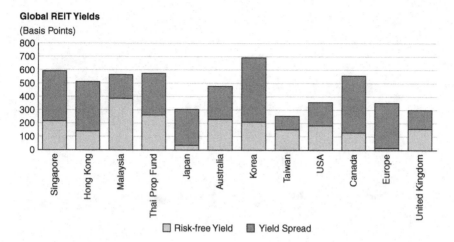

Global REIT Yields

Figure 8

Source: The Business Times dated April 20 2015 — "S'Pore still seen as a major Asia Reit hub".

Singapore, an advanced property market with diverse product offerings such as direct investments in properties, REITs, property funds and property indices, a still favourable tax environment when compared to neighbouring countries and a transparent and effective regulatory environment continues to be an attractive long term investment option. Singapore REITs continue to offer the highest risk adjusted returns in the region (Figure 8).

18

THE TALE OF TWO REITs

Real Estate Investment Trusts (REITs), though operating in the same industry as property developers and full service property companies, possess several distinguishing features. REITs are subject to closer regulatory oversight and in Singapore, are required to comply with Monetary Authority of Singapore's[1] (MAS) norms including at least 75% of the REIT's property being income generating in nature, a maximum loan to value ratio of 45%, a minimum distribution[2] payout of 90% and development activity restricted to 10% of property value.[3]

The performance of REITs tends to be more stable than property developers and full service property companies. Hence, investment in REIT units is ideal for those investors who seek stability and recurring income.

Investors in REIT units enjoy (recurring) rental income and capital gains from property without having to manage or own otherwise unaffordable real estate assets. A mandatory requirement to distribute 90%

---

[1] Source: Monetary Authority of Singapore's Code on Collective Investment Schemes effective 1 January, 2016.

[2] As REITs are incorporated as trusts, they issue units which are similar to shares/ common stocks issued by companies. The distribution paid by REITs is similar to dividends paid by companies.

[3] MAS allows an additional development allowance of 15% if the purpose is redevelopment of a property held by the REIT for at least three years.

of income to investors and ownership rights vested in an independent trustee are major factors distinguishing REITs from property stocks, which are also free to diversify away from real estate.

Genesis & Evolution

CapitaLand Mall Trust (CMT) and Ascendas Real Estate Investment Trust (A-REIT), both constituents of the Straits Time Index, are Singapore's largest REITs by portfolio value and market capitalization. But the two REITs are very different in terms of sector focus.

CMT, sponsored by CapitaLand Limited which holds a 29.31% stake in CMT and the first REIT incorporated in Singapore, invests in Singapore-based shopping malls that are rented out to international and local retailers. CMT, established as a property fund in 2001, launched an initial public offering the next year.

CMT, which started business with a portfolio of three malls spanning a gross floor area (GFA) of 800,000 square feet (sq ft) in 2002, grew its portfolio to sixteen shopping malls located in the suburban and downtown Singapore with an associated GFA of 10,863,768 sq ft by end-2015. Besides its shopping malls, CMT also has a 14.3% stake in CapitaLand Retail China Trust, a China-focused REIT, which owns 11 shopping malls across seven cities in China.

A-REIT, sponsored by Ascendas Pte Ltd which holds a 20.01% stake in A-REIT, invests primarily in business and science parks, industrial properties, data and logistics centres spread across Singapore, Australia and China. A-REIT was set up as unit trust scheme in 2002, the year in which it also launched an IPO. This REIT, which began operations with a portfolio of eight properties, grew its portfolio to 133 properties by end-March 2016. A-REIT's primary focus is on business and industrial sectors with a portfolio comprising 103 properties in Singapore, 27 properties in Australia and 3 properties in China with an aggregate S$9.7 billion value. A-REIT's customer base of 1,470 companies is drawn from a range of industries such as manufacturing, logistics service providers, electronics, telecommunications, manufacturing services and back-room support office in service industries.

Temasek Holdings is the ultimate shareholder of both CMT and A-REIT.

Please refer to Tables 11 and 12 in Appendix 1 for the key milestones in CMT's and A-REIT's evolution.

Business & Financial Review

CMT has since inception focused on shopping malls which have access to public transportation networks and located close to large population catchments or within popular shopping and tourist destinations. The REIT has also maintained a large and diversified tenant base of the portfolio, which has translated into high occupancy rates of over 94% during the last decade and steadily growing rental revenues. The granular nature of the portfolio is evident from no single tenant contributing more than 4% of gross rental income (GRI). The tenants are also drawn from over 16 industries, with food & beverages contributing the highest, accounting for 29% of GRI. This and the practice of entering into tenancies of three years minimize adverse rent reversion.

However, steadily rising supply of retail space and slowing macroeconomic growth, which translates into weaker consumer sentiment, has resulted in CMT negotiating lower increases in rental rates with its tenants. The percentage increase in current rental rates over previous rental rates (typically negotiated three years ago) has been slowing since 2015. In 1H 2016, the percentage increase in rental rate was just 1.7%; a ten-year trough which is lower than the 2.3% increase achieved in 2009 during the aftermath of the GFC (Figure 1).

CMT conducts proactive mall management which includes property development carried out to enhance its future income generation capacity. Though such capital expenditures reduce funds available for

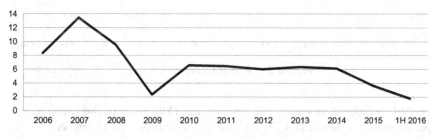

Figure 1. CMT: % Increase in Rental Rates.

distribution, they are essential to sustain rental income momentum and future distributions.

In contrast to the Singapore-centric CMT, A-REIT has pursued a strategy of acquisitions and geographical diversification to boost its earnings. This strategy of geographical diversification has enabled A-REIT counterbalance the earnings volatility arising from Singapore's flat to negative rental reversionary trends, by expanding overseas to Australia where rental volatility is subdued and occupancy is higher. Its expansion in China is a further diversification with the Shanghai business park catering to service sector industries like IT and software development and to headquarters of multi-national companies and large local corporations. A-REIT's 1,470 strong customer base occupies its 133 properties that include business & science parks, integrated development, amenities & retail properties, high specifications industrial properties & data centres, light industrial properties & flatted factories and logistics & distribution centres.

The increased supply of industrial properties in Singapore and slowing macroeconomic growth have contributed to the decline in A-REIT's occupancy rates; which are still robust. A-REIT's portfolio occupancy, which was at least 94% during the eight year period FY07[4] to FY13, progressively declined to a still robust 89.6% in FY14, 87.7% in FY15 and 87.6% in FY16 (Figure 2).

The earnings of both REITs are expected to see a boost in medium term but each one for different reasons. CMT with its trademark

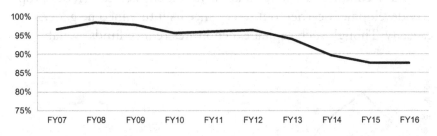

Figure 2.   A-Reit Occupancy Rates

---

[4] A-REIT's financial year ends of 31 March and FY07 refers to the twelve-month period ending 31 March 2007. CMT's financial year ends of 31 December.

strategy of asset revitalisation, is lifting the earning potential and value of its Funan Mall when it reopens in 2019. A-REIT's FY2017 earnings will feel the full year impact of the S$1.5 billion worth of acquisitions it made in 2015/2016.

CMT is currently redeveloping its Funan Mall into an integrated development comprising two office towers, service residences and a retail space, expected to cost S$560 million which will expand floor space by about 400,000 sq feet. Analysts expect its rental income to more than double and result in a S$600 million rise in its asset value. This will also help support its rental reversion rate which has declined steadily in recent times. In future, stepped-up marketing efforts to retain and boost shopper traffic could increase costs and possibly weigh on margins.

A-REIT's acquisitions include tenancies whose tenants are involved in sectors that are covered under Singapore's S$19 billion RIE2020 Plan (Research Innovation & Enterprise plan). Also 12% of vacancies are in the sectors covered by the plan, which would be of further boost to the trust.

Financial Review

Notwithstanding the recent macroeconomic pressures, both CMT and A-REIT by virtue of their strategically located high quality property portfolio and careful choice of tenants, have witnessed steadily growing revenues and stable net property income (NPI) margins.[5]

During the decade ending 31 December 2015, CMT's revenues have more than doubled to SGD669 million, while the REIT has maintained its NPI margin at around 70% (Figure 3). Note: Changed accounting policy excluded JV revenue and NPI since 2011.

Similarly, A-REIT during the decade ended 31 March 2016, reported a 169% growth in revenues to SGD761 million. NPI margin is healthy though it has declined to 70% in FY16 from the decade's peak of 77.4% in FY10 (Figure 4).

---

[5] NPI margin is net property income (NPI) expressed as a percentage of revenues.

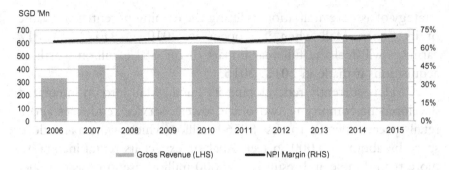

Figure 3. CMT: Revenue & NPI Margin.

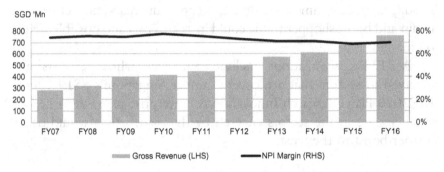

Figure 4. A-REIT: Revenue & NPI Margin

The growth in revenues and NPI has been driven by portfolio expansion on account of the sizable net investments both REITs have incurred. CMT has incurred SGD4.27 billion net investments[6] during the ten-year period, which drove the 83% growth in portfolio value to SGD8.37 billion as of 31 December 2015 (Figure 5).

A-REIT's net investments during the period FY07 to FY16 were SGD5.06 billion which resulted in a 193% growth in portfolio value to SGD9.60 billion as of 31 March 2016 (Figure 6).

Another factor that drove the rise in portfolio values has been the sharp increase in unrealised fair value of properties.

Both CMT and A-REIT have funded their portfolio expansion primarily through borrowings and equity raisings. So, while their balance

---

[6] Net investments = Capital expenditures + Acquisition expenditures Less Divestments.

SGD 'Mn

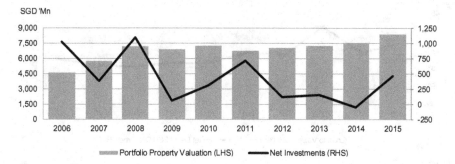

Figure 5. CMT: Portfolio Value & Investments.

SGD 'Mn

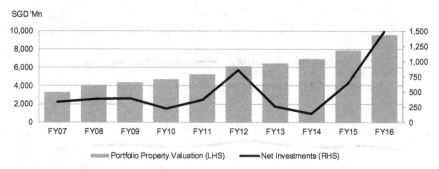

Figure 6. A-REIT: Portfolio Value & Investments

sheet leverage (the ratio of total borrowings to value of property portfolio) is well within the regulatory ceiling of 45%, their cash flow leverage (the ratio of net debt to EBITDA) is quite high at 6.0x for CMT as of 31 December 2015 and 7.8x for A-REIT as of 31 March 2016. Figure 7 indicates that while both REITs have moderate balance sheet leverage, their cash flow leverage is much higher than most non-property corporates covered in this book.

The risk arising from high cash flow leverage is partially offset by the medium tenor of debt contracted by both REITs (5.3 years to maturity for CMT and 3.4 years for A-REIT) and competitive borrowing costs of around 3.0% (Figure 8).

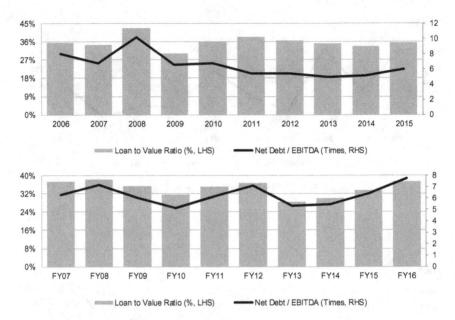

Figure 7. CMT: Leverage (top). A-REIT: Leverage (bottom).

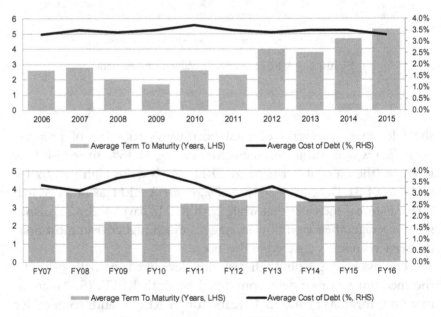

Figure 8. CMT: Debt Profile (top). A-REIT: Debt Profile (bottom).

	2006	2007	2008	2009	2010	2011	2012	2013	2014	2015
CMT	5.00	4.20	3.40	3.60	3.60	4.20	3.60	5.00	4.50	4.80
	FY07	FY08	FY09	FY10	FY11	FY12	FY13	FY14	FY15	FY16
A-REIT	6.18	5.12	4.60	4.70	4.50	5.30	4.90	6.00	6.10	5.50

Figure 9. EBITDA Interest Cover (Times).

The tenor of borrowings and competitive interest rates that both the REITs have been able to negotiate with lenders, reflects their high quality property portfolio and maintenance and the backing of a strong sponsor. The competitive borrowing costs have translated into healthy interest covers for both REITs (Figure 9).

MAS requires REITs to distribute at least 90% of their annual profits available for distribution. In line with this requirement, both REITs have distributed almost 100% of their adjusted net income[7] to unit holders, as indicated in Figure 10.

The REITs' reported income includes fair value (losses)/gains on its investment portfolio. These unrealized (losses)/gains represent the (depreciation)/appreciation in portfolio value arising from the valuation exercise the MAS requires REITs to conduct at least annually. Figure 10 indicates that while both REITs have distributed close to 100% of their cash profits as is evident from their adjusted distribution payout ratio, there have been fluctuations in the reported distribution payout ratio.

In 2009, in the aftermath of the GFC, CMT's fair value losses exceeded its cash net income resulting in a negative distribution ratio for a year. Similarly, A-REIT reported a positive net income which was much lower than its adjusted net income due to sizable fair value losses and the reported distribution ratio was close to 250%.

Relying on the reported net income would lead to investors overestimating/underestimating the distribution payout ratio. Hence investors would need to monitor the fair value (losses)/gains and the adjusted distribution payout ratio as two separate parameters.

---

[7]Adjusted Net income = Reported Net Income less Fair value (losses)/gains on investment properties

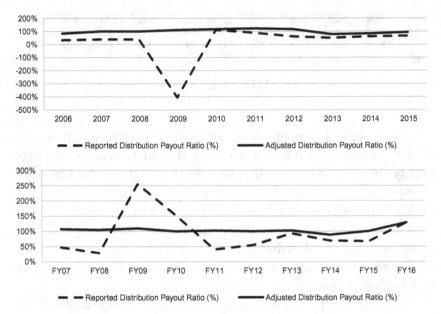

Figure 10.   CMT: Distribution Payout (top). A-REIT: Distribution Payout (bottom).
Source for Figures 1 to 10: A-REIT and CMT annual reports and authors' calculations

Challenges

The immediate challenges faced by Singapore-based REITs, including A-REIT and CMT, is tiding through the current phase of macroeconomic slowdown, which puts pressure on their occupancy rates and their ability to increase rents.

In the long term, the growth prospects of Singapore REITs are limited by their small size, high cash flow leverage and refinancing risk. The requirement to distribute at least 90% of annual cash profits results in the REITs inability to plough back funds into their core business. Hence they would necessarily have to raise debt or equity to fund expansion.

Raising equity is possible only when stock market conditions are favourable and the sponsor would have to subscribe to new shares in order to maintain their shareholding. Hence, REITs frequently finance portfolio expansion and upgradation through debt, resulting in high cash flow leverage.

REITs inability to pay down debt using operating cash flows is on account of their inability to declare lower distributions. Hence they would necessarily have to refinance maturing debt.

Certain REITs in Singapore have introduced the Distribution Reinvestment Plan (DRP), under which unit holders may opt to receive their distributions as units. But as REITs as an asset class are targetted as investors requiring recurring cash income, DRPs have met with modest success.

Takeaways

Moody's Investors Services has assigned investment grade ratings to both CMT and A-REIT. CMT is rated A2 with Stable Outlook and A-REIT, A3 with Stable Outlook, due to the backing of a strong sponsor, the highly regulated environment they operate in, high quality property portfolio, robust profitability, modest balance sheet leverage and healthy interest coverage ratio.

The ten-year dividend yield, assuming the dividends are not rein-vested, for A-REIT is 64% and for CMT, 48%. This translates to an average annual yield of 6.4% for A-REIT and 4.8% for CMT, much higher than the sub-1% interest rates offered on Singapore banks' fixed deposits. But as investors will observe in the final chapter, there are corporates whose annual dividend yield is much higher than REIT yields, although the non-REIT investments are exposed to higher stock price volatility.

Hence, investors would need to look at the risk-adjusted returns offered by financial instruments. The key difference between bank deposits and REIT units is that bank deposits are debt instruments while REIT units are equity. Banks have a contractual obligation to repay deposits with interest, irrespective of their performance. REITS are required to pay at least 90% of their post tax cash profits, which is an outcome of the REITs' performance.

Singapore bank deposits are covered by deposit insurance up to SGD50,000 per depositor and are less risky than REIT units, which in turn are subject to closer regulatory oversight than corporates and also offer greater visibility of earnings. Hence REIT units are exposed to lower earnings volatility than corporates.

19

GLOBAL LOGISTIC PROPERTIES

Global Logistic Properties (GLP) provides warehousing, logistics and supply chain facilities in China, Japan, Brazil and the USA to manufacturers, retailers and third party logistics companies. It is the market leader in all these countries except United States. In United States it is the second largest warehouse operator after Prologis. GLP's customers include Adidas, COFCO, H&M, Panasonic Logistics, Schenker, Amazon, Deppon, JD.com, Procter & Gamble, Unilever, Coca-Cola, DHL, FedEx, Rakuten, Walmart and Goodaymart (Haier).

GLP is a company in its growth phase; supply of logistic facilities and services continues to lag rapidly growing demand. In the words of the company CEO Ming Z. Mei, *"The overall China market faces a long-term undersupply of modern logistics facilities, with warehouse stock per capita in China only 1/13th the amount of the US"*. A study by Macquarie Research shows that even with China growing at seven percent and current warehouse pipeline growing at 41% CAGR, the shortage of warehouses in the world's second biggest economy will continue for at least three years.

A casual observer of stock and property markets would note that CapitaLand, CDL and GLP are all categorised as property companies. Yet GLP's business model is very different from CapitaLand's and CDL's. CapitaLand and CDL are engaged in property development across multiple real estate sub-sectors such as residential, retail, hospitality, industrial and office and have also sponsored REITs into which they inject their recurring income generating properties. GLP, on the other hand, owns and operates logistic facilities.

CapitaLand and CDL generate cyclical and potentially volatile revenues from property development as well as the relatively more stable recurring income from their investment properties and dividends from the REITs they have sponsored. GLP is a property owner, developer and fund manager focussing on the logistics sector. However GLP's revenues have tended to be more stable than CapitaLand and CDL as recurring rental revenues constituted 81% of its FY16[1] revenues followed by fund management fees (16%) and dividends (2%).

Genesis and Evolution

In 2010, GLP floated an USD2.7 billion IPO, then the largest ever real estate IPO globally, and now has a market capitalisation of SGD8.93 billion as of 15 July 2016, with the Government of Singapore Investment Corporation (GIC) as its largest shareholder owning 36.57% of the shares (June 2016).

Please refer to Table 13 in Appendix 1 for the key milestones in Global Logistic Properties' evolution.

Business & Financial Review

Starting with portfolio of logistic facilities in Japan and China in 2010 with a completed area of 6 million square metres GLP's portfolio now includes United States and Brazil with the total area rising to 38 million square metres as of end-FY16 (Figure 1). The average occupancy rate of GLP's global portfolio was 92% as of end-FY16.

GLP's core real estate assets of investment properties i.e., its logistics facilities and investments in jointly controlled entities have more than doubled during the period FY10 to FY16, with its logistic facilities accounting for most of its real estate assets. The company's foray

---

[1] GLP's financial year ending falls on 31 March

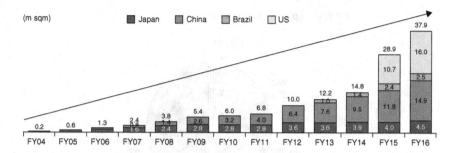

Figure 1

Source: Global Logistic Properties Company Overview, May 2015.

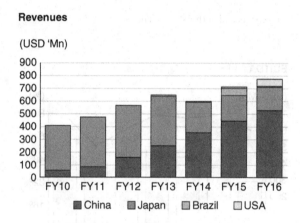

Figure 2

Source: GLP Annual Reports and authors' calculations.

into the US is recent. In 2014, GLP acquired an USD8.0 billion logistics property portfolio in the United States via its fund management platform. In 2015, GLP also entered into an agreement to acquire a US$4.55 billion US logistics portfolio from Industrial Income Trust, with the intention of injecting the portfolio into its fund management platform. In terms of net asset value (NAV), China and Japan continue to dominate the portfolio, accounting for 91% of revenues (Figure 2) and 82% of NAV in FY15 (Figure 3).

GLP, since its FY10 IPO, has generated a robust EBITDA margin mostly in excess of 70% (Figure 4). In FY15, its EBITDA margin

NAV: Geographic Breakdown

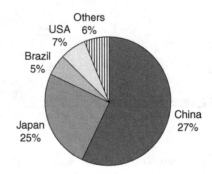

Figure 3

Source: GLP Annual Reports and authors' calculations.

EBITDA

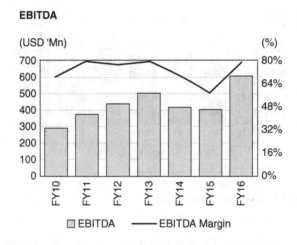

Figure 4

Source: GLP Annual Reports and authors' calculations.

declined to 57% due to the loss of rental income on account of the USD54.3 million losses incurred on sale of its investment properties and the higher operating expenses incurred on its expanded investment portfolio. The logistics business is a capital intensive business, especially since GLP is in its growth phase (Figure 5).

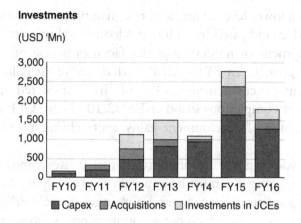

Figure 5

Source: GLP Annual Reports and authors' calculations.

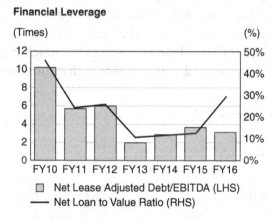

Figure 6

Source: GLP Annual Reports and authors' calculations.

With the successful expansion and stabilisation of GLP's portfolio, its cash flow leverage metric i.e. the ratio of net lease adjusted debt to EBITDA (Figure 6) has moderated significantly to 3.12x by end-FY16 from 10.24x as of end-FY10. Balance sheet leverage i.e. its net loan to value ratio continued to be low at 20% as of end-FY16. GLP is exposed to a lower level of financial risk than property developers like CapitaLand, as indicated by its low net loan to value ratio.

Development of modern logistics facilities is one of GLP's key engines of growth. In FY16, GLP started USD2.80 billion of new developments, representing 14% of its completed portfolio. Development completions stood at USD2.10 billion. GLP generated US$225 million of development gains, representing a profit margin of 27%.

While assessing the profitability of real estate companies at an after tax level, investors must be aware if the profit figure includes fair value changes. Fair value changes are changes in the market value of investment properties, which per accounting policy, property companies are allowed to report as a gain or loss in their income statement depending on whether their property portfolio has appreciated or depreciated in value. Figure 7 indicates that fair value changes have constituted a bulk of GLP's reported net income. So, the dividend payout ratio i.e. the percentage of dividends paid to net income seems low on a reported basis. If fair value gains are excluded from net income, the 'adjusted' dividend payout ratio is much higher as indicated in Figure 8. A second point to note is that the treatment of fair

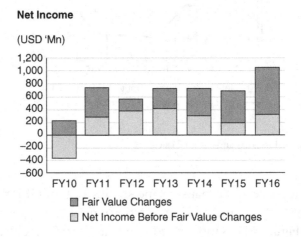

Figure 7

Source: GLP Annual Reports and authors' calculations.

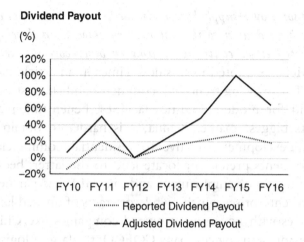

Figure 8
Source: GLP Annual Reports and authors' calculations.

value gains and losses is symmetric i.e., should the property portfolio depreciate in value, companies would have to report a fair value loss in their income statement as GLP did in FY10.

Challenges

GLP's exposure to China at 57% of its $36 billion is of concern to financial markets. Development starts and completions for 2017 were recently guided lower as tenants have turned cautious about renewals in a slowing environment. The weakness of the Chinese yuan and the Brazilian real currencies are also weighing on earnings. On the business front, competition has surfaced from insurance companies and e-commerce firms which are entering the logistics business.

The slowdown in the world's second largest economy and property oversupply in some cities are causes for concern. But GLP is upbeat about the growing contribution of domestic consumption and services to China's GDP and the fast expanding retail segment.

To tackle these threats the company has reined in its investments in parts of China. "*About 20% of the markets we are operating in*

China face some over-supply because in the last two years a lot of pension funds have been drawn to the sector, so we slow down development in those markets but we continue to grow in other core markets," CEO Ming Z. Mei was quoted in Business Times in an article dated June 20, 2016. The growing trend of e-commerce and chain stores is driving demand for modern logistics facilities, benefitting players like GLP. In its biggest market, China, it is harder to obtain land for warehouse development relative to residential/commercial. Local state governments prefer to allocate land to the latter, because they are bigger drivers of employment and tax. GLP has partnered with state-owned enterprises which own large tracts of unused land. It has joint ventures with government owned companies like China's biggest food manufacturing company COFCO; the largest logistics company Sinotrans, and automaker Brilliance Group. It can also potentially tap into 16 million square metres of land through its partners China Life Insurance, China Development Bank and Bank of China, which own around CNY17 billion worth "allocated" land use rights. These are typically allocated by the government on a gratuitous basis and do not have a specific lease term.

Takeaways

GLP has using the fund management platform to enhance returns and recycle capital once its assets are stabilised. Since the launch of the fund management platform in 2012, the company has lowered development risks by inducting more capital partners which also means better profit margins through recurring fees. It has unlocked capital in China by selling stakes to state owned enterprises and financial institutions and aims to use the REIT model to realise cash profit and generate higher recurring income from management fees..

The capital unlocking in its biggest market of China gives it the opportunity to recycle capital and grow its fund business in its biggest market, by offering REIT products to investors seeking yield products. The fund management business, in which the company leverages on external funds to improve returns and expand its property network, without increasing equity, remains a part of its key strategy. Its assets under management grew by 75% in the past financial year to USD35 billion and fee earnings are seen boosted as the USD11 billion uncalled capital gets deployed. The fund management business contribution to revenue could rise to one-third from the present 17%, CEO Mei was quoted in a Business Times article.

The company's entry into the new markets of United States and Brazil is lifting profitability and helping diversify its portfolio. Still, diversification is not a core strategy and, the company is more focused on growing its logistics property development and fund management platforms. The rise in occupancy rates and rental stability in the new markets is leading to reduced volatility and steady financials. The fund management business, in which the company leverages on external funds to improve returns and expand its property network, without increasing equity, remains a part of its key strategy. GLP is a major benefactor of the explosion in e-commerce and the rising domestic consumption in fast growing emerging markets of China and Brazil. Although e-commerce is already growing rapidly, the opportunity that lies ahead is even bigger.

Digital retail penetration is exploding in China, which overtook United States as the world's biggest digital retail market in 2013. E-commerce shoppers' purchases have grown at the pace of 70% each year since 2009. According to Bain & Co., China has leapfrogged ahead of its counterparts in the global digital market with online retailing accounting for 6% of all purchases, compared with 5% in Germany and 3.9% in Japan.

GLP's exposure to retail and consumer goods sectors is more than half the total in all the markets, a clear reflection of the growing importance of e-commerce in the group's strategy. Online sales in Asia Pacific are expected to reach $1.3 trillion by 2019, implying a compound growth rate of 18.5% over the next three years. The explosion in e-commerce should fuel GLP's growth in the next five years.

20

SINGAPORE TELECOMS: AN OVERVIEW

Telephones were first introduced in Singapore in 1879 by Bennett Pell, manager of the Eastern Extension Telegraph Company, with a trial connection made between Raffles Square and Tanjong Pagar using a telegraph line. Pell also set up a 50-line exchange made up of manual switchboards in 1881, giving Singapore a head start. The city state, then a British colony, was the first in the East to have a telephone system, barely three years after Alexander Graham Bell patented his invention.

This exchange was located at Collyer Quay, operating from the office of John Fraser & Co. From 1882, this exchange grew under a new owner, the Oriental Telephone and Electric Company (OTEC), and was marked by several milestones, including the opening of a Central Telephone Exchange in Hill Street in 1907 and the start of international services inaugurated by a Singapore-London call on 1 December 1937.

After World War II, the rate of subscribers overwhelmed OTEC's capacity and it could not cope with the increased load. This prompted the British colonial government to terminate its licence in 1954 and acquire its assets on 1 January the following year. The domestic telephone service then came under a new body, the Singapore Telephone

Board (STB), formed under the Singapore Telephone Board Ordinance, while another entity, the Telephone Department, took charge of trunk and international telephone services.

The Telephone Department was converted into a statutory board, the Telecommunication Authority of Singapore (TAS). On 1 April 1974, STB and TAS merged into a single statutory board known as Telecommunication Authority of Singapore, the Telecommunication Authority of Singapore (TAS) in a bid to streamline operations and provide higher quality and efficient services. The Postal Department was merged with Telecoms on 1 October 1982 with the objective of optimising resources from both organisations and provide the "*most efficient and cheapest service to the public.*"

On 1 April 1992, the telecommunications aspect of Telecoms was corporatised as Singapore Telecommunications Private Limited (Singapore Telecom) while its postal services was taken over by a newly formed subsidiary company, Singapore Post Pte Ltd. TAS was reconstituted as the regulator of telecommunications and postal industries.

Singapore Telecom's (Singtel) initial public offering opened on 12 October 1993 and the shares floated on the Stock Exchange of Singapore on 1 November. Its public listing made history as 1.4 million Singapore citizens became direct shareholders of a giant national utilities company for the very first time. The event also marked the largest floatation on the stock exchange — a company with a share capital of 15.25 billion shares.

In 1996, the government informed Singtel that it would end the company's monopoly in the telecommunications market on 1 April 2000. Singtel's license to be the sole provider in Singapore's mobile services market had been scheduled to end in 1997, while its monopoly on fixed line, IDD and other services was to end in 2007. The company received SGD1.5 billion in compensation from the government for the early implementation of full market liberalisation.

The telecommunications market in Singapore is highly organised, with three integrated info-communications operators providing landline, mobile phone, and cable TV and internet/broadband connections — Singtel, StarHub and MobileOne (M1). A fourth entrant in this market is expected to intensify competition as Australia's TPG Telecom launches mobile services in 2018 after it won spectrum rights in December 2016. However, this has not adversely affected consumer freedom. Consumers are free to opt for landline, mobile, cable TV and internet connections from different service providers, though this may not be a cost effective choice.

The trends in mobile penetration, wireless broadband subscriptions, residential wired broadband penetration rate and mobile data usage are characteristic of a developed nation. Mobile penetration has increased by 75% during the twelve year period 2003 to 2012 to 148% in 2014 from 84.5% in 2003. During the three year period 2012 to 2014, wireless broadband subscriptions have grown by 24% to 10.07 million from 8.11 million. The household wired broadband penetration rate has been at over 100% since 2012, with the figure reaching 106% in 4Q 2014. The monthly average of mobile data usage has almost trebled to 9.33 petabytes in 4Q 2014 from 3.38 perabytes in 2Q 2011.

Telecoms across the world are a highly regulated sector. Nitin Soni, Director — Telecom, Media and Technology at Fitch Ratings states:

"Singapore's telecom regulatory environment has gradually moved from a fairly monopolistic environment in 2000 to a competitive environment with emphasis on penalizing anti-competitive behaviour as of today.

In 2000, the telecom regulator, Information Development authority (IDA) opened up the sector to foreign and domestic companies to promote competition and efficiency in the sector, dominated then by Singapore Telecommunication Limited (Singtel). During the last 15 years, IDA has on several occasions, demonstrated its stance to promote competition and establish fair and transparent competitive environment. Also, during late-2011, Government of Singapore also amended the Telecommunications Act, giving it more power to curb monopolistic behaviour and to promote competition in the telecommunications sector.

In 2005, IDA conceptualized a fibre-based national broadband network (NBN), an alternative to Singtel's dominant copper-based network, under its Intelligent Nation 2015 masterplan (iN2015). IDA designed the NBN structure in three layers — OpenNet, Nucleus Connect and retail service providers to structurally separate the active and the passive infrastructure. OpenNet, owned by a consortium of Singtel, Canada' Axia Netmedia, Singapore Press Holding and SP telecommunications is responsible for the design, build and operation of the passive infrastructure including the dark-fibre network and ducts. Nucleus Connect — Owned by StarHub, is responsible to provide wholesale network services over their active equipment including switches and transmission to retail service providers at non-discriminatory and non-exclusive prices. The Retail Service Providers (RSPs), which formed the third layer, offered services over the NBN to end-users, including businesses and consumers.

During September 2013, IDA once again promoted competition by asking Singtel to divest its majority stake in NetLink Trust by April 2018. During November 2013, NetLink Trust, a business trust that owns the ducts and manholes, acquired 100% in OpenNet for SGD126m. IDA also ensured competition by establishing monitoring board consisting of government representatives to ensure Singtel does not influence any decisions on service price as well as terms and conditions."

21

STARHUB

Singtel is Singapore's largest info-communications company, both by revenues and market capitalization. Yet we chose to write about StarHub as the first chapter in the telecom section of this book as it is a pure play info-communications company. In other words, StarHub's operations are focussed on mobile, pay TV, broadband and fixed services for both consumer and corporate markets in Singapore. Hence readers would be able to better understand the business, growth potential and risks associated with an integrated info–communications operator.

Singtel, on the other hand, is an info-communications operator-cum-investor, offering info-telecom services both is Singapore and Australia through its subsidiary Optus and has invested in major telecom companies across Asia Pacific. The telecom section of this book analyses how this factor results in some interesting similarities and differences in the two companies' performance and possibly, growth trajectories.

Genesis

According to www.referenceforbusiness.com:

> "*In 1998, a consortium led by ST Telemedia, a unit of the Singapore state-owned investment agency Temasek Holdings, won its license bid*

and established StarHub Holdings. Other shareholders in the new com-
pany included BT Group, Nippon Telegraph & Telephone Corp...
StarHub began setting up its cellular and fixed line networks, including
building its own fiber optic network. The company's investment in this
effort topped $1.5 billion. StarHub expected to launch its cellular net-
work by 2000; the fixed line telephone sector was not expected to be
deregulated until 2002.

In 1999, StarHub brought in a new CEO, Steven Terrell (Terry)
Clontz, an American who had entered the telecommunications industry
as an engineer for Southern Bell in 1973.... Clontz led StarHub to its first
acquisition, Cyberway Pte., one of only three Internet service providers
(ISPs) in Singapore. The company rebranded its Internet service under
the StarHub brand, and then jump-started the market by offering the
city's first free dial-up service. This move helped establish the StarHub
brand among customers for the first time. The addition of Internet service
added an important component to its "hub" concept that of providing the
full array of telecommunications services.

StarHub officially launched its cellular phone operations in 2000.
The company quickly established itself as an aggressive competitor,
introducing customer services such as free incoming calls and per-
second billing... Another focus for the company at the beginning of the
new decade was the extension of its international service agreement
networks. By the end of 2000, the company had signed agreements with
partners in 16 countries, including mainland China, as well as the
United States and the United Kingdom. The company expected to build
out this network to more than 50 partners worldwide into the
mid-decade.

StarHub began preparing for its future expansion in 2001, bidding
for and winning one of the city's 3G cellular phone licenses. In the mean-
time, the company also had begun negotiations that would bring a major
extension to its "hub" concept. Those negotiations resulted in the company's
announcement that it had reached a merger agreement with Singapore
Cable Vision (SCV), the city's only pay-TV provider...

By 2003, StarHub Cable TV's subscriber base had topped 300,000,
with a penetration rate of nearly one-third. In that year, the company's
cable television operation received a new boost when the Singapore govern-
ment announced that the Singapore market was most likely not large
enough to support two pay-TV services. As a result, StarHub retained a
de facto monopoly on that market. By the end of that year, the company's

cable television service neared 400,000, lured by its expanded offering of 50 channels...

The company rolled out a digital television service in 2004, adding 11 digital channels as well as a series of interactive services. StarHub went public in October 2004, listing its stock on the Singapore Stock Exchange."

Interestingly, Temasek is the controlling shareholder of both StarHub and Singtel with effective stakes of 56.08% and 51% respectively. Nippon Telegraph and Telephone Corporation is StarHub's second largest shareholder with a 9.91% stake. The remaining stake is held by a host of institutional and retail investors.

Please refer to Table 14 in Appendix 1 for the key milestones in StarHub's evolution.

Business & Financial Review

During the eleven year period from 2005 to 2015, StarHub's revenues grew by 56% to SGD2.44 billion in 2015 from SGD1.57 billion in 2005, propelled by its four key businesses — mobile, pay TV, broadband and fixed network services (Figure 1). However, revenues have been stagnating since 2012 on account of the intensively competitive nature of the Singapore info-communications market.

StarHub's revenue growth has been fuelled primarily by a growth in its customer base across all businesses (Figures 2, 3 and 4) and customer loyalty as indicated by its business-wise churn rate hovering around a low 1% (Figure 5). Churn rate is defined as the percentage of subscribers to a service that discontinue their subscription to that service in a given time period.

The decline in the number of cellular subscribers in 2014 does not adversely impact StarHub as this decline was driven by a fall in the less remunerative prepaid cellular subscribers, whose average revenue per user (ARPU) was SGD17 per month. The more remunerative post-paid subscriber base that yields an ARPU of SGD72 per month grew.

Characteristic of highly penetrated and competitive info-communications markets, ARPU across business segments has stagnated and

Revenue Composition

(*SGD 'Mn)

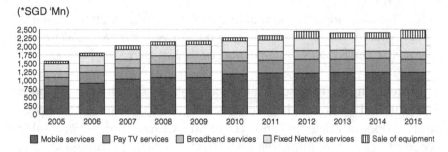

Figure 1

Source: StarHub Annual Reports & Authors Calculations.

Cellular Subscribers

(*000)

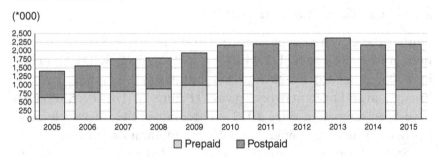

Figure 2

Source: StarHub Annual Reports & Authors Calculations.

even declined in the mobile prepaid and residential broadband businesses (Figure 6).

A steadily growing customer base coupled with stagnating ARPU has resulted in StarHub's EBITDA margin remaining stable and ranging from 29% to 32% during the last eleven years (Figure 7), though EBITDA in SGD terms has grown by 55%.

The stagnating trend in StarHub's EBITDA margin offers a sharp contrast to the declining trend in Singtel's EBITDA margin during the period 2005–2015. The EBITDA margin of Singtel's Singapore's

Broadband Lines

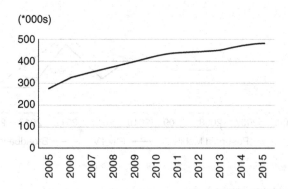

Figure 3

Source: StarHub Annual Reports & Authors Calculations.

Pay TV Subscriptions

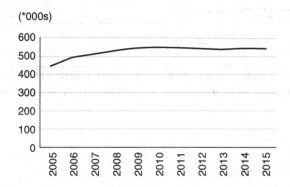

Figure 4

Source: StarHub Annual Reports & Authors Calculations.

business declined to 32% in FY14 from 47% in FY05. There are two contributory factors to this divergence in trend.

Firstly, the increasing competition in Singapore's info-communications landscape counterbalanced Singtel's first mover advantage in the mobile and land line businesses and led to a decline in its margin. Secondly, as StarHub and Singtel operate in a highly competitive

Churn Rates

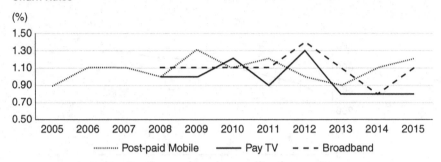

Figure 5

Source: StarHub Annual Reports & Authors Calculations.

Average Revenue Per User (ARPU)

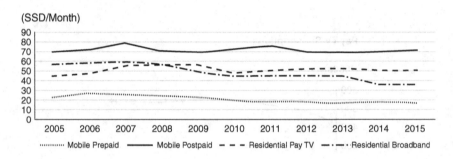

Figure 6

Source: StarHub Annual Reports & Authors Calculations.

EBITDA & EBITDA Margin

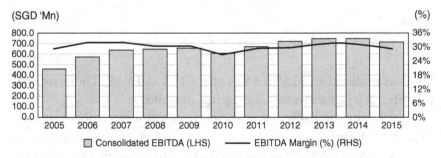

Figure 7

Source: StarHub Annual Reports & Authors Calculations.

industry their operating expenses, particularly customer acquisition costs are comparable. StarHub's traditionally lower EBITDA margin reflects its significantly smaller size than Singtel and the resultant lower bandwidth to absorb these costs.

At the current juncture, the EBITDA margins of StarHub and Singtel's Singapore business are almost on a par. Going forward, the EBITDA margins of Singapore's info-communication companies is likely to be under some pressure as the proportion of data in ARPU, particularly non-SMS data which is a low margin item, is increasing (Figure 8). While StarHub reports non-voice as a percentage of ARPU, Singtel reports the percentage of non-SMS data to ARPU. StarHub does not report the ratio of non-SMS data to ARPU but Singtel does. This trend is unlikely to be different for the two companies.

The info-communication business is capital intensive on account these companies' necessity to keep pace with the rapid technological advancements and constantly upgrades their product offerings. StarHub's capital intensity i.e., the ratio of its capital expenditure to revenues, during the period 2005 to 2015 has ranged from 10% to 16% (Figure 9), which is comparable to Singtel's capital intensity. However, the key difference between the two companies is that while

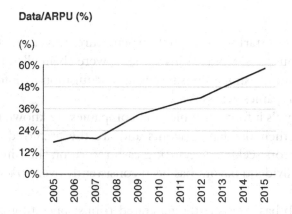

Figure 8

Source: StarHub Annual Reports & Authors Calculations.

Capex & Capex Intensity

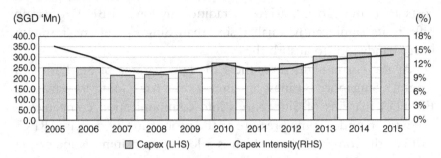

Figure 9

Source: StarHub Annual Reports & Authors Calculations.

Dividend Payout

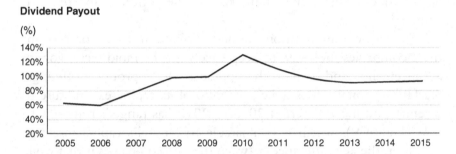

Figure 10

Source: StarHub Annual Reports & Authors Calculations.

almost all of StarHub's capital expenditure was incurred on its Singapore business, Singtel's investments were channelled towards its Singapore and Australian businesses and acquisition of info-communication companies across Asia.

Singapore's info-communication companies are known to be generous with their dividend payouts and are the preferred choice for equity investors seeking a recurring cash return on their investments. StarHub's dividend payout has been consistently over 90% since 2008 (Figure 10).

StarHub has consistently generated robust operating cash flows, which has financed its sizable capex and dividends. This has resulted

Financial Leverage

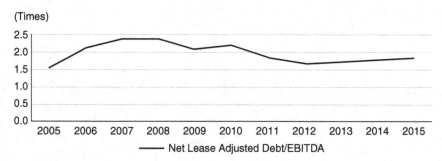

Figure 11

Source: StarHub Annual Reports & Authors Calculations.

in its financial leverage, as measured by the ratio of net lease adjusted debt to operating EBITDA, being moderate and ranging from 1.50x to 2.50x during the last ten years (Figure 11).

StarHub's strong market position, consistent operating and financial performance and a high dividend paying track record make it an apt investment for long term investors seeking predictable dividend payouts.

22

SINGAPORE TELECOMMUNICATIONS

The evolution of Singtel from a government owned statutory board to Singapore's largest info-communications operator and a multinational telecom investor is an interesting illustration of a Singapore company nimbly adapting to the giant strides taken by the info-communication industry during the last few decades and consolidating its market leading position while simultaneously being a successful investor in overseas telecom companies.

Singtel is among the foremost home grown multinational companies and represents Temasek's single largest investment accounting for 13% of its SGD242 billion portfolio as of 31 March 2016. Temasek is also Singtel's largest shareholder holding a 51% stake in the company.

Please refer to Table 15 in Appendix 1 for the key milestones in Singtel's evolution.

Singtel's business drivers are its info telecom businesses in Singapore and Australia and a portfolio of investments in the telecom space in India, The Philippines and Thailand.

Business & Financial Review

During the eleven year period FY06[1] to FY16, revenues have grown to approximately SGD17 billion in FY16 from SGD13 billion in FY06 driven by business growth in Singapore and Australia, through its wholly owned subsidiary and Australia's largest telecommunication company Optus (Figure 1). Revenues from Singapore operations steadily grew by 80% during the eleven year period ended FY16. Consolidated revenues peaked to SGD18.82 billion in FY12 before moderating to the current levels, mirroring the trend in Optus' revenues and the SGD/AUD exchange rates.

But the growth drivers have changed drastically over the years. While land lines was Singtel sole business at the time of inception, mobiles, data and internet services drive revenues and margins at the current juncture. The average collection rate per minute of international calls has plummeted to less than SGD0.10 during the last decade (Figure 2)[2] and the number of land line connections has decreased on account of the reduction in the number of residential connections (Figure 3).

The substitution of land lines with mobile phones is evident in the number of cellular subscribers more than doubling during the last decade (Figure 4). But due to the competitive environment of

Revenues

(SGD 'Bn)

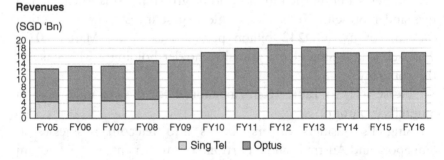

☐ Sing Tel   ■ Optus

Figure 1

Source: Singtel Annual Reports & authors' calculations.

---

[1] Singtel's financial year ending is 31 March.
[2] Figures 2 to 11 relate to Singapore only.

International Telephone

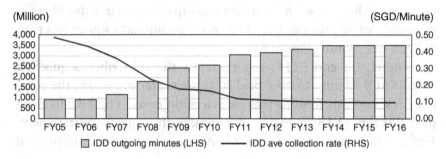

Figure 2

Source: Singtel Annual Reports & authors' calculations.

National Telephone Lines

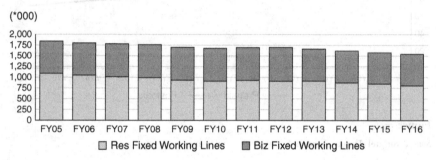

Figure 3

Source: Singtel Annual Reports & authors' calculations.

Cellular Subscribers

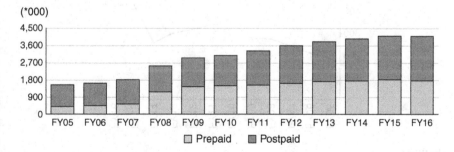

Figure 4

Source: Singtel Annual Reports & authors' calculations.

Singapore's info-telecommunication industry, the average revenue per user (ARPU) per month from postpaid cellular subscribers is declining, while prepaid ARPU has been traditionally low at less than SGD20 per month (Figure 5).

Singtel, till end-FY14, reported just the subscriber acquisition costs (SAC) relating to post-paid customers. Starting FY15, the company restated this item to include retention costs. The hike in post-paid SAC in FY15 in Figure 6 indicates the expense restatement. Figure 7 indicates that the restated SAC i.e., the cost of acquiring and

Cellular ARPU

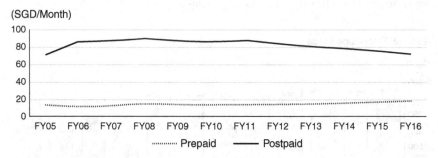

Figure 5

Source: Singtel Annual Reports & authors' calculations.

Postpaid SAC

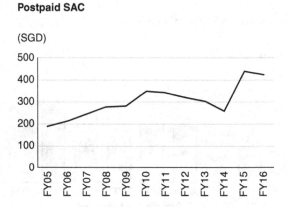

Figure 6

Source: Singtel Annual Reports & authors' calculations.

Restated Postpaid SAC

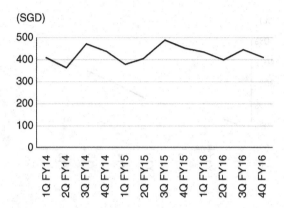

Figure 7

Source: Singtel Annual Reports & authors' calculations.

Data/ARPU (%)

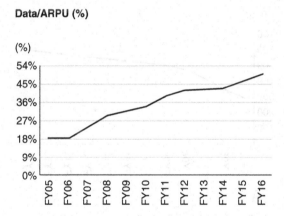

Figure 8

Source: Singtel Annual Reports & authors' calculations.

retaining post-paid mobile customers has been range bound from SGD400 to SGD500 since FY14.

With the convergence of information and communication and the increased use of messaging services and apps, the share of data in ARPU (Figure 8) has steadily risen over the years accompanied by a

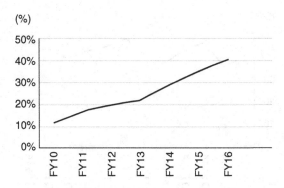

Figure 9

Source: Singtel Annual Reports & authors' calculations.

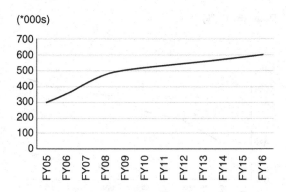

Figure 10

Source: Singtel Annual Reports & authors' calculations.

corresponding decline in voice usage. Since 2010, the share of non-SMS data in ARPU has also increased (Figure 9). Non-SMS data is low margin revenue, as it is provided by third party service providers using info-telecom companies as the medium.

Other key sources of revenue for info-telecom operators like Singtel are broadband (Figure 10) and TV subscriptions (Figure 11), which are steadily increasing.

Sing Tel TV Subscriptions

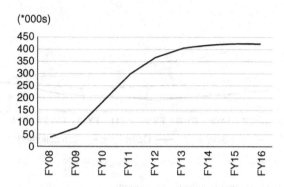

Figure 11

Source: Singtel Annual Reports & authors' calculations.

EBITDA

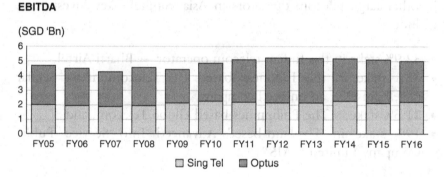

Figure 12

Source: Singtel Annual Reports & authors' calculations.

The rising post-paid mobile customer acquisition and retention costs and the increasing share of non-SMS data in ARPU has contributed to the compression in Singtel's EBITDA margin though there has been a modest increase in EBITDA in SGD terms (Figure 12). EBITDA margins of 25% to 30% appear to be the new normal for Singapore-focussed info-communication companies going forward (Figure 13).

EBITDA Margin

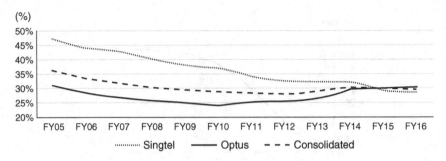

Figure 13
Source: Singtel Annual Reports & authors' calculations.

However, for Singtel the decline in EBITDA margin has been counterbalanced by a robust growth in dividends from its investments in other large telecom operators in Asia. Singtel's key investments include:

- 32.9% stake in the Indian telecom operator — Bharti Airtel,
- 35% stake in the Indonesia-based PT Telekomunikasi Selular ("Telkomsel"), an unlisted company,
- 21.5% stake in The Philippines-based Globe Telecom, and
- 19% stake in Thailand-based Advanced Info Service Public Company Limited ("AIS")

The book value of these associates and joint ventures has been fairly stable at around SGD10 billion (Figure 14), the market value of Singtel's stake in the listed entities is an estimated SGD16 billion (Figure 15).

During the eleven year period FY06 to FY16, dividends from associates and joint ventures has more than doubled to SGD1.2 billion in FY16 from SGD505 million in FY06 (Figure 16).

Characteristic of info-communication companies, Singtel started operations by providing telephone services and keeping abreast of technological advancements expanded its product suite to offer mobile communication, cable TV, broadband and digital services

Key Associates & JVs: Book Value

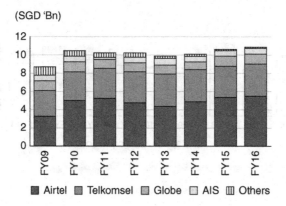

Figure 14

Source: Singtel Annual Reports & authors' calculations.

SGD 'Bn	Market Capitalization (1)	Stake (2)	Market Value of Singtel's Holding
Airtel	30	32.9%	10
Globe	9	21.5%	2
AIS	19	23.3%	5
Total	59		16
(1) As of 15 July 2016			
(2) As per FY16 Annual Report			

Figure 15

Source: Singtel Annual Reports & authors' calculations.

Associates & Joint Ventures

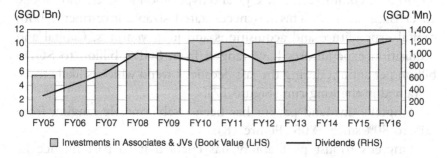

Figure 16

Source: Singtel Annual Reports & authors' calculations.

Capex & Acquisitions

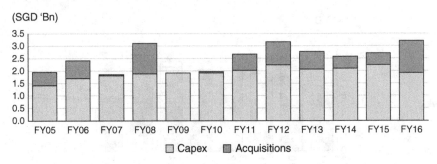

Figure 17
Source: Singtel Annual Reports & authors' calculations.

Dividend Payout

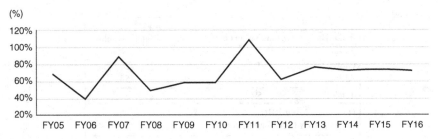

Figure 18
Source: Singtel Annual Reports & authors' calculations.

including e-commerce, concierge and hyper-local services, and mobile advertising services. This has necessitated sizable investment, both capital expenditure and acquisitions and joint ventures. Capital and acquisition expenditures have ranged from SGD2 billion to SGD3 billion per annum during the last decade, a trend which is likely to be sustained in the long run (Figure 17).

Singtel's dividend payout has been sizable mostly ranging from 60% to 80% since FY05 (Figure 18).

Singtel's robust profitability has enabled it to part finance its sizable investments and dividend payouts. Hence, its financial leverage as measured by the ratio of net lease adjusted debt to EBITDA

Financial Leverage

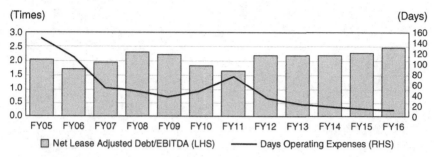

Figure 19
Source: Singtel Annual Reports & Authors' Calculations.

has been moderate at less than 3.0x since FY06. However, it must be noted that financial leverage has been increasing since FY12.

The decline in the company's cash balance from SGD2.8 billion as of 31 March 2006 to SGD462 million as of 31 March 2016 has been stark. In other words, a decade ago Singtel used to hold cash equivalent to about five months of operating expenses, while it holds cash equivalent to 14 days of operating expenses as of 31 March 2016 (Figure 19). Whether rising financial leverage and lower cash balances are indications of Singtel's increasing risk appetite remains to be seen.

The decline in cash balance is not necessarily a negative development. While Singtel earns an EBITDA margin of about 30% from its core business, banks pay an interest rate in the low single digit on its cash balances. With a strong market position and a robust financial profile, the company could easily tap capital markets and bank financing should the need arise. Hence by reducing its cash holdings, Singtel has reduced its 'negative carry' i.e., it has redirected its low return generating cash balances to the higher return generating info-communication business and compensating its shareholders.

23

INVESTING IN SINGAPORE TELECOMS: TAKEAWAYS

Telecommunications in Singapore is an industry at a crossroads. The strengths of the three operators, Singtel, StarHub and M1 are strong controlling shareholders, a demonstrated track record in offering integrated info-telecom services, stable market share and strong financials. Singtel has established its market leadership in the mobile telecommunications business, StarHub in Pay TV and M1 is a stable third operator.

But this industry faces several headwinds. Firstly, the profitability of these operators is likely to witness a declining trend. This is because with technological advancements in the info-telecom space telecom companies are increasingly becoming a channel to provide data and services to subscribers as opposed to being service providers. This has resulted in the share of the low margin non-SMS data to ARPU increasing; a trend that is likely to be sustained.

Secondly, telecoms is a capital intensive business as info-telecom operators need to constantly keep abreast of technological advancements and upgrade their product suite to maintain their market position. The capital expenditure would have to be funded through a combination of debt, operating cash flows and equity. This would lead to some increase in the telecom operators' financial leverage,

231

which is an indicator of their financial risk, and interest expenses. A partial mitigant to this risk is that all three operators are moderately leveraged at the moment and have the flexibility to increase their financial leverage to some extent without impairing their viability.

Thirdly, Singapore is a mature market characterised by high levels of info-telecom penetration. Hence, the growth prospects of StarHub, M1 and the Singapore division of Singtel are low. We believe that Singtel's growth prospects are the brightest among the three operators and will be fuelled by its investments in foreign telecom companies.

TPG Telecom, an Australian firm, made the winning bid of S$105 million in the New Entrant Spectrum Auction (NESA) which concluded in December 2016. MyRepublic, the other contender in the two-horse race, exited the NESA with a S$102.5-million bid. TPG will be provisionally allocated the full 60 MHz of spectrum made available in the NESA, comprising 20 MHz in the 900 MHz, and 40 MHz in the 2.3 GHz spectrum bands. The new spectrum rights are expected to commence earliest on April 1, 2017. The new entrant has a larger allocation of the coveted 900MHz would mean existing players would raise their capex investments in the next two years, opines Fitch Ratings. The lower frequency band is more cost-efficient for 4G deployment because of its wider coverage and better penetration within buildings.

Notwithstanding these risks, all three telecom operators have generated robust EBITDA margins in excess of 30%. The competitive nature of the industry is evident from the convergence of the EBITDA margins of the three operators, despite the disparities in their scale of operations. The healthy EBITDA and financial leverage of less than 2.0x points to these operators' underlying financial strength. These companies have returned handsome stock returns, both dividend yield and capital gains during the last decade. Additionally, Singtel, StarHub and M1 have also returned capital to their investors.

24

COMFORTDELGRO

Singaporeans and tourists to the city state, by observing the ubiquitous blue Comfort cabs and yellow CityCabs, would have deduced that the company that plies these cabs is the market leader in Singapore. ComfortDelGro, in addition to operating the largest taxi fleet of 16,997 cabs in Singapore, also operates a fleet of 3,656 public buses through its listed subsidiary SBS Transit Ltd, 350 private buses including buses owned by subcontractors, the North East and Downtown Mass Rapid Transit (MRT) train lines, the Light Rail Transit (LRT) systems in Punggol and Sengkang, and offers automotive engineering services and inspection and testing services.

ComfortDelGro is interesting from an investor's standpoint for multiple reasons. Firstly, it is a home grown multinational corporation (MNC) with operations in the UK, Ireland, Australia, China, Vietnam and Malaysia and is among the largest land transport companies in the world. Like Singtel, the company embarked on its overseas expansion plans soon after its listing on the SGX, as it realised that restricting its operations to Singapore would limit its growth and earnings prospects.

Secondly, its substantial shareholders include the financial services firm The PNC Financial Services Group, Inc.[1] with a 6% stake as per the 2015 Annual Report and the investment manager Capital

---

[1] One of The PNC Financial Services Group, Inc's key investments is BlackRock, Inc. in which it has a stake of about 20%

Research and Management Company with a 5.94% stake. Comfort-DelGro's free float at 88.06% is one of the highest among companies listed on the SGX. Thirdly, with purely financial investors as key shareholders and a professional management, the company's stock has generated amongst the highest total returns on the SGX. It would be interesting to explore if ComfortDelGro will be able to sustain such returns going forward given its scale and market position and the long term challenges it faces at the current juncture.

Genesis

"In 1970, the NTUC[2] set up a taxi co-operative called NTUC Comfort which helped to break the pirate (unlicensed) taxi racket rampant in the 1960s. It started with 200 Morris Oxford taxis and 200 British Austin minibuses paid for out of British loans out of their aid package. By 1994, with 10,000 taxis and 200 school buses, it was corporatized and listed on the Stock Exchange of Singapore as Comfort Group Limited."

In 2003, the company emerged in its present form with the merger of the Comfort Group Limited and DelGro Corporation.

Please refer to Table 16 in Appendix 1 for the key milestones in the evolution of Comfort DelGro.

ComfortDelGro, which started exclusively as a cab operator, swiftly expanded and diversified its services and area of operations. By year-end 2015, buses and bus stations accounted for 41% of operating profits (2005: 40%), followed by taxis at 36% (2005: 45%), automotive engineering services at 9% (2005: 8%), rail at 1% (2005: loss of 2%) and other services at 12% (2005: 9%).

While Singapore continues to be ComfortDelGro's revenue and profit driver, its share in operating profits has reduced to 54% in 2015 from 68% in 2005. Other key markets include UK and Ireland which contributed to 20% of 2015 operating profit (2005: 22%), Australia —14% (2005: 2%) and China to 11% (2005: 9%). Vietnam and Malaysia are minor markets for ComfortDelGro whose combined

---

[2] National Trade Union Congress

contribution to operating profits stagnated at less than 1% during the decade ended 2015.

Financial Review

During the eleven year period ended December 31 2015, ComfortDelGro's revenues and assets grew steadily at a CARG of over 5% (Figure 1) and the company's EBITDA margin was healthy and mostly ranged from 20% to 23% (Figure 2).

Running a land transport business requires sizable investments to maintain, upgrade and expand the vehicle fleet. ComfortDelGro has

Assets & Revenues

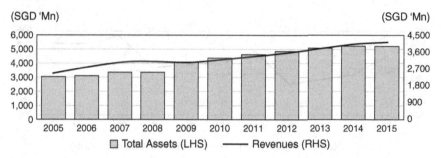

Figure 1
Source: ComfortDelGro Annual Reports.

EBITDA

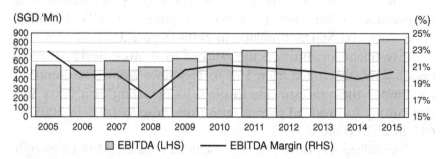

Figure 2
Source: ComfortDelGro Annual Reports.

Investments

(SGD 'Mn)

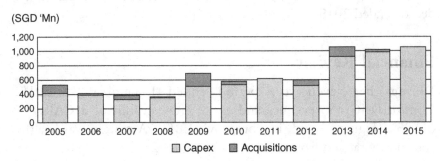

Figure 3

Source: ComfortDelGro Annual Reports.

Dividend Payout & Investment Intensity

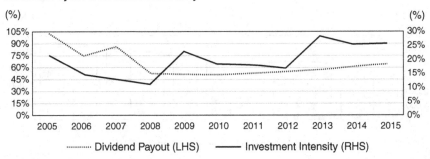

Figure 4

Source: ComfortDelGro Annual Reports.

expanded its business through capital expenditures and acquisitions. Its investment outlay almost doubled to slightly over SGD1 billion in 2015 from over SGD500 million in 2005 (Figure 3).

Investment intensity i.e. the ratio of total investments[3] to revenues has mostly ranged from 15% to 25% since 2005. The company has funded these investments through its operating cash flows and also cutting its dividend payout ratio from close to 100% in 2005 to 64% in 2015 (Figure 4).

The willingness of the management and shareholders to plough back profits into the business has resulted in ComfortDelGro's financial

---

[3] Total investments is the sum of capex and acquisition expenditure

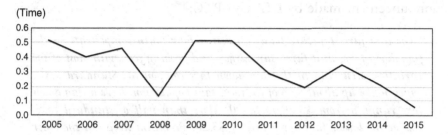

Net Lease Adjusted Debt To EBITDA

Figure 5
Source: ComfortDelGro Annual Reports.

leverage i.e. the ratio of net lease adjusted debt to EBITDA to remain at less than 1.0x during the past decade (Figure 5). This implies that the company is exposed to a low level of financial risk.

Notwithstanding ComfortDelGro's obvious strengths of a demonstrated track record of efficient operations, a diversified business profile both in terms of service and geography, a professional management and healthy financials, the company is exposed to certain long term risks.

Challenges

The cab industry is undergoing a fundamental change. The traditional model of owning and operating cabs is being overhauled with the entry of operators of operators like Uber, Lyft, Curb and Sidecar. These companies connect commuters to private, standalone cab operators through a mobile app. In the new 'transportation network' business model, heavy investment is not required to purchase and maintain vehicle fleets, which significantly reduces barriers to entry.

In March 2015,[4] Singapore's Land Transport Authority (LTA) and Public Transport Council (PTC) have proposed to standardise

---

[4] "Joint release by the Land Transport Authority & PTC — Some Parts Of Taxi Fare Structure To Be Standardised To Prevent Further Fare Complexity" dated March 31 2015

taxi fares with effect from 2H 2015. According to the joint announcement made by LTA and PTC:

> *"The taxi fare structure today consists of four main components — the flag down fare, unit fares, surcharges, and booking fees, with most of the variation occurring in the flag down fare component. Standard taxis, which make up about 95% of the total taxi population, have a flag down fare ranging from $3.20 to $3.90. More than half of standard taxis charge the lowest flag down fare of $3.20. Premium taxis, on the other hand, charge a flag down fare ranging from $3.50 to $5.00.*
>
> *LTA and PTC will adopt a balanced approach, which focuses on preventing taxi fares from becoming even more complex in the future. As mandating the harmonisation of flag down fares may lead to higher flag down fares for commuters, we will leave them as they are for now. Over time, taxi companies may, on their own accord, adjust and harmonise flag down fares within their own fleets in response to market conditions.*
>
> *The PTC will, however, require taxi companies to standardise the other taxi fare components, namely, the unit fares, surcharges, booking fees and additional passenger fees. This will prevent taxi fares from becoming even more complex for commuters in the future, like what has happened for flag down fares today, and facilitate comparison across taxi companies. As these fare components do not differ greatly within each taxi company today, taxi companies should not revise rentals or make significant adjustments to fares in order to comply with the new requirements."*

LTA and PTC's decision to leave the flag down fares unchanged but equalise the other fare components will allow cab companies to compete on the basis of price and commuters stand to benefit. But for cab companies, this might result in some decline in profitability. The situation may be exacerbated by ComfortDelGro losing a few of its bus routes in Australia to competition.

The UK and Ireland account for 20% of ComfortDelGro's operating profits. The impact of the UK voting to exit the European Union on the company remains to be seen.

Takeaways

The above risks are partially counterbalanced by the low crude oil price that prevails at the current juncture which will enable ComfortDelGro control its operating expenses and the stable prospects for public transport in Singapore.

Public transport is a cost effective and convenient commuting option in Singapore with the continuous expansion of the MRT network and bus fleet over the years. Singapore transportation statistics reveal certain interesting trends. The number of private vehicles (including taxis) has been steadily increasing, albeit at a slowing rate, during the last thirteen year, 2002 to 2014 (Figure 6).

Also, the annual average mileage per private car has declined by almost 14% during the period 2002 to 2014 (Figure 7) and the average daily passenger trips by public transport improved by a whopping 38% during the same period (Figure 8).

Private Vehicles In Singapore

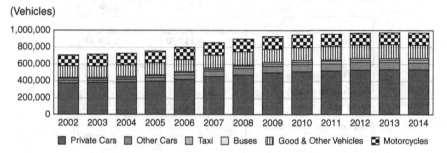

Figure 6
Source: Singapore Land Statistics in Brief 2004 to 2015.

Average Annual Km Travelled Per Private Car

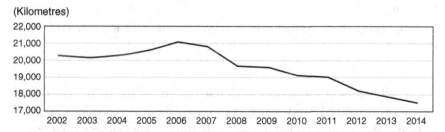

Figure 7
Source: Singapore Land Statistics in Brief 2004 to 2015.

Average Daily Riderships

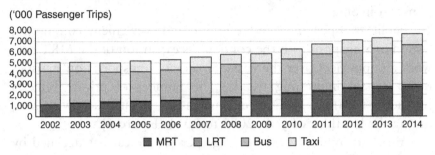

Figure 8

Source: Singapore Land Statistics in Brief 2004 to 2015.

SGD 'Mn		Comfort Delgro	SMRT (1)
	Singapore	2,468.70	1,296.60
	Overseas	1,642.80	
Revenue		**4,111.50**	**1,296.60**
EBITDA		840.00	342.10
EBITDA Margin (%)		20.4%	26.4%
Dividend Payout (%)		63.8%	55.6%
Total Assets		5,216.30	2,720.00
Net Lease Adjusted Debt /EBITDA (x)		0.06	2.26
Market Capitalization (2)		6,489.00	2,358.00
Current P/E (2)		21.02	21.55

(1) SMRT's finanical years ending is on 31 March
(2) As of July 15, 2016

Figure 9

Source: ComfortDelGro and SMRT Financial Statements, www.bloomberg.com and authors' calculations.

A comparison of ComfortDelGro's financials with the other Singapore-focussed land transport major, SMRT Corporation Ltd, indicates that ComfortDelGro is clearly the market leader with a more diversified business model and stronger financials (Figure 9).

Peer Comparison

This distinction is particularly interesting when one considers the fact that Temasek Holdings has a 54.10% stake in SMRT and underscores one of the reasons for Singapore's emergence as a leading global financial and business hub i.e., the city state provides in most industries an even playing field for government linked and private sector entities.

25

SINGAPORE AIRLINES

Singapore Airlines (SIA) has established itself as a leading global airline not only in terms of fleet and service quality, but also by registering a consistent financial performance in an industry in which bankruptcies and reorganisations have not been uncommon. Much larger airlines, like American Airlines, US Airways, Delta, United and Southwest who have had the advantages of catering to both domestic and international markets and larger fleets, have been through periods of financial distress and reorganisation.

SIA is interesting from an investor's standpoint as it is an example of how maintaining efficient operating metrics and financial discipline coupled with disciplined fleet upgradation and expansion can translate into meaningful long term returns for shareholders in an otherwise volatile industry.

Genesis

The British Imperial Airways, Straits Steamship Company and Ocean Steamship Company of Liverpool together incorporated the Malayan Airways in 1937. As the promoters were unsure of the commercial viability of the Malayan Airways, the airline lay dormant and was revived only after World War II.

Reflecting the political developments of the time, the airline's name was changed to Malaysian Airways in September 1963 and subsequently to Malaysia-Singapore Airlines (MSA) in May 1966. That month, the Singapore and Malaysia governments injected fresh capital into the carrier, bringing their shareholdings to 42.79% each. The rest of the shares were held by the Brunei government, BOAC, Qantas, the Straits Steamship Company and the Ocean Steamship Company.

By 1971, differences arose between the governments of Malaysia and Singapore over MSA's corporate direction and the alliance came to an end. MSA's assets were divided, with Singapore receiving all the Boeing aircraft, airline headquarters building, aircraft hangars and maintenance facilities at Paya Lebar Airport, computer reservation system and most of the overseas offices. Malaysia received the Friendship Fleet, Britten-Norman aircraft, equipment in Malaysia and some overseas offices, and Singapore paid compensation for the imbalance in the divided assets.

Evolution

The newly-named Singapore Airlines became Singapore's flag carrier and inherited MSA's international route network, which connected over 20 airports across 18 destinations including Europe, the Middle East, Australia and parts of South, Southeast and North Asia. The lack of a domestic air-travel market meant that from the start, SIA and the Singapore government had to focus on the expansion of the airline's international route network. Between 1973 and 1997, the government signed air services agreements with the governments of Australia, New Zealand, Indonesia, Malaysia, Japan, India, Taiwan, Korea and the Philippines. These agreements helped pave the way for future negotiations for air traffic rights. Other routes were added via codesharing agreements and strategic alliances.

Other facets of SIA's strategy included the growth of a modern aircraft fleet, the development of the then-newly inaugurated Changi Airport as an air traffic hub, and the promotion of Singapore as a travel destination. A key factor in SIA's growth was Singapore's development as a hub for Southeast Asian business.

To develop its service culture, SIA opened seven schools to train staff in the core functional areas of cabin crew, flight operations, commercial training, information technology, security, airport services and engineering. An SIA Management Development Centre was also incorporated. The company benchmarks its customer service not only against other airlines, but also against those in other industries such as hotels, restaurants and car rental companies. These measures helped transform SIA into an airline that has won several awards and accolades.

From its inception, SIA has invested substantially in its brand. In 1972, SIA worked with an advertising agency, Batey Inc., to *"present Singapore Airlines as a competent, modern, international airline of Asian origin, offering the best in-flight service in the world"*. In its early days, the airline would run between three to four commercials per year based on the Singapore Girl concept of a stewardess-driven service culture. The Singapore Girl is now one of the airline's most recognisable trademarks despite some criticisms of sexism and subservience in the image.

SIA is now one of the largest companies listed on the SGX, with Temasek Holdings having a majority stake of 55.3% in the company.

Please refer to Table 17 in Appendix 1 for the key milestones in SIA's evolution since 2000.

An examination of SIA's milestones since 2000 indicates that the airline has adopted a multi-pronged strategy to maintain its market position. These include maintaining a state of the art fleet, entering into code share arrangements to expand network, acquiring and divesting companies guided entirely by commercial considerations, enhancing passenger travel experience through a slew of online and in-flight facilities, rationalising its workforce when necessary and divesting assets.

Currently, SIA's passenger portfolio comprises four airlines:

- The flagship Singapore Airlines which is a long haul full service airline,
- Scoot, a long haul low cost airline,
- SilkAir, a regional full service airline, and
- Tiger Air, a regional low cost airline

In FY16, East Asia accounted for 44% of SIA's consolidated revenues (FY06: 44%), Europe 9% (15%), South West Pacific 9% (12%), the Americas 4% (8%), West Asia & Africa 3% (7%) and non-scheduled services and incidental revenue 30% (15%).

Operating Performance

SIA has sought to consolidate its market position through product differentiation rather than expansion. The airline has taken a conscious decision to maintain its overall capacity i.e. the product of total capacity production (in tonnes) and distance flown (in kilometres), while ensuring optimal passenger experience. This has resulted in SIA maintaining its overall load (Figure 1), i.e. the product of total load carried (in tonnes) and distance flown (in kilometres) even through the global financial crisis of 2007–08.

The 'overall' statistics presented in Figures 1 to 3 are a consolidation of the flagship carrier Singapore Airlines, SilkAir and SIA Cargo.

SIA's overall yield i.e. the ratio of passenger revenue from scheduled services divided by revenue passenger-km grew by a modest 15.4% during the nine year period FY06[1] to FY15. But the carrier's

Load & Capacity

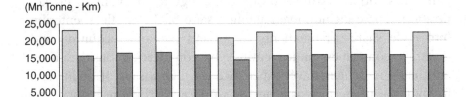

Figure 1

Source: SIA Annual Report and authors' calculations.

---

[1] SIA's financial year ending is on 31 March

Unit Yield & Cost

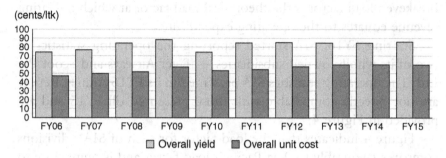

Figure 2
Source: SIA Annual Report and authors' calculations.

Overall Load & Breakeven Load Factors

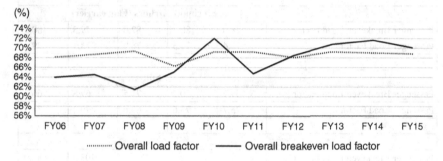

Figure 3
Source: SIA Annual Report and authors' calculations.

overall unit cost i.e., operating expenditure divided by available seat-km outstripped yield growth at 26.6% during the same period (Figure 2).

SIA has maintained a healthy load factor i.e. revenue passenger-km expressed as a percentage of available seat-km, of about 70% (Figure 3). This indicates that occupancy rates of SIA's flights are quite high. The International Air Transport Association (IATA) estimates Asia Pacific's load factor to be 66.6%. But the overall breakeven load factor i.e. overall unit cost expressed as a percentage of overall yield has increased to 71.6% in FY14 from 63.9% in FY06 due to the growth in unit costs exceeding the unit yield momentum. The overall breakeven load factor is the theoretical load factor at which operating revenue equates to the operating expenditure.

Starting FY16, SIA started reporting the operating statistics of two of its wholly-owned subsidiaries — Tiger Airways and Scoot Pte Ltd. The operating statistics SIA presented in its FY16 Annual Report are not directly comparable with those presented till FY15 and are provided in Figure 4.

Figure 4 indicates that the load factor for each of SIA's divisions compares favourably to Asia Pacific's load factor and is quite close to the breakeven load factor.

	FY12	FY13	FY14	FY15	FY16
Singapore Airlines (Flag carrier)					
Passenger Breakeven Load Factor	78.0	80.7	82.0	79.5	80.2
Passenger Load Factor	77.4	79.3	78.9	78.5	79.6
Silk Air					
Passenger Breakeven Load Factor	69.7	70.2	71.5	69.8	66.7
Passenger Load Factor	75.7	73.6	69.6	70.2	71.5
Scoot					
Passenger Breakeven Load Factor				103.6	83.9
Passenger Load Factor				82.2	84.5
Tiger Airways					
Passenger Breakeven Load Factor				88.2	82.9
Passenger Load Factor				82.1	83.3
SIA Cargo					
Cargo Breakeven Load Factor	67.3	69.5	67.0	65.2	65.2
Cargo Load Factor	63.8	63.4	62.5	63.3	61.9
Group Airlines (Passenger)					
Passenger Load Factor	77.4	79.0	78.3	78.5	79.8

Figure 4

Source: SIA Annual Report and authors' calculations.

Revenue & EBITDA Margin

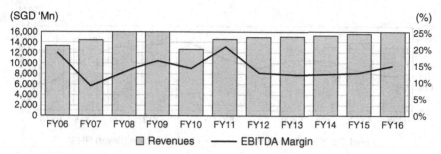

Figure 5

Source: SIA Annual Report and authors' calculations.

Jet Kerosene & Crude Oil Prices

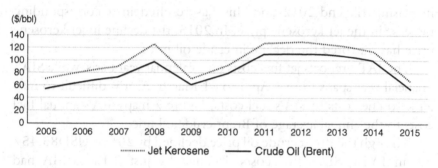

Figure 6

Source: IATA Industry Facts & Statistics downloaded from www.iata.org.

Rising breakeven load factor and high crude oil prices (and jet fuel prices as a result) till end-FY14 resulted in an EBITDA margin compression for SIA. EBITDA margin improved marginally to 12.7% in FY15 and significantly to 14.8%, underpinned by low crude oil prices (Figure 5).

An alternate way of analysing the trend in SIA's EBITDA margin is to examine its cost structure. Fuel costs and staff costs are the two largest components of an airline's operating expense.

As is evident from Figure 6 jet kerosene and Brent crude oil prices are closely correlated. Crude oil have been almost continuously

Fuel Cost & Crude Oil Price

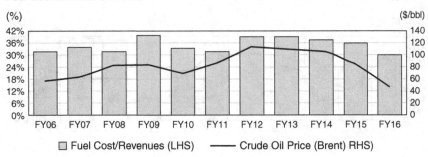

Figure 7

Source: SIA Annual Report and authors' calculations.

increasing till end-2012 and this has resulted in a corresponding increase in the jet kerosene price. In 2015, the decline in jet kerosene price has mirrored the decline in crude oil price.

The IATA reports jet fuel costs on a calendar year basis, while SIA's financial year spans from 1 April to 31 March. As it is difficult to map jet kerosene costs to SIA's fuel costs, Figure 7 maps SIA's annual fuel costs to the annual average of Brent crude oil price.

Though the Brent crude oil price declined by 20% to USD85.45/bbl in FY15, SIA's fuel costs declined by just 2.1% as SIA had hedged its fuel purchases. Hence the savings on the fuel bill were offset by the loss on its hedging contracts. In FY16, a 44% decline in crude oil prices resulted in a 19% decline in SIA's fuel costs. The IATA estimates the average jet kerosene price to further decline to USD45/bbl during calendar year 2016. This should result in all airlines including SIA saving on their fuel bills and improving their EBITDA margins, though the extent of savings achieved is a function of the extent to which their fuel bills are hedged and the tenor of the hedging contracts.

By rationalising its workforce over the years (Figure 8), SIA has reduced its staff cost both in absolute terms by almost 6% since FY06 and as a percentage of revenues to 16% in FY16 from 18.6% in FY06 (Figure 9).

Average Number Of Employees

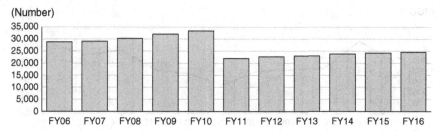

Figure 8

Source: SIA Annual Report and authors' calculations.

Staff Costs

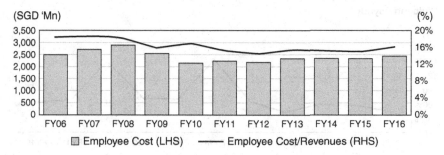

Figure 9

Source: SIA Annual Report and authors' calculations.

SIA's pre-eminent market position as a leading passenger and cargo carrier stem from the constant fleet upgradation. This has resulted in an investment intensive business model (Figure 10), although it does result in better flight safety standards. Investments are defined as the sum of capital expenditures and acquisitions. In SIA's case, capital expenditures constitute 98% of its investments and acquisitions have been minor in relation to its scale of operations.

Characteristic of a Temasek portfolio company, SIA's dividend payout has traditionally been high (Figure 11).

SIA has traditionally maintained a liquid balance sheet. Unrestricted cash as of 31 March 2016 was SGD3.97 billion equivalent to 50% of

Investments

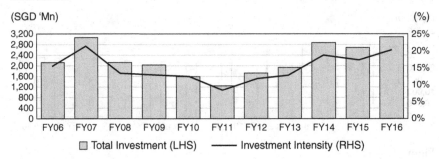

Figure 10

Source: SIA Annual Report and authors' calculations.

Dividend Payout

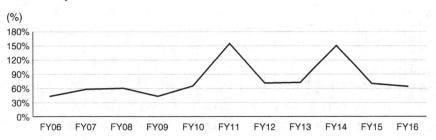

Figure 11

Source: SIA Annual Report and authors' calculations.

Financial Leverage

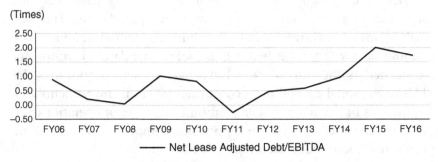

Figure 12

Source: SIA Annual Report and authors' calculations.

the sum of its debt and debt equivalent of leased aircrafts. Financial leverage, defined as the ratio of net lease adjusted debt to EBITDA, was 1.74x as of 31 March 2016 (Figure 12), exposing SIA to a moderate level of financial risk. The rise in financial leverage is on account of the increase in SIA's fleet of aircrafts on operating leases.

Challenges

Major risks Asia Pacific carriers face include over capacity, negative currency translations arising from a strengthening US Dollar and the macroeconomic slowdown in China which could put load factors under pressure. SIA's key challenge in the medium term is to maintain its market position without compromising its inherent financial strength. SIA has adopted a multipronged strategy to counter these risks. Key elements of which include optimising fuel costs aided by the low fuel price environment, introduction of premium economy class, fleet renewal, creation of a new hub at New Delhi with a fleet of nine planes through its joint venture with Tatas — Vistara and creating new revenue sources by expanding the KrisFlyer programme and establishing a flight training joint venture with Airbus.

The year 2014 witnessed several flight accidents and fatalities. According to IATA's June 2015 Safety Fact Sheet, flight-related fatalities touched a four year peak in 2014. This tragic trend was sustained in 2015 with thirty sixty eight flight accidents reported; though fatalities were much lower (Figure 13). Maintaining its flight safety record would remain SIA's priority.

	2009	2010	2011	2012	2013	2014	2015
Yearly Flights (Millions)	33.2	34.0	35.0	35.6	36.2	38.0	37.6
Total Accidents	90	94	92	75	81	73	68
Fatal Accidents	18	23	22	15	16	12	4
Fatalities	685	786	490	414	210	641	136

Figure 13. Global Airlines Accidents Trend
Source: IATA Safety Fact Sheet.

Takeaways

Despite operating in a cyclical and capital intensive industry that is getting increasingly competitive especially in the low cost segment, SIA's operating and financial metrics have been consistently sound. Singapore's flag carrier started operations with significant handicaps such as the absence of a domestic market to cater to and a small fleet size. However, the airline has demonstrated that it's possible for a mid-sized airline to carve out a significant market position and generate attractive shareholder returns, by ensuring sound operations, prudent financial policies and a disciplined approach to fleet expansion.

26

AND THE CURTAINS FALL...FOR NOW

A review of the twenty companies covered in this book highlights the diversity of their businesses, the differentiated strategies they have adopted to build their market position and how these home grown companies have spread their wings to prosper in the most opportune markets globally. Singapore's business friendly policies, effective rule of law, robust intellectual property regime and low-corruption environment have combined to create a culture of corporate excellence and discipline. The city-state's policies have enhanced economic freedom transforming its workforce into one of the most skilled globally, and helped boost prosperity across the corporate landscape.

To put Singapore's competitive advantages, cyclical risks and system specific challenges in perspective, we have summarized below the stock performance of listed companies included in the book. The companies covered in this book but excluded from Figure 1 below are the unlisted Temasek Holdings and Marina Bay Sands. Also excluded is Fraser & Neave, which is no longer a STI constituent.

Stock Performance of Select Singapore-based Blue Chips

Figure 1 offers a few interesting pointers for investors. Firstly a large company in terms of market capitalisation does not necessarily translate into a high share price. Singtel's SGD68.40 billion market

Company	Industry	Ownership Major Shareholder	52 Week Share Price Range(SGD) (a)	Current P/E	Price / Book	10-year Stock Returns Dividend Yield	10-year Stock Returns Capital Gains	10-year Stock Returns Total Return
Golden Agri Resources	Agri-Business	Massingham International Ltd.	0.31 - 0.45	58.33	1.17	1%	-96%	-95%
Olam International (b)	Agri-Business	Temasek Holdings Pte. Ltd.	1.555 - 2.170	-55.91	1.01	56%	124%	179%
Wilmar International (c)	Agri-Business	Kuok Brothers Sdn. Bhd.	2.61 - 3.750	18.74	1.34	27%	37%	64%
DBS	Bank	Temasek Holdings Pte. Ltd.	13.01 - 17.60	9.34	0.97	47%	30%	77%
OCBC Bank	Bank	Lee Foundation (Singapore)	7.410 - 9.45	9.89	1.05	64%	83%	147%
United Overseas Bank	Bank	Wee (Cho Yaw)	16.800 - 20.46	9.53	0.99	77%	105%	182%
Singapore Exchange Limited	Financial Services	SEL Holdings Pte. Ltd.	6.610 - 8.05	22.62	8.95	175%	355%	529%
Keppel Corporation	Conglomerate	Temasek Holdings Pte. Ltd.	4.640 - 6.59	7.43	0.89	217%	172%	389%
SIA Engineering	Engineering	Temasek Holdings Pte. Ltd.	3.31 - 3.91	23.95	2.84	84%	54%	138%
Sembcorp Industries	Engineering	Temasek Holdings Pte. Ltd.	2.160 - 3.28	10.90	0.79	66%	36%	102%
ST Engineering	Engineering	Temasek Holdings Pte. Ltd.	2.630 - 3.45	20.49	4.71	61%	21%	82%
Genting Singapore	Gaming	Genting Bhd	0.660 - 0.99	402.50	0.99	16%	124%	140%
CapitaLand	Property	Temasek Holdings Pte. Ltd.	2.80 - 3.40	12.42	0.75	31%	12%	43%
CapitaLand Mall Trust	REIT	CapitaLand Limited	1.85-2.25	11.05	1.03	48%	-14%	35%
Ascendas Real Estate Investment Trust	REIT	Ascendas-Singbridge Pte. Ltd.	2.09-2.57	19.57	1.15	64%	10%	75%
Global Logistic Properties (d)	Property	GIC Private Limited	1.595 - 2.620	13.44	1.03	13%	3%	15%
Singtel	Telecom	Temasek Holdings Pte. Ltd.	3.38 - 4.36	17.74	2.71	75%	93%	168%
StarHub	Telecom	Temasek Holdings Pte. Ltd.	2.73 - 3.97	17.59	23.99	95%	90%	184%
Comfort Delgro	Transportation	Capital Research Global Investors	2.39 - 3.12	20.77	2.67	55%	136%	191%
Singapore Airlines	Transportation	Temasek Holdings Pte. Ltd.	9.60 - 11.67	15.86	1.03	49%	-2%	47%

Source: Thomson Reuters & Yahoo Finance

(a) As of November 30 2016

(b) Olam changed its financial year ending to Dec 31 from Jun 30. So a 10.5 year return has been provided.

(c) 3 year stock returns

(d) Five year stock returns ending 31 Dec 2015 provided

Figure 1

Source: www.bloomberg.com, www.sg.finance.yahoo.com and authors' calculations.

capitalisation is the highest among the companies covered, but its share price has ranged from SGD3.38 to SGD4.41 during the last one year. United Overseas Bank's share price is the highest ranging from SGD16.80 to SGD23.37 during the last year, but its SGD30.22 billion market capitalisation is the fourth highest.

Secondly, a high share price is not synonymous with a high share value. One of the indicators of the 'value' a share is the price earnings ratio (P/E ratio). All other factors remaining constant, the stock with a lower P/E is considered a 'cheap' stock and hence, a more attractive buy.

The P/E ratios of companies with similar business profiles tend to trade within a close range. For example the P/E ratios of DBS, OCBC and UOB trade between 9.3x to 10.0x and the telecom companies — Singtel and StarHub trade between 17.5x to 17.75x.

Though GAR, Wilmar and Olam are categorised as agribusiness companies, their business profiles are very different. So the P/E ratios trade in a very wide band. Similarly, the engineering companies — ST Engineering, Sembcorp and SIA Engineering run very different businesses. So their P/E ratios range from 10.0x to 24.0x.

Price to book (P/B) is another metric used to make investment decisions. If a company's fundamentals are sound, a lower P/B ratio implies that the stock is undervalued. It is interesting to note that the P/B ratios of the Singapore banks, property companies and Keppel Corporation and Sembcorp Industries are close to 1.0x i.e., the market value per share (the share price) is close to the book value per share.

Successful long term investors are conversant with companies' fundamentals and prospects and hold definitive views on stocks. If investors believe that the fundamentals and long term prospects of the above-mentioned companies are sound despite the low P/B ratios, then these stocks present an attractive buying opportunity.

Historical returns may also be used as a guide for making investment decisions. But investors must be aware that there is no guarantee that a company's stock may sustain its historical returns. Hence historical returns must always be viewed in conjunction with a company's fundamentals and prospects and the performance of a company's competitors while making an investment decision.

Also, understanding a company's business and associated risks are essential pre-requisites to successful investing. Investors who do not have the time or wherewithal to understand companies' business models are better off investing in index tracking exchange traded funds. The STI delivered a total return of almost 175% during the decade ended 31 December 2015.

The five companies that have delivered the highest ten year total return are Singapore Exchange (529%), Keppel Corporation (389%), ComfortDelGro (191%), United Overseas Bank (182%) and Olam International (179%). Temasek Holdings is the controlling shareholder of two of these companies — Keppel Corporation and Olam International.

While total return indicates how much dividend yield and capital gains a stock has delivered, a stock delivering high total return will not necessarily suit all types of investors. Investors seeking recurring income would prefer investing in stocks that provide a high dividend yield while those seeking to grow their investment portfolio and do not require recurring dividends would prefer stocks that are likely to appreciate in value i.e. generate capital gains.

Keppel Corporation stock has provided the highest ten year dividend yield of 217%, followed by Singapore Exchange (175%), StarHub (95%), SIA Engineering (84%) and United Overseas Bank (77%). Temasek Holdings is the controlling shareholder of three of these companies — Keppel Corporation, StarHub and SIA Engineering.

The companies, whose share prices have appreciated the most in ten years i.e. provided the maximum capital gains are Singapore Exchange (355%), Keppel Corporation (172%), ComfortDelGro (136%), Genting Singapore and Olam International (both 124%). Temasek Holdings is the controlling shareholder of two of these companies — Keppel Corporation, and Olam International.

The total returns of eighteen of the nineteen companies covered in this book are much higher than the low single digit interest rates term deposits fetch in Singapore. But investors must remember that the risk profiles of term deposits and stock returns are very different. Hence, investors must diversify their investments across multiple asset classes including deposits, stocks and property. Barring Golden Agri

Resources that has generated a negative total return, on account of falling CPO prices and a still evolving business model, the average annual total return for the remaining nineteen stocks ranges from a 3% for GLP to a maximum of 52.9% for the Singapore Exchange.

Does this imply that these companies (excluding Olam which is no longer an STI constituent) would continue to be the face of STI in the long run? Probably not. As the global macro economy and Singapore evolve and ebb and flow of business cycles continue, product and services offered by even the major companies may diminish in relevance or completely lose their relevance or the company's performance may deteriorate to an extent that its inclusion in the STI is not warranted or the company may be acquired by a larger/stronger company.

The book highlights how land lines which were initially a major source of revenue for Singtel are now a very small part of Singtel's business. Singtel expanded and upgraded its product suite in line with the technological developments and consolidated its market leadership in the Singapore telecom industry. Shipping major, Neptune Orient Lines, hit by falling freight rates, high debt levels and consequently poor financial performance, made way for Hutchison Port Holdings in the STI. Erstwhile index constituent and conglomerate Fraser & Neave was acquired by ThaiBev, after its one-time joint venture partner Heineken bought back its flagship brewery business. So, STI's composition has evolved over time and may be very different from its current composition ten years down the road.

Moreover, stocks are not the only investment instrument through which investors may gain an exposure to a company. Singapore has a small (in relation to bank loans) but growing bond market. According to Asia Bond Monitor, Singapore's bond market grew by 135% to SGD314 billion in 1Q 2016 from SGD133.12 billion in 2004. In 1Q 2016, the share of Singapore Government and corporate bonds outstanding was 59% and 41% respectively. To facilitate small investor participation in bond issues, the Government of Singapore introduced the Singapore Savings Bonds in 2015. The minimum investment in the Singapore Savings Bonds was just SGD500.

Bond returns are generally lower than stock returns as the coupon payable on a bond is a contractual commitment a government or a company makes and hence entails a lower level of risk. On the other hand, a company has the option to pay dividends on its stock out of its after tax profits and is perceived to be a riskier investment instrument than bonds. According to Thomson Reuters data, the average yield on sovereign and corporate Singapore bonds in 2015 were 2.43% and 2.70% respectively.

Notwithstanding the mode of investment — stocks or bonds, all corporates are exposed to a set of cyclical risks and system specific challenges. The cyclical risks and system specific challenges the Singapore corporate sector is exposed to and how equipped the corporates are to tide over these risks and challenges determines their long term prospects. Singapore corporates are exposed to the following cyclical risks:

- An uncertain global macroeconomic environment exacerbated by a macroeconomic slowdown in China and the contagion-like effect from sovereign defaults such as those in Europe and Latin America reverberating across the globe;
- Rising corporate debt levels in Singapore coupled with an interest rate hike would translate into higher interest expenses and lower profits for companies. According to data published by the Bank for International Settlements, Singapore's corporate debt to GDP ratio has increased to 142.7% in 2015 from 111.1% in 2008;
- Sustained low commodity and crude oil prices that depress the performance of agri-business companies and engineering firms. However companies for whom commodities and fuel are inputs would benefit from lower production costs and higher profits;
- Tourist arrivals to Singapore in 2015 registered an annual growth of just 0.9% due to the macroeconomic slowdown and anti-corruption crackdown in China, the depreciating Indonesian Rupiah and the uncertainty in global markets. While tourist arrivals have been improving in 2016, a robust tourist traffic is essential for tourist dependent industries such as hotels, serviced residences, medical tourism and gaming; and

- Singapore property prices continue to be low on account of the government imposed cooling measures and banks tightening their lending norms. In view of the unsold private residential units from launched projects and un-launched projects with prerequisites for sale, the prospects for Singapore's property sector is muted. According to Ms. Chia Siew Chuin, the director of research and advisory at Colliers International, "*Developers will adopt a restrained stance on new launches, while homebuyers adopt a wait and see attitude, given the substantial supply*".

The UK voting to exit the European Union is unlikely to have a material impact on Singapore as the UK accounts for 1.6% of Singapore's merchandise imports in June 2016 and less than 1% of merchandise exports. According to the Straits Times, the UK is ranked only 22nd among Singapore's trading partners.

The US Federal Reserve is widely expected to make multiple hikes in 2017, although the pace of increment will be gradual. This will exert mild downward pressure on the profit margins of some Singapore corporates in the near term.

Singapore corporates face a set of system specific challenges. Foremost among these is "*Enhancing the Entrepreneurship*" landscape of the country. Singapore is home to several industries that were built from the scratch such as agribusiness, airlines, banks, engineering and gaming. But the government's role in facilitating innovation and entrepreneurship has been significant. In a bid to foster private sector entrepreneurship the government sponsored Entrepreneurship Review Committee (EnRC) has engaged over 100 members of the start-up community, comprising entrepreneurs, angel investors, venture capitalists, and incubators to achieve three objectives — drive more private sector involvement, provide greater market access opportunities and improve the quality of start-ups. The success of the EnRC in motivating the private sector to spear head Singapore's corporate sector innovation is a long term goal. The government is moving in the right direction to promote private sector entrepreneurship.

Singapore's labour market is tight at the current juncture with unemployment declining to 1.9% in January 2016 from 2% in July

2013. Businesses have, of late, ranked manpower as their single biggest concern, especially in the services sector. The situation is exacerbated by Singapore's tightening immigration laws. The inability of certain businesses, especially service businesses, to hire adequate Singaporeans and Permanent Residents is incentivizing them to move their manufacturing facilities overseas.

Job outlook, which is defined as the difference between the percentage of employers looking to increase recruitment and those looking to decrease recruitment, is better in other Asian countries such as Taiwan (42%), India (37%) and Japan (23%). China's and Singapore's job outlook is ranked on a par at 13%.

Falling labour productivity is another systemic challenge Singapore faces. As indicated in Figure 2, Singapore's unit labour cost index has risen by 19% to 124.4 in 1Q 2016 from 104.6 in 2012. But the percentage change in value added per worker has been consistently lower than the percentage change in unit labour cost (Figure 3). In other words, the incremental value added per worker has been lower than the increase in labour cost.

Limited gender diversity on the boards of Singapore's listed companies is another challenge. Women's share of directorships inched up to 8.8% in 2014 from 6.6% in 2008. Most of the increase in representation by women directors has come from their role as independent directors. But it still is much lower than in Norway (40.5%), UK FTSE

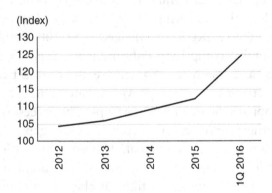

Unit Labour Cost

Figure 2

Source: Economic Survey of Singapore 1Q 2016.

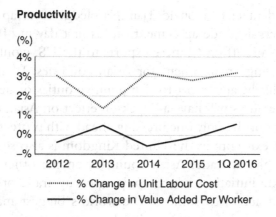

Figure 3

Source: Economic Survey of Singapore 1Q 2016.

100 (23.5%), Australia ASX 200 (19.9%), US S&P 500 (19%), New Zealand Top 100 (14.8%), China Top 100 (13.2%), Indonesia (11.6%), Hong Kong HSI 50 (11.1%), India (10.6%) and Malaysia (10.2%).

While Singapore topped the global league tables for greenfield FDI in 2014, it has slipped to the 15th rank in 2015 in the AT Kearney FDI Confidence Index from the 9th rank in 2014. Industry observers attribute this to MNCs shifting their attention to the more familiar markets in the west in the face of the prevailing global macroeconomic uncertainty. This merely indicates that no country, least of all Singapore, is insulated from global developments. Singapore has been the world's second freest economy behind Hong Kong[8] for several years now and this will exacerbate the impact from shifts in global economic balances.

Most corporates covered in this book have emerged stronger from both the AFC and GFC. The experience of encountering two major crises should stand Singapore corporates in good stead in encountering the risks mentioned above. However, China is a major market for several Singapore corporates. Some analysts and industry observers contend that Singapore corporates are driven by a single engine that is China and that this concentration risk could pose risks to the country's long-term prospects. A healthy balance in terms of country-wise exposure would be prudent.

US President elect Donald Trump's pledge to scrap the Trans-Pacific Partnership trade agreement on his first day in office and his threat to levy a tariff on Chinese exports to the US, would create an uncertain trading environment for Asian countries. While a drastic change is unlikely, any effort to slap punitive duties or deploy trade-restricting measures will have a knock-on effect on Asian companies.

Trump is not the only one pressing ahead with protectionist policies — the Brexit vote in the United Kingdom is also seen posing a challenge to global trade. Asian countries on the other hand have launched trade initiatives which could open up trade opportunities and increased access to some of the world's biggest markets. The 16-nation Regional Comprehensive Economic Partnership agreement, gives potential access to three of the world's largest market blocs: China, India and the 10 countries of ASEAN. China's One Belt One Road initiative, a modern day Silk Road, is a drive for an integrated economic area based on new infrastructure and increased trade links. These developments present opportunities to Singapore companies which are among the most globalised in the region.

Also, with the OPEC agreeing to a 1.20 billion barrels output cut from January 2017, crude oil prices are likely to witness some appreciation. This may improve the prospects of Keppel O&M and Sembcorp Marine, but squeeze the margins of transportation companies like Singapore Airlines and ComfortDelGro.

Courtesy the soft interest rate environment that has prevailed since 2008, Singapore corporates increased their borrowing. Hence investors with a limited appetite for risk should take into account the significance of China as a market to a company and its financial leverage, in addition to the risks mentioned in the company specific chapters, before making an investment decision.

Global central banks are no longer in sync with the US Federal Reserve which is seen making multiple interest rate hikes in 2017 at a time many others are still keeping monetary conditions easy. This could make funding costs volatile, forcing many companies to deleverage given the economic slowdown.

Interesting times lie ahead for investors in Singapore Blue Chips. To sum up, we would like to quote legendary investor Peter Lynch — "Know what you own, and know why you own it."

APPENDIX 1

MILESTONES

Table 1 Golden Agri Resources (GAR)

2005	GAR expanded its businesses to soybean processing in China by acquiring Asia Integrated Agri Resources
2010	• GAR adopted policy of no development on peat land regardless of depth • Government of Liberia and Golden Veroleum (Liberia) Inc, a subsidiary of the Verdant Fund LP, to form partnership in US$1.6 billion Sustainable Palm Oil project
2011	• GAR received RSPO membership • GAR launched pioneering Forest Conservation Policy • GAR published its inaugural Sustainability Report • GAR expanded its downstream business in Indonesia • Received first RSPO certification covering 14,955 hectares of plantations and one mill under SMART (subsidiary) in North Sumatra. • Nestlé and Unilever resumed oil palm purchases from SMARTGAR launched Social and Community Engagement Policy
2012	• GAR and SMART launched Yield Improvement Policy (YIP) to reduce impact on land • GAR and SMART published High Carbon Stock Forest Study Report Stena Weco and GAR created new joint venture on shipping company to provide an overall solution for GAR's international transportation of its palm oil products

(Continued)

Table 1   (*Continued*)

2013	GAR and SMART implemented pilot on High Carbon Stock forest conservation in PT Kartika Prima Cipta, West Kalimantan, Indonesia
2014	• GAR Declared Strong Commitment to the New York Declaration on Forests at the UN Climate Summit 2014
	• GAR formed a 50:50 equity participation company with Louis Dreyfus Armateurs Group, to collaborate in Indonesian based shipping and logistic business
	• GAR and CEPSA establish a 50:50 joint venture to jointly develop, formulate, produce, distribute and sell fatty alcohols at a global level, joint venture completed in September
2015	• GAR acquires 28.08% in Duta Anugerah Indah, an Indonesian company involved in television broadcasting which focuses on education and humanitarian fields, which are part of GAR's corporate social responsibility initiatives in Indonesia.
	• GAR buys company owning land next to its Dumai unit in Indonesia for USD53.6 million
2016	• GAR completes mapping its supply chain to the mill, which tracks the location and other relevant details of all the 489 mills which supply Crude Palm Oil (CPO) and Palm Kernels (PK) to its processing facilities in eight different locations in Indonesia.

Table 2   Wilmar International

1995	• Established first oil palm milling plant with a capacity of approximately 40 MT per hour
	• Purchased first liquid bulk vessel with cargo capacity of 6,500 deadweight tonnage (DWT) to provide logistics and transportation support to business operations
1996	Expanded refinery operations into Malaysia with the acquisition of one oil palm refinery plant and one fractionation plant in Butterworth, Malaysia. Both plants were upgraded from a daily capacity of 500 MT to 1,000 MT upon commissioning.
1998	Expanded into the production of higher value-added downstream products through the establishment of the first specialty fats plant with a capacity of 100 MT per day.

(*Continued*)

Table 2 (*Continued*)

2000	• Began developing and marketing own brand of Sania edible oil consumer pack in Indonesia to create brand awareness • Acquired three copra crushing plants in Sulawesi with an aggregate daily capacity of 900 MT
2002	Established first compound fertilizer manufacturing plant with a production capacity of 120,000 tonnes per year
2004	First oleochemical plant commenced operation in Shanghai
2005	Acquired a controlling interest in Jakarta Stock Exchange listed PT Cahaya Kalbar Tbk, a producer of specialty oils and fats for the chocolate, cocoa confectionery industry, bakery and cakes ingredient industry, and beverage and food industry

2006	• Renamed Wilmar International Limited on 14 July 2006 upon completion of the reverse takeover of Ezyhealth Asia Pacific Ltd
	• Re-listed on the Singapore Exchange on 8 August 2006 after a successful equity placement exercise at S$0.80 per share, which raised approximately US$180 million
	• Concluded a major capacity expansion drive through the completion of:
	  • three refineries with an aggregate daily capacity of 4,500 MT
	  • three fractionation plants with an aggregate daily capacity of 4,500 MT
	  • four palm kernel crushing plants with an aggregate daily capacity of 800 MT
	  • four oil palm milling plants with an aggregate hourly capacity of 200 MT
	  • one compound fertiliser manufacturing plant with a daily capacity of 1,000 MT
	  • one refinery (daily capacity of 2,500 MT) and one fractionation plant (daily capacity of 2,000 MT) in East Malaysia, in a joint-venture with TSH Resources Bhd
	• Expanded oil palm plantation acreage through the acquisitions of
	  • Five plantation companies with a combined land bank of 85,000 hectares in Kalimantan, Indonesia
	  • 25,000 hectares land bank by two existing subsidiaries
	  • A plantation company with a land bank of 30,000 hectares in Jambi, Sumatra

(*Continued*)

Table 2   (*Continued*)

2007	• Completed the merger with Kuok Group's palm plantation, edible oils, grains and related businesses in a deal worth US$2.7 billion, as well as a restructuring exercise to acquire the edible oils, oilseeds, grains and related businesses of Wilmar Holdings Pte Ltd (WHPL), including interests held by Archer Daniels Midland Asia Pacific (ADM) and its subsidiaries in these businesses, for US$1.6 billion
	• Formed a joint venture (JV) with Olam International Ltd and SIFCA Group, one of Africa's largest agro-industrial groups with significant interests across oil palm, cotton seed oil, and natural rubber and sugar sectors in Africa. The JV was aimed at developing a regional leadership position in oil palm, natural rubber, sugar and potentially in other agricultural plantation crops in Africa
	• Successfully launched the inaugural US$600 million convertible bonds issue due 2012
	• Entry into the Philippines with the setting-up of two coconut oil mills and refineries in Roxas, Zamboanga del Norte and Gingoog, Misamis Oriental
2008	Formed a joint venture with Nizhny Novgorod Fats & Oils Group and Delta Exports Pte Ltd to spearhead expansion in Russia and the CIS countries
2009	• Establishment of Adani Wilmar Pte. Ltd., a 50:50 joint venture between Wilmar and Adani Global Pte Ltd
	• Establishment of Wilmar Consultancy Services Pte. Ltd., a joint venture company held by Wilmar, Karry Management Services Pte. Ltd. and Uniland Investment (Singapore) Pte Ltd
2010	• Expanded into the sugar business through the acquisition of Sucrogen Limited (now known as Wilmar Sugar Australia Limited), the largest raw sugar producer and refiner in Australia, and PT Jawamanis Rafinasi, a leading sugar refinery in Indonesia
	• Acquired Natural Oleochemicals, a leading oleochemicals producer with significant market share in Europe and Asia and a growing presence in USA
	• Formation of Joint Venture with Elevance Renewable Sciences, to construct a world sale biorefinery to produce green olefins, multifunctional esters and acids, and premium mixture of oleochemicals and advanced biofuels
	• Acquisition of business of Windsor & Brook Trading Pte Ltd, a Singapore sugar trading company, by Wilmar's wholly owned subsidiary, Wilmar Trading Pte Ltd
	• Joint Venture between Wilmar and PZ Cussons to establish an oil palm refinery and food ingredients business in Nigeria

(*Continued*)

Table 2 *(Continued)*

2011	• Further expanded into the sugar business through the acquisition of PT Duta Sugar International in Indonesia and Proserpine Mill in Australia
	• Expanded its African footprint to Ghana through the acquisition of Benso Oil Palm Plantations Limited, a company listed on Ghana Stock Exchange
	• Established South African subsidiary, Wilmar Continental Edible Oils and Fats (Pty) Limited ("Wilmar Continental"). Wilmar Continental is an indirect 54.61% owned subsidiary of Wilmar held through Wilmar Resources Pte Ltd and Equatorial Trading Limited. The principal activities of Wilmar Continental include oilseed crushing, refining and bottling of edible oils and distribution to manufacturers, wholesale and the retail markets.
2012	• Formed strategic partnership with Archer Daniels Midland Company (ADM) in tropical oils refining in Europe, global fertiliser purchasing and distribution, and global ocean freight operations. Launched Olenex CV. headquartered in Rolle, Switzerland to handle the sales and marketing of refined vegetable oils and fats to European Area and Switzerland.
	• Established a 50:50 joint venture company, Yihai Kerry Kellogg Foods (Shanghai) Company Ltd, with Kellogg Company for the manufacture, sale and distribution of breakfast cereals and savoury snacks in China
	• Formed a 50:50 Joint Venture with Clariant Ltd for production and sales of amines and selected amines derivatives
	• Acquired approximately 30,000 hectares of land in Nigeria for expansion of oil palm plantations
	• Establishment of Dongguan Yihai Kerry Syral Starch Technology Co., Ltd, a 51:49 joint venture between Yihai Kerry Investments Co., Ltd, an indirect wholly-owned subsidiary of Wilmar, and Syral China Investment, a wholly-owned subsidiary of Tereos Internacional, part of the French cooperative agro-industrial group Tereos. The principal activities of DYKSS will be the development, promotion, marketing, manufacturing and sale in China and export from China of wheat starch and derivatives (including sweeteners), and wheat gluten.
2013	• Acquired 27.5% stake in Cosumar S.A., the sole sugar supplier in Morocco. The company is also the third largest sugar producer in Africa, with ownership of one of the largest refineries in the world
	• Extension of the partnership with Tereos, to include corn and potatoes, and the formation of new Joint Venture in a corn starch facility in Tieling (Liaoning Province), northern China
	• Acquisition of 35% equity interest in Estate Management Services (Private) Limited ("EMSPL") by Pyramid Wilmar Plantations (Private) Limited (an indirect 87.5% owned subsidiary of Wilmar). EMSPL's principal activities are managing and superintending estates and plantation property in Sri Lanka.

(Continued)

Table 2 (*Continued*)

- Joint venture with Elevance Renewable Sciences, Inc. began shipping commercial products including novel specialty chemicals from their first world-scale biorefinery located in Wilmar's integrated manufacturing complex in Gresik, Indonesia. The biorefinery is the first to utilise Elevance's proprietary metathesis technology.
- Joint venture with Clariant International Ltd, The Global Amines Company Pte Ltd, commenced production of amines in Lianyungang, China
- First venture in the United States, Wilmar Oils & Fats (Stockton), LLC, commenced operations
- Pledged commitment to an integrated policy of "No Deforestation, No Peat and No Exploitation" that aims to advance an environmentally and socially responsible oil palm industry

2014
- Formed joint venture company in Myanmar with Great Wall Food Stuff Industry Company Limited which shall acquire two sugar mills, a bioethanol plant and an organic compound fertiliser plant
- Acquired an ethoxylation facility in Lavera, France from Huntsman Corporation
- Entered into an agreement to acquire a strategic stake in Mumbai-based Shree Renuka Sugars Limited. Subject to relevant regulatory approvals, this investment will allow the Group to establish a significant presence in India and Brazil, the two most important sugar markets
- Established footprint in Ethiopia through a joint investment agreement with Repi Soap and Detergent S. Co. for the upgrading of an existing manufacturing facility and building of a new integrated manufacturing complex

2015
- Wilmar and Hong Kong based investment management and holding company First Pacific, through a 50:50 joint venture, acquire the Australian food company, Goodman Fielder (GF).
- Formed joint venture with Volac International to develop animal feed fat business
- Entered into an agreement whereby Olenex, a partnership with ADM to market oils and fats in Europe
- Established Nam Duong International Foodstuff Corporation, a joint venture company with Saigon Union of Trading Cooperatives, for the manufacture of sauces and condiments for both the domestic and export markets.

2016
- Wilmar enters into two conditional joint venture agreements with Singapore Food Industries to supply certain safe and high quality food to the Chinese market

---

Table 3 Olam International

1989–1991	• Established in Nigeria by the Kewalram Chanrai Group. First venture was to export cashews from Nigeria into India • Added cotton to portfolio • Started exporting shea nuts from Nigeria to Europe • Moved headquarters to London
1992–1994	• Traded the first parcel of cocoa beans from Nigeria • Set up operations in Benin, exporting raw cashew to India and cotton to Nigeria • Expanded to other countries in West Africa, Tanzania and India • Set up the coffee, rice and wood products businesses • Employee strength increases to 500
1995	• Established offices in Burkina Faso and Uganda • Added sugar and sesame to the product portfolio
1996	• Olam headquarters moved from London to Singapore • Set up the company's first South East Asian operations in Indonesia • Established offices in Senegal and Uzbekistan
1997	• Started operations in Gabon exporting tropical hardwood logs to Asia and Europe
1998	• Expansion into France and Vietnam • Became the first international Licensed Buying Company for cocoa in Ghana
1999	• Set up operations in Mozambique, Madagascar and Thailand • Consolidated our origin processing operations in cotton, cocoa and coffee
2000	• Set up operations in Papua New Guinea
2001	• Commenced operations in South Africa • Employee strength increased to 1,500
2002	• AIF Capital, IFC and Temasek Holdings invest in Olam (Private Equity investments) • The Spices and Vegetable Ingredients business started in Vietnam with pepper processing and trading
2003	• Continued geographic expansion by establishing operations in Russia, USA, Brazil and the Middle East • Expanded the Edible Nuts business and set up a peanut trading business • Became the largest shipper of robusta coffee in the world

(*Continued*)

Table 3   (*Continued*)

2004	• First Non-Executive and Independent Directors joined the Board of the Company • We created a Board Corporate Social Responsibility and Sustainability (CR&S) Committee to formalise the company's sustainability strategy
2005	• Listed on the Main Board of The Singapore Exchange, with the IPO oversubscribed 16 times • Employee strength reached 5,000
2006	• Launched strategy of growing inorganically through acquisitions in addition to our organic growth • Expanded into Central America and Andean Region by setting up coffee operations in Colombia and Peru
2007	• Independent CR&S function established and resourced • Acquired Queensland Cotton Holdings in Australia and a peanut blanching company Universal Blanchers in USA • Entered China with Spices and Vegetable Ingredients through the acquisition of Key Food Ingredients • The sugar business entered refining through the acquisition of PT. Dharmapala Usaha Sukses in Indonesia
2008	• Awarded the World Business and Development Award in support of the Millennium Development Goals of the United Nations Development Programme • Acquired De Francesco in the USA and expanded the scale of the dehydrated onion business • Geographic footprint expanded to 60 countries and employee strength crossed 10,000
2009	• Launched six year strategic plan for entering selectively into the upstream and mid/downstream parts of the value chain • Temasek Holdings re-invested in the company with an equity investment of S$300m • Began the specialty fats business through the acquisition of Britannia Food Industries in the UK • Set up the soluble coffee manufacturing plant in Vietnam • Listed in Forbes Asia's Fabulous 50 for first time, and again in 2010 and 2012
2010	• Acquired SK Foods and Gilroy Foods in the USA to grow the Spices and Vegetable Ingredients business

(*Continued*)

Table 3 (*Continued*)

	• Started growing almonds in-house with the acquisition of Timbercorp's almond orchards in Australia • Entered the sweeteners business through the investment in PureCircle • Employee strength expands to 15,000
2011	• The wood business acquired Congolese Industrielle des Bois in the Republic of Congo and the world's largest contiguous FSC® certified forestry concession • Entered the hazelnut business through the acquisition of Progida in Turkey
2012	• Won the Asian Human Capital Award for innovative and impactful people practices • Expanded the Packaged Foods Business downstream operations with the acquisition of OK Foods • Crossed 10 million metric tonnes of traded volume
2013	• Sale And Lease-Back Of Its Australian Almond Orchards For A\$200M
2014	• Acquires US Peanut Sheller McCleskey Mills at Enterprise Value of USD176 million • Acquires the global cocoa business of Archer Daniels Midland Company at an enterprise value on a cash and debt free basis of US\$1.3 billion,
2015	• The Grains platform plans to expand into animal feed and related businesses in Nigeria. • Olam Palm Gabon enters into a USD130 million sale of long term lease rights of land and a sale and lease-back of plantation and milling assets
2016	• Olam acquires Amber Foods which owns the wheat milling and pasta manufacturing assets of the BUA Group in Nigeria, for a total enterprise value of US\$275.0 million.

Table 4 The Singapore Exchange

2000	• Launch of the SGX's IPO • Introduced the SGX, S&P, CNX Nifty Index Futures contract
2003	• Reached agreement with Nihon Keizai Shumbun to trade the Nikkei Futures and Options on Electronic Trading System • Introduced a unit share market which allowed trading of odd lots with a minimum size of one share
2004	• Added Nikkei 225 Futures onto the Mutual Offset link with the Chicago Mercantile Exchange, creating a single marketplace around-the-clock, where customers only need to put up one margin for each position

(*Continued*)

Table 4   (*Continued*)

2005	• Announced the development and proposed implementation of an over-the-counter clearing facility, which will cover energy derivatives and forward freight agreements.
	• Closed the Nikkei 225 and Japanese Government Bond open outcry trading pits. Both contracts are traded entirely on SGX QUEST
2006	• Launched the new futures trading rulebook and clearing rules to meet new market initiatives
	• Announced the listing of the first China "A" share index futures (FTSE/Xinhua China A50 Index)
	• Launched SGX AsiaClear a facility for the clearing of OTC oil swaps and forward freight agreements
2007	• SESDAQ transformed into Catalist[1] board, Asia's first sponsor supervised listings platform for fast-growing companies
	• Tokyo Stock Exchange acquired a 4.99% stake in the SGX
	• Announced the transfer of oversight of corporate governance for listed companies from the Council of Corporate Disclosure and Governance to the Monetary Authority of Singapore and the SGX
2008	• Acquired SICOM
	• First IPO on Catalist board
	• SGX Beijing Representative Office officially opened
	• Introduced "watch-list" for listed companies on SGX Mainboard
	• Singapore Press Holdings, the SGX and FTSE Group launched the revamped STI and 18 new sub-indices
2009	• Conducted electronic poll voting for all resolutions passed at the FY2009 AGM. Poll voting works on the principle of one-share one-vote, as opposed to the previous practice of a 'show of hands' or 'one-person-one-vote'
	• SGX AsiaClear launched the world's first clearing of OTC Iron Ore Swap contracts
	• Introduced new measures to facilitate secondary fund raising by listed companies
2010	• The SGX becomes first in Asia to clear OTC traded financial derivatives
	• The SGX and NASDAQ OMX launch ADRs, bringing US-listed Asian companies to Asia
	• Established a London office
	• Moved 130 companies to Catalist

(*Continued*)

[1] Catalist refers to fast growing companies listed on the secondary board and not the Mainboard of SGX

Table 4 (*Continued*)

2011	• The SGX successfully launches clearing service for OTC Traded Asian FX Forwards • The SGX's Reach world's fastest trading engine, goes live • Southeast Asia's Largest IPO HPH Trust lists on the SGX
2012	• The SGX starts trading MSCI Indonesia Futures • The SGX opens Chicago and London hubs • The SGX starts dual currency trading in its Securities market • The SGX introduces 'My Gateway' portal to enhance investor education
2013	• Proposed circuit breakers for securities market • Launched depository services for Renminbi bonds • Launched AsiaClear futures for iron ore and oil
2014	• Proposed introduction of a new set of Asian currency futures contracts on Chinese renminbi, Japanese yen and Thai baht • Introduction of circuit breakers an additional market safeguard to be applied initially to Straits Times Index and MSCI Singapore Index component stocks and all those securities priced $0.50 and above. • SGX proposes the first electricity futures to be introduced in Asia
2015	• Standard board lot size of securities listed on SGX reduced from 1,000 to 100 units from 19 January 2015, volumes rise • SGX Bond Pro began trading Asian corporate bonds in G3 currencies, with Asian local currencies to follow. It is the first Over-The-Counter (OTC) trading venue dedicated to Asian bonds. • Plan to add new Asian currency futures contracts on the Taiwanese dollar (TWD/USD) and Renminbi crosses (SGD/CNH, CNY/SGD, EUR/CNH) to expand its current suite of foreign exchange (FX) futures in the third quarter of 2015, subject to regulatory approval.
2016	• SGX ties up with Taiwan Stock Exchange whose unit will join SGX as a remote trading member, allowing TWSE member brokers to directly trade SGX-listed securities • SGX and India's National Stock Exchange plan to introduce futures on Indian sector-specific index futures on SGX. This is the first time that derivatives on Indian sector indices are being launched outside India.

Table 5 Keppel Corporation

1968	The Dockyard Department of the Port of Singapore Authority corporatised to form Keppel Shipyard (Pte) Ltd
1972	Keppel Shipyard acquires 39% interest in the listed Far East Shipbuilding Ltd (renamed FELS in 1972).

(*Continued*)

Table 5   (*Continued*)

1972	Singaporeans took over Keppel Shipyard's management from the British ship repair group, Swan Hunter.
1973	Keppel Shipyard increases stake in FELS to 61.3%
1975	Keppel Philippines Shipyard was set up in partnership with Filipino investors.
1976	Acquisition of Singmarine Shipyard, a medium-size shipbuilder and repairer.
1978	Shin Loong Credit (renamed Shin Loong Finance) established to provide factoring to marine contractors
1980	Keppel Shipyard listed on the Singapore Stock Exchange. 30 million shares of $1.00 each was offered to the public at $3.30 per share.
1983	Keppel Shipyard diversifies into property by acquiring a 82% stake in Straits Steamship Company
1986	• Keppel Corporation incorporated. Keppel Shipyard becomes a division of Keppel Corporation • Acquisition of the 12 hectare ex-Mitsubishi Yard, which became a cornerstone in the growth of FELS
1989	Straits Steamship Company renamed Straits Steamship Land following the restructuring of the company to focus on property development. The non-property businesses grouped under Steamers Maritime Holdings (Steamers).
1990	Keppel Corporation acquired Asia Commercial Bank and renamed it as Keppel Bank
1991	Keppel Corporation acquired a 20% stake in Arab Heavy Industries (AHI), a shipyard in the United Arab Emirates. Interest in AHI has since increased to 33%.
1992	Rationalisation of Engineering Business under Keppel Integrated Engineering (KIE).
1993	• Keppel leads the Singapore consortium in the development of the Suzhou Industrial Park. • Straits Steamship Land develops the first global-class commercial building in Vietnam • FELS develops two Build-Own-Operate floating power barges which supplied a total of 180MW of electricity to the Philippine power grid addressing brownout problems in the country.
1994	• Steamers (now Keppel Telecommunications & Transportation) spearheads the Keppel Group's participation in 1997 in MobileOne (now M1), a consortium formed with SPH, Cable & Wireless and Hong Kong Telecom. • FELS sets up a technology company for R&D of jackup rigs.

(*Continued*)

Table 5 (*Continued*)

1995	• Subic Shipyard & Engineering Works inaugurated in The Philippines following the acquisition of the former Philseco yard.
	• Straits Steamship Land begins construction of its first property in Shanghai, and signs agreement to develop a golf resort with residential development in Kunming, Yunnan Province.
1997	• The Keppel name adopted across the Group.
	• The Caspian Shipyard in Baku, Azerbaijan, set up to meet demand for oil rigs in the new frontier for oil and gas industry.
	• Keppel Bank acquires the Asian financial crisis hit Tat Lee Bank. The enlarged bank is renamed Keppel TatLee Bank in 1998.
1998	• Keppel removes cross-shareholdings in its Group of companies and rationalises the businesses which include the merger of Keppel FELS (previously FELS) and KIE into Keppel FELS Energy & Infrastructure (KFEI).
1999	• Keppel acquires about 77% interest in the Singapore Petroleum Company (SPC).
	• Keppel Shipyard acquires Hitachi Zosen and was named Keppel Hitachi Zosen (KHZ).
	• Keppel Land (previously Straits Steamship Land) increases its regionalisation thrust, re-balances its Singapore trading assets and investment properties and starts the property fund management fee-based business.
	• Keppel Shipyard moves out of Telok Blangah, paving the way for the redevelopment of a 32hectare site into Keppel Bay, Singapore's premier waterfront precinct.
2000	• k1 Ventures: Formerly Singmarine Industries, then Keppel Marine Industries, the company changes its mandate to become a diversified investment company.
	• Positioning SPC as an Integrated Oil and Gas Company: Against the backdrop of US$10 oil per barrel, SPC begins its upstream business with the acquisition of the offshore Kakap gas field in Indonesia.
	• Keppel acquires BrasFELS yard in Angra dos Reis, Brazil, and develops it into the most established offshore and marine facility in Latin America.
2001	• Banking and financial services division divested
	• Ship yard operations consolidated and KHZ delisted
	• Keppel Land, together with HK partners, successfully bids for a prime site in the New Downtown at Singapore. The 1.14hectare site is developed as One Raffles Quay to yield a total of 1.32 million square feet of prime office space.
2002	• Shipyard operations consolidated. Keppel Offshore & Marine (Keppel O&M) established to become one of the world's largest offshore and marine groups.

Table 5   (*Continued*)

- Keppel O&M completes the acquisition of Dutch offshore shipyard and renames it Keppel Verolme BV.
- Acquisition of Keppel Seghers Technology (formerly Seghers Better Technology) contributed to the securing of the NEWater and Waste-to-Energy projects on Build-Own-Operate basis from the Singapore Government in 2005.

2003
- Keppel O&M established Keppel Kazakhstan, an offshore engineering and construction facility (which has been divested in 2014).

2005
- Secures Marina Bay Financial Centre at Singapore, an iconic 4.7 million square feet integrated development with office, commercial, residential and entertainment offerings.
- Keppel O&M acquires a shipyard in Nantong, China.

2006
- Keppel Seghers secures from the Qatari government a QR3.9 billion (about SGD1.7 billion) solid waste management project and in the following year, a QR3.6 billion (about SGD1.5 billion) wastewater treatment plant.
- Keppel Land sponsors the establishment of a new office property focused REIT now known as Keppel REIT (formerly K-REIT Asia).

2007
- Keppel O&M Technology Centre and Keppel Environmental Technology Centre set up with seed money of SGD150 million and SGD50 million respectively.

2008
- The Keppel Group enters into an agreement to lead the Singapore consortium in developing an Eco-City project in Tianjin.

2009
- Divestment of 45% stake in SPC

2010
- Established and listed K-Green Trust (renamed as Keppel Infrastructure Trust in 2014) to invest in *"green"* infrastructure assets in Singapore and globally.
- Keppel O&M partners Qatar Gas Transport Company to jointly develop the Nakilat-Keppel Offshore & Marine yard in Qatar, and separately acquires a yard for specialised shipbuilding in Santa Catarina, Brazil
- Keppel Land China established to own and operate all of Keppel Land's properties in China.
- The Securus Data Property Fund jointly formed by Keppel Telecommunications & Transportation (Keppel T&T) and AEP Investment Management to invest in a global portfolio of income-generating, green field data centres in Europe, Middle East and Asia. This is the world's first Shariah-Compliant Data Centre Fund.

(*Continued*)

Table 5 (*Continued*)

2011	• Keppel T&T enters into a joint venture with Sinotrans Ltd to jointly develop and operate a river port along Yangtze River, China.
	• Keppel O&M acquires a 27.8% stake in topside module fabricator Dyna-Mac Holdings Ltd via an equity placement.
2012	• Keppel O&M Technology Division established to further strengthen technological expertise and operational processes of the Group's offshore and marine business.
	• Keppel T&T forms joint ventures to develop the Sino-Singapore Jilin Food Zone International Logistics Park in Jilin Province, and Keppel Wanjiang International Coldchain Logistics Park in Lu'an City, Anhui. It also makes its first foray into Indonesia in partnership with PT Puninar Jaya.
	• Keppel Corporation acquires a stake in independent upstream oil and gas company, KrisEnergy, and gradually increases its interests to 31.4%.
2013	• Re-organisation of Keppel Energy and Keppel Integrated Engineering under the newly-incorporated Keppel Infrastructure.
	• Keppel Infrastructure completes the 800MW capacity expansion at Keppel Merlimau Cogen, bringing its total power generation capacity in Singapore to 1,300MW.
	• Baku Shipyard LLC, Keppel's second shipyard in Azerbaijan inaugurated.
	• Keppel Logistics acquires a 60% stake in Sanshui Port, in Foshan, China. It also embarks on developing the new Tampines Logistics Hub in Singapore, which caters to demand for critical-component logistics.
2014	• Keppel unit Ocean Mineral Singapore gets approval from the International Seabed Authority (ISA) for its first seabed mineral recovery licence.
	• Keppel Logistics expands Australia footprint and to manage a 10,000 square metre warehouse in Brisbane, Australia.
2015	• Keppel offers to buy all shares of subsidiary Keppel Land which will lifte net assets and earnings per share by 4% and 13%
	• Keppel plans to develop its fourth data centre in Singapore
	• Keppel DC REIT acquires its first data centre in Germany
2016	• Keppel Corp restructures investment division, to consolidate its interests in business trust management, real estate investment trust (REIT) management and fund management businesses under Keppel Capital Holdings Pte. Ltd. (Keppel Capital), a wholly-owned subsidiary of Keppel Corporation.

Table 6   Fraser & Neave (F&N)

1883	John Fraser and David Chalmers Neave form The Singapore and Straits Aerated Water Company
1898	The Singapore and Straits Aerated Water Company is renamed Fraser & Neave Limited upon issuing its shares to the public
1931	F&N enters into a joint venture with Holland-based Heineken N.V. to form Malayan Breweries Limited to produce beer. Malayan Breweries is subsequently renamed Asia Pacific Breweries Limited ("APB").
1932	Tiger Beer, Singapore's first home grown beer is launched
1936	F&N is awarded the Coca-Cola bottling franchise for Singapore and Malaysia
1959	The region's first sweetened condensed milk plant is built in Petaling Jaya, Malaysia as a JV with Beatrice Foods of Chicago
1963	The condensed milk facility starts operations
1968	Dairy production commences in Singapore
1974	• F&N launches its corporate logo to better reflect its growing group of businesses and international expansion • A state-of-the-art ice cream manufacturing plant is built in Singapore
1983	F&N launches 100PLUS, a carbonated isotonic drink to commemorate its centenary
1985	F&N's breweries and soft drink plants in Singapore are relocated for the relocated lands to be developed by F&N as it enters the property business
1987	F&N together with Goodman Felders Watties assumes control of the retail chain Cold Storage Holdings
1990	F&N acquires Centrepoint Properties and the Singapore-based dairy operations of Cold Storage Holdings. Centrepoint Properties is subsequently renamed
1995	F&N forms Myanmar Brewery Limited to gain a foothold in the country's developing beer market
1999	F&N acquires a 20.1% stake in Times Publishing Group
2000	F&N assumes majority stake of Times Publishing Group, thereby establishing the third major business of the group after food and beverage and breweries
2002	• F&N delists Times Publishing and Frasers Centrepoint through two voluntary conditional cash offers in 2001. • F&N returns capital of SGD0.80 per share to shareholders and cancels 1 ordinary share for every 10 ordinary shares

(Continued)

Table 6 (*Continued*)

2006	• F&N launches its retail REIT, Frasers Centrepoint Trust • F&N announces the acquisition of Nestlé's canned and liquid milk business in Malaysia and Thailand, becoming the largest canned milk producer in Southeast Asia on completion of the acquisition in 2007
2008	Acquires a 17.7% stake in the SGX-listed commercial REIT, Allco Commercial Trust, which was subsequently renamed as Frasers Commercial Trust
2012	F&N divests its entire stake in APB for a cash consideration of SGD5.60 billion
2013	• F&N becomes part of the Thai conglomerate, the TCC Group • F&N distributes SGD3.28 per share in cash to shareholders aggregating SGD4.73bn, almost 85% of the cash consideration it received from the APB divestment
2014	• F&N demerges its property business through a distribution in specie of all the issued shares in FCL to F&N shareholders, and relisting of FCL by way of introduction on the Singapore Stock Exchange • F&N returns capital of SGD607mn (SGD0.42 per share) to shareholders
2015	• F&N signs 22-year agreement with Nestle to manufacture and distribute Carnation, Bear Brand, Bear Brand Gold, Ideal Milk and Milkmaid in ASEAN • F&N sells 55% stake in Myanmar Brewery at USD560 million
2016	• F&N expresses interest to acquire the Peroni and Grolsch beer brands.

Table 7 Sembcorp Industries

1998	• SembCorp Engineering Clinches Multi-Million Malampaya Contract • SembCorp Industries sells its stake in FCC
1999	• Participation In The Equity Of SembCorp Gas Pte Ltd • The proposed acquisition of the remaining 33.33 per cent of the issued and paid up share capital of Singapore Offshore Petroleum Services Pte Ltd not already owned by SembCorp Logistics Ltd; and The proposed disposal of the entire issued and paid up share capital of SML Shipyard Pte Ltd. • Proposed Acquisition of SML Shipyard Pte Ltd • SembCorp Industries to receive SGD139 million from sale of Pacific Internet shares • Acquisition of the Remaining 51 per cent Equity Interest in the Capital of Industrial IMEX Pte Ltd

(*Continued*)

Table 7   (*Continued*)

- Proposed Reorganisation of the SHARE Capital of Sembawang Resources Limited for the Purpose of the Privatisation of Sembawang Resources Limited Pursuant to a Scheme of Arrangement (The Scheme)
- Singapore Food Industries Initial Public Offer
- Proposed Divestment of Ventura Development by SembCorp Industries
- Restructuring of Jurong Shipyard
- Jurong Shipyard: (1) Proposed Sub-Division of each ordinary SHARE of $0.50 into five ordinary shares of $0.10 each (2) Proposed change of name to SembCorp Marine Ltd
- Proposed sale of 40.55 per cent shareholding in Singapore Computer Systems Limited

SembCorp Waste Management set to acquire 40 per cent of Pacific Waste Management, Australia's second largest waste management company

2000	• SembCorp energy becomes first Singapore energy company to participate in Australia's power generation; acquires 30% of Edison Mission Energy's power plant in Western Australia
	• Formation of SembSita
	• SembCorp Waste Management bags SEMAC — the largest waste management company in Singapore — for SGD120 million
2001	• SembCorp Marine acquires a 50 per cent equity stake in PPL Shipyard for SGD16 million
	• Jurong Shipyard will invest SGD16 million for a 70 per cent Equity Stake In Maua Jurong, Brazil
	• Secured a USD80 million FPSO Conversion Project
	• Establishment Of A New Subsidiary Semac Recycling
	• Jurong Shipyard's Brazilian Joint Venture Secures First Contract Of SGD270 million
	• SembCorp Waste Management Bags SGD3.3 million Contract for Waste Collection and Environmental Services
	• SembCorp Utilities INVESTS USD38 million in a 717MW power plant in Vietnam
2002	• SembWaste's Australian Associate Secures aUSD151 million Contract For Waste Collection Services
	• SembCorp Industries divests Singapore Food Industries (SFI) for SGD262.5 million cash
2003	• SMOE clinches two contracts worth SGD460 million
	• SembEnviro forms joint venture company in Malaysia

(*Continued*)

Table 7 (*Continued*)

- SMOE clinches SGD175 million offshore platform contract in Thailand
- SembEnviro takes 60 per cent stake in leading China waste management and environmental services company, Shanghai Sincere
- SembCorp Utilities invests in a 605 MW power plant in Shanghai — The largest gas-fired cogeneration plant in China
- SembCorp Utilities expands to Europe with strategic acquisition
- SembEnviro adds comprehensive cleansing BUSINESS to its environmental services portfolio
- SembCorp Industries Divests its Entire Stake in Cathay International Water for USD44.8 million (SGD77 million)
- SembCorp Industries subscribes 655, 000 redeemable preference SHARES in the capital of SembCorp Utilities
- SembWaste won SGD11 million lawsuits brought by TRI
- SembCorp Industries divests its building materials companies for SGD39 million
- Chumpol NaLamLieng steps down as Director of SembCorp Industries' Board
- SembCorp Industries establishes in-house treasury unit- SembCorp Financial Services
- SembCorp Marine ups stake in PPL Shipyard
- SembCorp Industries makes a SGD16.6 million GAIN from open-market sale of 1,000,000 shares in Pacific Internet
- SembCorp Industries divests its China leisure companies for SGD10.9 million in cash
- SembCorp Marine's subsidiary, Jurong Shipyard clinches shipbuilding contract worth S$110 million
- SembCorp Marine plans to build giant shipyard in Tuas
- SembCorp Marine's subsidiary Jurong Shipyard secures another two ship-building contracts worth SGD110 million
- SembEnviro Alex Fraser opens Southeast Asia's first integrated construction and demolition waste materials recovery facility
- SembWaste Cleantech Implements Conservancy Owner Operator Scheme
- SembWaste Cleantech Clinches SGD24.8 million Worth of New Cleaning Contracts
- SembCorp Utilities Increases its Stake in Nanjing SembCorp SUIWU to 75 %
- SembCorp Industries Divests its Entire Stake in Vietnam Service Apartment, Resulting in FY 2003 gain of SGD8.6 million

(*Continued*)

Table 7   (*Continued*)

2004	• Disposal of entire interest in Joint Venture Company, Bohai Sembawang Shipyard (Tianjin)
	• SembWaste Cleantech awarded SGD45 million Public Cleansing Contract
	• SembCorp Officially opens Indonesia's newest Offshore Engineering Fabrication Yard
	• SembCorp Marine's subsidiary PPL Shipyard secures USD117.6 million Rig Building Contract
	• Jurong Shipyard Secures Letter of Intent for USD628 million (SGD1.068 billion) P-54 FPSO EPC Turnkey Project
	• SembCorp Marine's subsidiary Jurong Shipyard signs Acceptance Of Notice Of Award for USD628.8 million (SGD1.068 billion) P-54 FPSO EPC Turnkey Project
	• SembCorp Marine acquires 30% Equity Stake in Cosco Shipyard Group to grow its Marine Business in China
	• SembCorp Industries disposes entire 30% equity interest in Sime SembCorp Engineering Sdn. Bhd.
	• SembCorp Marine's Subsidiary Jurong Shipyard secures USD84 million (SGD140 million) Shipbuilding Contract
	• SembCorp Marine's Subsidiary Jurong Shipyard secures Rig Building Deal Worth USD131 million
	• SembCorp Marine's Subsidiary Jurong SML bags USD32 million Shipbuilding Deal
	• SembCorp Marine's Subsidiary Jurong Shipyard secures two Shipbuilding Contracts worth SGD143 million from Wan Hai Lines
2005	• SembCorp Marine's Subsidiary PPL Shipyard secures s USD133.7 million Rig Building Contract
	• SembCorp Marine's Subsidiary PPL Shipyard secures a Second Rig Building Contract worth USD119.6 million
	• SembCorp Marine's Subsidiary PPL Shipyard secures another Rig Building Contract worth USD121 million
	• PPL Shipyard secures another Rig Building Contract worth USD129 million
	• Jurong Shipyard secures USD127.1 million Rig Building Contract
	• PPL Shipyard secures USD130 million Rig Building Contract from Japan Drilling Co., Ltd
	• Jurong Shipyard secures a USD131 million Rig Building Contract

(*Continued*)

Table 7 (*Continued*)

- Completion of SembCorp's Divestment of 28.8% equity interest in Pacific Internet
- SeaDrill Confirms OPTION to build Second Unit Of Ultra Deep Water Semi-Submersible Rig with Jurong Shipyard at USD404 million & Signs Option for a Third Unit
- SembCorp Industries Unwinds its Interest in Pt Bintan Lagoon Resort

2006
- PPL Shipyard secures 1st Rig Building Contract worth USD175 million
- SembCorp Marine Injects Capital into Cosco Shipyard Group to grow its Ship Repair and Ship Conversion Business in China
- SembCorp Industries to accept offer by Toll Holdings for its entire stake in SembCorp Logistics
- PetroMena orders 2nd Semi-Submersible Drilling Unit from Jurong Shipyard for USD480 million
- Acceptance of Voluntary Conditional cash offer by Toll Holdings for SembCorp Logistics
- SembCorp Inks Waste-To-Resource JV with China's Largest Lead Recycler, Jiangsu Chunxing
- Jurong Shipyard secures USD165.5 million Rig Building Contract
- SembCorp Industries to receive an additional SGD44 million for the sale of its stake in SembCorp Logistics
- SembCorp Marine divests its entire interest in Deep Driller I Jackup Rig for a net profit of SGD13.3 million
- SembCorp Utilities Submits Final Revised Proposal for Fujairah IWPP Project
- SembUtilities acquires 40% interest in Fujairah Independent Water and Power Plant in UAE
- SembCorp Marine acquires an Additional 50% Stake in Jurong Marine Services Pte Ltd
- SembCorp Marine's Brazilian Shipyard Mauá Jurong secures USD550 million Gas Platform Construction Contract
- SembCorp Marine's subsidiary Sembawang Shipyard awarded Drillship Upgrading Contract by Neptune Marine Oil & Gas Limited
- Fujairah Independent Water and Power Plant achieves Financial Close

2007
- Sembcorp Marine's Subsidiary, PPL Shipyard, secures Repeat Rig Building Contract at USD190 million from Offshore Group Corp
- Sembcorp Marine's Jurong Shipyard secures third Newbuild Deepwater Semi-Submersible Drilling Rig at USD524 million (SGD802 million) from Petromena

(*Continued*)

Table 7 (*Continued*)

- Sembcorp Utilities signs 20-Year Contract with Lucite International for the Supply of Utilities and Services
- Sembcorp Marine's subsidiary, SMOE, secures USD300 million Contract for the Construction of an Offshore Platform Integrated Deck
- Sembcorp Marine's subsidiary, Sembawang Shipyard, awarded SGD150 million FPSO Conversion from Bluewater Energy Services B.V., Holland
- PT SMOE Indonesia secures USD80 million contract to build Offshore Platforms for Total E&P Indonesie
- Sembcorp Marine's Jurong Shipyard secures third Ultra-Deepwater Semi-Submersible Rig from Seadrill at USD535.5 million (SGD814 million)
- Sembcorp Utilities to Divest its 35% stake in Shenzhen Chiwan Offshore Petroleum Equipment Repair & Manufacture Co Ltd to SMOE
- Sembcorp Marine's Jurong Shipyard secures USD442 million Contract to build a Harsh Environment Jackup Rig
- Sembcorp Marine's Jurong Shipyard secures USD88 million Conversion Contracts
- Sembcorp Marine's subsidiary, Sembawang Shipyard secures USD221 million contract to Design, Construct, Outfit and Commission a 5,000 Tonnes DP3 Heavy Lift Crane Vessel from Nordic Heavy Lift ASA, Norway
- Sembcorp enters Northeast China with Industrial Water Supply Joint Venture
- Sembcorp Marine's PPL Shipyard secures 3rd Jackup Rig Order from Offshore Group Corp at USD190 million Sembcorp's Industrial Park business enters North Vietnam with a Third VSIP Project

2008
- SembCorp Marine's PPL Shipyard secures 4th Jackup Rig Order from Offshore Group Corp at USD198 million
- Sembcorp Marine's PPL Shipyard secures Rig Order from Egyptian Drilling Company at USD201 million
- A gain of SGD230 million from Sale of Quoted Investment in Cosco Corporation (Singapore) Ltd
- Divestment of Sembenviro KK Asia Pte Ltd
- SembCorp Marine's subsidiary, Sembawang Shipyard secures a SGD300 million Contract
- SembCorp Marine's Jurong Shipyard acquires a 70% Equity Stake in Shanghai Jurong Marine Engineering & Technology Co. Ltd

(*Continued*)

Table 7 (*Continued*)

2009	• Sembcorp NEWater to start building Changi NEWater Plant in April
	• Sembcorp Seals Gas Deal worth USD5.5 billion
	• Sembcorp Marine's Jurong Shipyard Secures Letter of Intent From Seadrill to Build a Deepwater Semisubmersible Drilling Rig at USD640 million (SGD870 million)
	• Sembcorp Marine's PPL Shipyard secures USD430 million Contract to Build Two Units of Jackup Rigs for Seadrill
	• Order from Larsen OIL & Gas to Build a Deepwater Semisubmersible Drilling Rig at USD640 million (SGD870 million)
	• A 2nd Jackup Rig Order for Sembcorp Marine's PPL Shipyard from Egyptian Drilling Company at USD220 million
	• Sembcorp Marine's Subsidiary, Sembawang Shipyard, secures SGD99 million Contract to Convert a Tanker into a DP Floating Drilling, Production, Storage and Offloading (FDPSO) Vessel, with Extended Well-testing Drilling Capability, for Petroserv S.A., Brazil
2010	• Sembcorp Commences Construction of USD1 billion Salalah Independent Water and Power Plant in Oman
	• Sembawang Shipyard secures Longevity, Upgrading and Damage Repair Contracts worth SGD130 million and renews Long-Term Contract with Eitzen Group
	• Sembcorp Marine's Jurong Shipyard secures SGD130 million Pre-FPSO conversion Contract from Petrobras
	• Sembcorp proposes Voluntary Tender Offer to acquire shares in Cascal, a Leading Provider of Water and Wastewater Services
	• Opening of Singapore's Fifth and Largest NEWater Plant, The Sembcorp NEWater Plant
	• Sembcorp commences Tender Offer to acquire all Outstanding Shares of Cascal for USD6.75 per Share in cash
	• Sembcorp Establishes First Power Project in India
	• Sembawang Shipyard secures Upgrading and Repair Contracts worth SGD110 million
	• Sembcorp Marine's Sembawang Shipyard secures FPSO Conversion and Upgrading Contracts worth SGD75 million
	• Sembcorp Marine's PPL Shipyard secures USD364 million Contract to Build Two Jackup Rigs with OPTIONS for another Three Jackup Rigs from Atwood Oceanics Pacific Limited
	• Sembcorp Marine's Jurong Shipyard Secures SGD351 million FPSO Conversion Contract

(*Continued*)

Table 7   (*Continued*)

- Sembcorp Marine's Jurong Shipyard secures USD384 million Contract To Build Two Jackup Rigs with OPTIONS for another Four Jackup Rigs from Seadrill
- Sembcorp Marine's PPL Shipyard announces a USD195 million Contract to sell a Jackup Rig to Transocean Ltd
- Sembcorp Marine's Jurong Shipyard secures USD400 million Contract To Build Two Premium Jackup Rigs with OPTIONS for another Four Jackup Rigs from Noble Corporation

2011
- Sembawang Shipyard secures Newbuilding and Upgrading Contracts worth SGD215 million
- Sembcorp Completes Acquisition of 49% Stake in Thermal Powertech Corporation India
- Sembcorp Marine's Jurong Shipyard Secures USD450 million Contract To Build a Harsh-Environment Jackup Rig From Seadrill
- Sembcorp Marine's Jurong Shipyard to Build Two More Premium Jackup Rigs at USD427.6 million for Noble Corporation
- Sembcorp Marine's Subsidiary SMOE secures close to SGD600 million Contract for an Integrated Processing and Living Quarters Platform
- Sembcorp Successfully Completes First Phase of USD1 billion Salalah Independent Water and Power Plant in Oman
- Sembcorp Marine's Sembawang Shipyard Exercises OPTION to Increase Shareholding Stake in Sembmarine Kakinada Ltd, India to 40% and Extends the Technical Management and Services Agreement to 10 Years
- Sembcorp Marine's Jurong Shipyard signs USD444 million Contract To Build Two Premium Jackup Rigs and Secures Additional OPTIONS To Build Another Two Jackups of Similar Design for Noble Corporation
- Sembcorp Co-Develops New Singapore-Sichuan Hi-Tech Innovation Park In Chengdu, China
- Sembcorp Marine's Jurong Shipyard secures a USD291.6 million Contract To Build an Accommodation Semi-submersible Rig with Options for another Two Units from a Subsidiary of Prosafe SE
- Sembcorp Marine's Sembawang Shipyard secures a USD140 million Contract to Convert a Ropax Vessel to DP2 accommodation and repair vessel from equinox offshore accommodation limited

2012
- Sembcorp Signs Agreement to Explore Developing a 1,200 Megawatt Power Plant In Vietnam

---

(*Continued*)

Table 7 (*Continued*)

- Sembcorp Marine's Wholly Owned Brazilian Shipyard Estaleiro Jurong Aracruz Secures a USD792.5 million Drillship Contract from Sete Brasil
- Sembcorp Marine's PPL Shipyard Secures a USD213 million Contract To Build a Pacific Class 400 Jackup Rig
- Sembcorp's 1,320-Megawatt Power Plant in India Secures Multi-Year Coal Supply Contract
- Sembcorp Marine's Jurong Shipyard secures a USD385.5 million Contract To Build a Semi-submersible Well Intervention Rig
- Sembcorp Marine's Jurong Shipyard secures a USD568 million Contract to Build a Harsh-environment Ultra-deepwater Semi-submersible Drilling Rig from North Atlantic Drilling Limited
- Sembcorp Marine's PPL Shipyard Secures USD218.5 million Contract to Construct a Jackup Rig for Gulf Drilling International Ltd (Q.S.C.)
- Sembcorp Acquires Power Assets in China for USD85.5 million and Grows Renewable Energy Portfolio
- Sembcorp Marine's Ppl Shipyard secures a USD208 million Contract to Construct a Pacific Class 400 Jackup Drilling Rig from Perisai (L) Inc.
- Sembcorp Marine's Sembawang Shipyard Secures FSO Repair & Upgrading and LNG Carriers' Life Extension Contracts worth SGD130 million
- SMOE's Indonesian Subsidiary Secures Contract worth about USD63 million for Engineering and Construction of Two Wellhead Platforms
- Sembcorp Marine secures USD4.032 billion Drillship Contracts from Sete Brasil
- Sembcorp Marine's Jurong Shipyard secures New Deep Water Capacity Ocean Apex Project from Diamond Offshore Drilling, Inc. for USD135 million
- Sembcorp Marine's Subsidiary Jurong Do Brasil Secures a Contract Worth USD674 million for Modules Construction and Integration of FPSOs P-68 and P-71
- Sembcorp Marine Secures its 7th Drillship Contract worth USD806.4 million from Sete Brasil
- Sembcorp Marine's PPL Shipyard secures Rig Orders worth USD434million to Build Two JackUp Rigs for Oro Negro

2013
- Sembcorp Marine's PPL Shipyard secures a Repeat Order for a Jackup Rig worth USD208 million from Perisai (L) Inc.
- Sembcorp Marine's PPL Shipyard secures Repeat Rig Orders from Oro Negro to Build Two Jackup Rigs at USD417 million

(*Continued*)

Table 7   (*Continued*)

- Sembcorp's 1,320-Megawatt Power Plant in India Secures 25-Year Power Purchase Agreement
- Sembcorp to Develop its First Overseas Energy-from-Waste Facility in the UK
- Sembcorp Celebrates the Official Opening of its USD1 billion Salalah Independent Water and Power Plant in Oman
- Sembcorp Marine's PPL Shipyard Secures USD220.5 million Contract to Construct a Jackup Rig for BOT Lease Co., Ltd
- Sembcorp Secures 20-year Coal Supply Agreement for its 1,320-megawatt Power Plant in India
- Sembcorp Expands Energy-from-Waste Capacity in Singapore with a New Steam Production Facility worth over SGD250 million
- Sembcorp Marine signs MOU with Partners Saudi Aramco and Bahri
- Sembcorp's Joint Venture, Sembcorp Salalah Power & Water Company, to Launch Initial Public offering in Oman
- Sembcorp Marine's Jurong Shipyard to Build a Second Semi-submersible Well Intervention Rig at USD346 million for Helix Energy Solutions
- Sembcorp Marine's PPL Shipyard secures USD211.5 million from Perisai (L) Inc.

2014
- Sembcorp Marine's Jurong Shipyard secures USD$1.08 billion in Contracts from Transocean to Build Two Drillships with OPTIONS for Three Additional Drillships
- Sembcorp Begins Construction of its Largest Energy-from-Waste Project in Singapore
- Sembcorp Marine's Jurong Shipyard secures a USD$236 million Contract to Build a Friede & Goldman JU 2000E Jackup Rig for Hercules North Sea Ltd
- Sembcorp Marine acquires Stake in GraviFloat AS
- Sembcorp Marine's Sembawang Shipyard secures Contract worth about SGD600 million from Saipem SA for the Conversion of Two FPSOs for Kaombo Project in Offshore Angola
- Sembcorp Marine Subsidiary Jurong Shipyard secures USD$696 million Libra FPSO Conversion Contract
- Sembcorp Marine's Subsidiaries secure Two Contracts Totalling SGD222 million in Value
- Sembcorp Marine's PPL Shipyard secures USD$240 million Contract to Build a Jackup Rig for Repeat Customer BOT Lease Co., Ltd with Japan Drilling Co., Ltd as Project Coordinator

---

(*Continued*)

Table 7 (*Continued*)

2015	• Sembcorp to Acquire a Renewable ENERGY Company in India with a Wind and Solar Portfolio • Sembcorp Completes Acquisition of Renewable Energy Company, Green Infra, in India • Sembcorp's First Power Plant in India Commences First Phase of Commercial Operation • Sembcorp gets USD$300 million contract to develop and operate a 225-megawatt gas-fired power plant largest gas-fired independent power plant in Myanmar. • Sembcorp Marine signs contract worth approximately USD$1 billion with Heerema Offshore Services B.V. (HOS) to build a new DP3 semi-submersible crane vessel (NSCV). • Sembcorp awarded USD$390 million contract to develop a 426-megawatt power plant in Bangladesh • Sembcorp invests 49% in joint venturue to invest in a mine-mouth 1,620-megawatt coal-fired power project in Chongqing municipality.
2016	• Launch of 2,640-megawatt Sembcorp Gayatri Power Complex in India • Signs long-term power purchase agreement (PPA) with Myanma Electric Power Enterprise (MEPE) for the supply of 225 megawatts of power for a period of 22 years.

Table 8 ST Engineering

1968	• Incorporation of Singapore Shipbuilding & Engineering Pte Ltd, now known as ST Marine, on 7 May 1968
1969	• Incorporation of Singapore Electronic & Engineering Pte Ltd (SEEL), forerunner of ST Electronics, providing electronics support at Sembawang
1971	• Singapore Technologies Automotive Pte Ltd. (ST Auto) formed
1975	• Incorporation of Singapore Aerospace Maintenance Company (SAMCO, [today known as ST Aerospace)
1990	• ST Aerospace and ST Marine publicly listed
1991	• ST Electronics and ST Auto publicly listed
1997	• ST Aerospace, ST Electronics, ST Auto, and ST Marine merged to form Singapore Technologies Engineering (ST Engineering), a SGD2 billion listed holding company. The newly formed Group provides solutions and capabilities in the aerospace, electronics, land systems and marine sectors for both defence and commercial companies.

(*Continued*)

Table 8   (*Continued*)

2000	• ST Engineering acquired Chartered Industries of Singapore (CIS) through ST Auto to form Singapore Technologies Kinetics (ST Kinetics), its land systems arm • ST Engineering established US headquarters, VT Systems, in Virginia to position itself for growth and expansion in the US.
2001	• ST Kinetics' Bronco All Terrain Tracked Vehicle was commissioned into service with the Singapore Army
2002	• Began expansion in the US in the aerospace and marine sectors • Formed VT Halter Marine following the acquisition of Friede Goldman Halter Marine, a world renowned builder of naval and commercial vessels; • Formed San Antonio Aerospace with the acquisition of Dee Howard Aerospace, one of the US' premier independent aircraft maintenance and modification facilities
2003	• Established US presence in the electronics sector through acquisition of Miltope Group Inc., a US manufacturer of militarised and rugged equipment for military and commercial applications. • First foray into China for its land systems sector through a joint venture with Beijing Zhonghuan Kinetics Heavy Vehicles Co. Ltd., to design and produce specialised heavy commercial and industrial vehicles for the construction industry in China • ST Kinetics' Primus self-propelled howitzer commissioned into service with the Singapore Artillery
2004	• Continued to expand presence in China through the setting up of Shanghai Technologies Aerospace Company Limited, a joint venture company with China Eastern Airlines, in Shanghai, China
2005	• Established US presence in the land systems sector through acquisition of Specialized Vehicles Corporation, a US manufacturer of specialised truck bodies and trailers • Continued expansion into China with joint venture company, Guizhou Jonyang Kinetics Co., Ltd, to design, manufacture and distribute excavators and specialty vehicles for the construction, mining and related industries • Made further inroads into the US with acquisition of iDirect, a leading US manufacturer of two-way internet protocol-based broadband satellite networking solutions
2006	• Delivered the first locally-built "RSS Intrepid" to Republic of Singapore Navy • Acquired US-based leading manufacturer of road construction and maintenance equipment, now known as VT LeeBoy

(*Continued*)

Table 8 (*Continued*)

	• ST Kinetics and Singapore's DSO National Laboratories incorporate joint venture for R&D
2007	• iDirect set up wholly owned subsidiary, iDirect Government Technologies (iGT) in the US to expand government business
	• ST Aerospace set up ST Aviation Training Academy (STATA) to offer commercial pilot training in Australia
	• US shipyard VT Halter Marine won first of several contracts totalling more than US$800m from the US Navy for the Egyptian Navy's Fast Missile Craft (FMC) project under the Foreign Military Sales (FMS) programme.
2008	• Achieved first military vehicle sale to a developed country with the award of a £150m (about S$330m) contract by the UK Ministry of Defence (UK MOD) for the supply of over 100 All Terrain Tracked Carriers (ATTC)
	• Launched the RoRo vessel — First in Singapore's history
	• ST Marine set up wholly-owned subsidiary in China to focus on environmental engineering
2009	• Acquired two leading companies in China's road construction and maintenance equipment market. The acquisitions, its third and fourth in China, were in line with its strategy to grow its specialty vehicle business
	• ST Electronics secured its first project in Tanzania with a contract to install a Tower Simulator for the Tanzania Civil Aviation Authority
2010	• Land Systems sector ventured into India with the set up of specialty vehicles company in Bangalore to market and manufacture a range of construction equipment
	• Scored its first contract with the Royal Australian Navy (RAN) to convert its 157.2m long combat logistics vessel, HMAS Success, which was double hulled to meet the International Maritime Organisation standards for environmental protection against oil spills.
	• Unveiled new hangar complex at Pudong International Airport in Shanghai. The facility, Shanghai Technologies Aerospace Company Limited (STARCO), is a joint venture company between China Eastern Airlines (CEA) and ST Aerospace.
2011	• Named one of six World Class Winners of the 'Global Performance Excellence Awards 2011' within the 'Large Manufacturing category'. The World Class Award, an international quality award, is bestowed on the Group for its outstanding quality framework and performance. The Awards were announced by the Asia Pacific Quality Organization (APQO) in Chicago, USA.

(*Continued*)

Table 8 (*Continued*)

- ST Kinetics entered the city bus segment by winning contract to supply MAN A22 buses to SMRT Buses Ltd
- Completed the delivery of over 100 ATTCs, named Warthog, to the UK Ministry of Defence_
- US subsidiary, iDirect Government Technologies received US government's approved Proxy Agreement, enabling it to pursue classified government and military contracts
- Expanded into engine leasing business, set up Total Engine Asset Management (TEAM), a joint venture company with Marubeni Corporation
- Established ST Aerospace (Guangzhou) Aviation Services Company, a joint venture with Guangdong Airport Management Corporation

2012
- Delivered the 141m Landing Platform Dock (LPD), which it designed and built for the Royal Thai Navy
- Secured its single largest naval export contract with the award of a shipbuilding contract worth about S$880m from the Royal Navy of Oman, to design and build four patrol vessels
- Launched the ExtremV, an advanced all-terrain tracked emergency vehicle specially customised for disaster relief and rescue missions
- Launched AERIA Luxury Interiors to mark expansion into VIP completion market
- Launched A330P2F conversion programme with Airbus and EFW.
- ST Kinetics in partnership with Science Applications International Corporation was accepted by the US Marine Corps to provide a customised version of its TERREX for the demonstration phase of the Marine Personnel Carrier Program.
- Extended the reach of its rail electronics solutions to the US and Malaysia — partnered GE Transportation to implement the SmarTrip Card Dispensers for the Washington Metro; and won first contract (through consortium) from MRT Corporation Sdn Bhd to provide Facility Supervisory Control & Data Acquisition Systems, to control and monitor the MRT facilities in the stations and depots.

2013
- Acquired Brazilian automotive MRO provider, Technicae Projetos e Serviços Automotivos Ltda., to further its defense business in Brazil and the rest of South America
- Acquired assets of Turbo Mach in San Antonio, Texas, a designer and manufacturer of composite components and assemblies for the aerospace industry to advance the sector's plan to develop its own manufacturing and repair capabilities to support the current and next generation of aircraft, as well as provided the sector with added capabilities to enhance its MRO competitiveness

(*Continued*)

Table 8 (*Continued*)

- ST Electronics (Satellite Systems) Pte Ltd, a subsidiary of ST Electronics, started the design and development of Singapore's first commercial remote sensing satellite. Named TeLEOS-1, this made-in-Singapore earth observation satellite is targeted to be launched into commercial service in 2015
- Awarded a contract to design and build eight naval vessels for the Republic of Singapore Navy
- Added shiprepair capability to its US shipyard, a 12,000 MT Floating Drydock,
- ST Kinetics' 40mm ammunition, known for its effectiveness and reliability, was selected for use in the Canadian Armed Forces' Tactical Armoured Patrol Vehicle programme and by the US Army. The same year, Australian Munitions partnered ST Kinetics to cooperate in Australia and New Zealand to develop, manufacture and market the 40mm low velocity, extended range and air bursting ammunition.
- Expanded rail electronics solutions into Toronto, Canada — ST Electronics' platform screen doors used by Merolinx Air Rail Link Spur Line.

2014
- ST Electronics expanded presence in Brazil, set up subsidiary to pursue potential projects in the areas of urban solutions relating to large scale electronics systems like intelligent transport and metro rail
- Opened a new aviation centre at Seletar Aerospace Park, Singapore
- ST Engineering's aerospace arm became an approved Airbus Corporate Jet service centre and Boeing Business Jet completion centre
- Acquired US flight school Aviation Academy of America to grow pilot training business
- Set up an aircraft maintenance, repair and overhaul (MRO) facility at the Pensacola International Airport in Florida
- ST Kinetics strengthened its market leading position in 40mm ammunition, with its partnership with General Dynamics-Ordnance and Tactical Systems for the US market.

2015
- ST Engineering and NTU launch laboratory for advanced robotics and autonomous systems ST Engineering's Subsidiary Develops The AIR+ Smart Mask, a new protective mask (the Smart Mask) and a micro ventilator (the AIR+), that involved breakthrough innovations that better protect mask wearers against airborne contaminants.
- ST Aerospace moves upstream in aircraft cabin interior value chain, set up ST Aerospace Aircraft Seats for the end-to-end design and manufacturing of a range of aircraft seating solutions.
- ST Aerospace strengthen its conversion portfolio, added A320/A321P2F to its programme

(*Continued*)

Table 8 (*Continued*)

- Launched the first Littoral Mission Vessel *"Independence"*, built for the Republic of Singapore Navy.
- Singapore Aerospace signs six-year engine maintenance contract worth approximately USD$350m (approximately S$472m) with India's second largest airline Jet Airways and its subsidiary JetLit

2016 • ST Kinetics progresses on contract awarded by the US Marine Corps to SAIC is worth USD$121.5 million

---

Table 9   SIA Engineering

2000 • Secures major maintenance contract with Polar Air Cargo
- SIA Engineering, P&W and TPC announce joint ventures
- SIA Engineering & P&W expand repair capabilities in Singapore
- SIA Engineering to join HAECO venture
- SIA Engineering floats an IPO
- Acquires stake in Messier Services Asia Pte Ltd (MSA)
- SIA Engineering announces joint Aerostructure repair venture
- SIA Engineering & Region Air announces signing of a long term "Total Support" Aircraft Maintenance Contract
- Announces joint venture with United Technologies & Singapore Technologies Aerospace Ltd

2001 • Breaks ground for third hangar
- Acquires 30% stake in Aerostructure Repair & Overhaul facility
- Announces signing of 3-Year contract with DragonAir

2002 • SIA Engineering invests USD4 million in aerospace tubes joint venture
- Signs service agreement with SALE
- Increases stake in Rohr Aero Services — Asia to 40%
- Rohr Aero breaks new ground with largest autoclave facility in Asia
- Signs MOU for line maintenance at Indonesian airport

2003 • MOU on engineering maintenance cooperation signed between SIA Engineering and CAL
- Acquires 49% stake in Indonesian joint venture

2004 • Invests SGD120 million to increase maintenance capacity
- Embarks upon B747-400 freighter conversion business
- Sets up Aircraft Interior Modification Centre in Singapore
- SIA Engineering Company sets up Aircraft Interior Modification Centre in Singapore

---

(*Continued*)

Table 9 (*Continued*)

	• SIA Engineering and Tiger Airways seal SGD110 million maintenance contract
	• Announces divestment of 5% stake in Taikoo (Xiamen) Aircraft Engineering Company Limited
	• Signs MOU for joint venture with hydraulics parts specialist Parker Hannifin
2005	• Forms line maintenance joint venture with Cebu Pacific Air
	• SIA Engineering and Parker Hannifin from Asia-Pacific hydraulic equipment service centre joint venture
2006	• ACE Services, the first non-OEM hydraulics repair facility in the world, officially opens in Singapore
	• Opens Two New Hangars & Announces Plans for 6th Hangar
2007	SIA Engineering Company signs MOU for Vietnam joint venture
2008	• Secures SGD116 million Cebu Pacific Contract to cover 18 more A320/A319
	• Wins USD21 million Gulf Air Contract
	• Establishes Philippines Base To Capture Increased MRO Work Flowing Into Asia
	• Secures SGD90 million FM contract from V Australia
	• Secures Airbus Contract
2009	• Establishes line maintenance foothold in Vietnam
	• Secures long-term fleet management contract from Gulf Air
	• The company's unions Agree On No-Pay Leave To Manage Surplus Manning Capacity
	• SIA Engineering and Sagem (Safran Group) Establishes Joint Venture for Avionics Components Maintenance, Repair and Overhaul
	• Secures 10-year contract from Panasonic Avionics Corporation
	• Restores wage cut and no-pay leave
2010	• Invests in Pratt & Whitney New-Generation Engines to Propel Growth
	• Signs MOU with Gulf Technics To Set Up Base In the Middle East
	• Signs MOU with Panasonic Avionics Corporation to explore joint venture opportunity
	• Adopts NTUC's Cheaper, Better, Faster strategy
	• Signs SGD2.2 billion Services Agreement with Singapore Airlines
	• Adds Royal Brunei Airlines to its Customer Base
	• Gives SGD0.6 million to staff in productivity gain-sharing
	• Signs A340 contract with Airbus
	• Forms Joint Venture With Panasonic Avionics Corporation
	• Opens 6th overseas line maintenance joint venture
	• Signs $300 million Services Agreement with SilkAir

(*Continued*)

Table 9　(*Continued*)

2011	• SIA Engineering & Sagem open SAFRAN's first avionics Centre of Excellence in Asia • Signs SGD358 million Services Agreement with SIA Cargo • Secures 6-Year Contract from AIRBUS
2012	• SIA Engineering Company & Panasonic Avionics Corporation Open First IFEC Centre of Excellence in Asia • Appointed by Messier-Bugatti-Dowty as Wheels and Brakes Authorised Repair Centre • Secures MRO contract for Scoot B777 fleet, opens line maintenance unit in San Francisco, secures VietJet Air's contract and SGD166 million Cebu Air Contract
2014	• Signs SGD350 million Services Agreement with SilkAir • SIA Engineering to form Joint Venture with Boeing
2015	• Signs Maintenance Training Services Agreement with Airbus • Signs SGD2.9 billion Services Agreement with Singapore Airlines • SIA Engineering Signs $197 million Services Agreement with SilkAir
2016	• Signs agreement with Airbus S.A.S (Airbus) to form a joint venture based in Singapore, which will provide airframe maintenance, cabin upgrade and modification services for Airbus A380, A350 and A330 aircraft to airlines in Asia-Pacific and beyond • SIA Engineering renews Fleet Management Programme (FMP) Agreement with Tigerair Taiwan, with a term of 5 years and covers a broad spectrum of inventory and technical management services for Tigerair Taiwan's fleet of A320 aircraft.

Table 10　CapitaLand

2000	• Announced merger plans between DBS Land and Pidemco Land to create the largest listed property company in Southeast Asia. Also announced concurrent merger plans between The Ascott and Somerset Holdings. • Trading commenced for shares of CapitaLand and The Ascott on the main board of Singapore Exchange. DBS Land and Somerset Holdings were de-listed on the same day. CapitaLand officially launched and corporate logo unveiled. • Embarked on first commercial investment in Japan with the acquisition of 11 floors of office space in Shinjuku Square Tower, Tokyo.

(*Continued*)

Table 10 (*Continued*)

2001	• Launch of icFox Singapore, a joint venture internet hub that provides business-enabling solutions for the construction industry. icFox is a joint venture between pFission, Davis Langdon & Seah Group, BruVest Limited, BuildVest (Holdings) Pte Ltd and icFox International. • Official opening of CapitaLand Tokyo office • Official launch of CapitaLand China Holdings Group in Shanghai. • Establishment of the first wholesale property fund denominated in Singapore dollars by CapitaLand Commercial and ERGO Insurance Group through the launch of a SGD875 million office property fund
2002	• Successful Initial Public Offering of CapitaMall Trust, Singapore's first listed real estate trust (REIT). • Joint venture formed between Ascott and Mitsubishi Estate Co Ltd, one of Japan's largest developers, to own, manage and develop serviced residences in Japan
2003	• CapitaLand divested in Indonesia, its entire 50% stake in the issued capital of PT Tropical Amethyst, in line with its strategy to focus on its core business. • CapitaLand Commercial set up a private retail property fund, CapitaRetail Singapore, to hold three suburban malls in Singapore. These malls, collectively worth about SGD500 million, are Lot One Shoppers' Mall, Bukit Panjang Plaza and Rivervale Mall. • Raffles Holdings completed the acquisition of the balance 43.33% shareholding in Raffles Hotel.
2004	• CapitaRetail Singapore successfully closed a SGD506 million issue of Commercial Mortgage Backed Securities (CMBS). This was Singapore's first CMBS issue with Euro-denominated Notes. • PREMAS International set up a joint venture, Tricon PREMAS LLC, to provide integrated facility management services and capitalise on facilities management opportunities in the United Arab Emirates. • PREMAS International formed a joint venture, PREMAS Total Asset Services Sdn. Bhd., in Malaysia. • CapitaLand launches operations in Beijing. • CapitaLand Commercial was restructured into two business units — CapitaLand Commercial and Integrated Development, and CapitaLand Retail — to ensure greater management focus on high growth areas. • CapitaLand Residential signed a Subscription Agreement for a 90% equity stake in Ghim Li Property Pte Ltd, a company which owns a 6,519 square metre condominium site in Tanjong Rhu, Singapore.

(*Continued*)

Table 10   (*Continued*)

2005	• CapitaLand established its first Shari'ah compliant property JV with Bahrain-based investment banking group, Arcapita Bank B.S.C.(c). ARC-CapitaLand Residences Japan will invest in Japanese rental apartments. Its target asset size is JPY30 billion (SGD423 million).
	• CapitaLand and Keppel Land jointly acquired, inter alia, a combined 39 per cent economic interest in the share capital of Bugis City Holdings Pte Ltd held by OCBC and The Great Eastern Life Assurance Company Limited for S$157 million.
	• CapitaLand divested its stakes in Bugis Junction (retail component) and Bugis Junction Tower (office component). Bugis Junction was divested to CMT via an asset sale for S$580.8 million, while Bugis Junction Tower was divested to Keppel Land Properties Pte Ltd via a share sale based on an asset value of SGD140.0 million.
	• Raffles Holdings entered into a transaction with Colony Capital, LLC for the sale of its entire hotel business, which included 41 hotels (14 owned and 27 managed) for an enterprise value of SGD1.72 billion. The transaction was completed on 30 September 2005.
	• CapitaLand set up and closed its eighth private equity fund, the USD400 million (SGD677 million) CapitaLand China Development Fund (CCDF).
	• CapitaLand set up a new business unit, CapitaLand Amanah Pte Ltd, to grow its Shari'ah compliant real estate financial business in Asia.
2006	• CapitaLand enters into a subscription agreement for a 20% stake in Hong Kong-listed Lai Fung Holdings, which has approximately one million sq m of landbank, mainly in Shanghai and the Pearl River Delta.
	• Ascott divests its last non-core asset in Singapore, Liang Court Shopping Centre, for
	• SGD175 million. This divestment is part of Ascott's strategy to focus on its core business in the serviced residence industry.
	• CapitaLand forms a joint venture with India's largest listed retailer, Pantaloon Retail (India) Ltd. It concurrently commits to invest up to USD75 million in Pantaloon's retail property fund and establishes a 50-50 joint venture for retail and fund management businesses in India.
	• Ascott enters India by signing an MDA with The Rattha Group to acquire and develop seven properties in four southern Indian states by 2010 at a joint total estimated investment of USD220 million.

(*Continued*)

Table 10 (*Continued*)

- ART enters into a sale and purchase agreement with Ayala Hotels Inc. and Ocmador Philippines BV to purchase their respective 60% and 40% stakes in Oakwood Premier Ayala Center in Makati City. The serviced residence will be named Ascott Makati, the first Ascott branded serviced residence in Manila.
- Ascott enters Bahrain and Qatar by signing management contracts with MENA Serviced Residence Holding BSC (C) for two serviced residences.

2007
- CapitaLand, together with Malaysia's Quill Group, listed Quill Capita Trust (QCT), Malaysia's first new listing on the Main Board of Bursa Malaysia Securities Berhad for the year
- CapitaLand completed its acquisition of a 95% stake in Shanghai Guang Nan Real Estate Development Co., Ltd,
- Malaysia Commercial Development Fund purchased a 40% stake in Lot J, Kuala Lumpur Sentral and a 39% stake in Lot D, Kuala Lumpur Sentral
- CapitaLand signed a Co-operative Agreement with Vanke, China's largest residential developer
- CapitaLand successfully established the CapitaRetail China Development Fund II with a fund size of approximately USD600.0 million (SGD900.0 million)
- The Ascott Group entered Georgia through a contract from Amtel Properties Development to manage the 65-unit Citadines Tbilisi Freedom Square.

2008
- CapitaLand, through Somerset Capital Pte Ltd, a wholly-owned subsidiary, launched a voluntary unconditional cash offer for the remaining shares in Ascott. The privatisation will strengthen Ascott's leadership position in the market, maximise CapitaLand's competitive advantage and increase cost savings.
- CapitaLand successfully divested its entire 50% stake in Savu Investments Pte. Ltd. which owns Hitachi Tower, a Grade A office building located in Singapore's prime Raffles Place, at an agreed value of SGD811 million. CapitaLand recorded a gain of SGD111.4 million from the sale.
- CapitaLand made key organisational changes to flatten the Group's organisational structure so as to support business growth. The new business units are CapitaLand Residential Singapore and CapitaLand China Holdings.
- In addition, the CapitaLand Commercial business unit now includes overseas businesses in India, Vietnam, Malaysia and Thailand.

(*Continued*)

Table 10   (*Continued*)

2009	• CapitaLand launched the 'Raffles City' brand in Ningbo. Raffles City Ningbo is CapitaLand's fifth integrated development in China after Shanghai, Beijing, Chengdu and Hangzhou.
	• CapitaLand deployed about SGD1 billion from its rights issue proceeds to its China, Vietnam and serviced residence businesses.
	• The public offer of CapitaMalls Asia was 4.9 times subscribed while the placement tranche received aggregate demand of approximately 2.5 times. Trading of CMA shares on the Singapore Exchange commenced on 25 November. Post-listing, CapitaLand's effective interest in CMA stands at 65.5%.
2010	• Ascott entered Vietnam's fourth largest city, Danang, through securing a contract to manage the 121-unit Somerset Danang Bay.
	• CapitaLand divested its entire 50% stake in Sichuan Zhixin CapitaLand Co., Ltd for a net gain of approximately SGD33 million, in line with its ongoing strategy of capital productivity.
	• Europe and Asia into Ascott Reit with divestment proceeds of SGD974 million. This move gave Ascott financial capacity to capture new growth opportunities and has transformed Ascott Reit into a larger and stronger platform which complements Ascott's global growth strategy
	• CapitaLand established a USD200 million joint venture fund with Mitsubishi Estate Asia and GIC Real Estate to invest in residential developments in Vietnam.
2011	• Ascott expanded into Germany's second largest city, Hamburg, through acquiring a turnkey project to be developed into Citadines Michel Hamburg
	• CapitaMalls Asia launched SGD200.0 million worth of 1-year and 3-year retail bonds to the public
	• CapitaLand divested its entire 40% stake in its joint venture company, TCC Capital Land Limited, for a cash consideration of THB2,340.8 million (approximately SGD97.1 million).
	• Ascott acquired its first serviced residence in the German city of Frankfurt, Citadines Messe Frankfurt, and entered Macau SAR in China through clinching a contract to manage Ascott Paragon Macau.
	• Ascott signed a lease agreement for Citadines Richmond Bangalore, its first serviced residence to open in India.
	• CapitaMalls Asia launched its secondary listing by introduction on the Main Board of the Hong Kong Stock Exchange (HKEx).

(*Continued*)

Table 10 (*Continued*)

2012	• CapitaMalls Asia raised SGD400.0 million through an issue of 10-year step-up retail bonds
	• CapitaMalls Asia acquired the remaining 73.71% stakes each in three malls in Japan — La Park Mizue in Tokyo, Izumiya Hirakata in Osaka and Coop Kobe Nishinomiya-Higashi in Hyogo for about JPY13.2 billion (on a 100% basis).
	• CapitaMalls Asia established CapitaMalls China Development Fund III (CMCDF III) with a fund size of USD1.0 billion, its largest private equity fund to date and fourth one in China. The fund will invest in the development of shopping malls and properties predominantly used for retail purposes in China.
	• CapitaMalls Asia issued SGD250.0 million of 10-year corporate bonds under the SGD2.0 billion Euro-Medium Term Note Programme
	• CapitaLand Treasury Limited, a wholly-owned subsidiary of CapitaLand successfully priced USD 400 million fixed rate notes.
2013	• The Group simplified its organisational structure into four main business units :CapitaLand Singapore, CapitaLand China, CapitaMalls Asia and The Ascott Limited, to sharpen its focus on key markets
	• Ascott entered Saudi Arabia by securing a management contract of its first premier serviced residence in Riyadh, Saudi Arabia. The 230-unit Ascott Olaya Riyadh is slated to open in 2015.
	• CapitaLand divested its non-core asset of Technopark@Chai Chee for a cash consideration of SGD193.0 million.
2014	• CapitaLand placed out its remaining stake of 39.1% in Australand for SGD970.1 million.
	• Ascott secured contracts to manage the 153-unit Somerset Kabar Aye Yangon, its first property in Myanmar
	• CapitaLand announced a voluntary conditional cash offer of SGD3.06 billion, with a view to delist CMA. CapitaLand achieved a 97.1% stake in CMA and CMA was suspended from trading on 10 June.
	• Ascott formed a strategic alliance with Vanke, the country's biggest developer, to drive its expansion plans in China.
	• Ascott secured a contract to manage its first Citadines Apart'hotel in South Korea. The 468-unit Citadines Haeundae Busan is slated to open in 2015.
2015	• Ascott opens its first serviced residences in Cyberjaya, Malaysia; Sri Racha, Thailand and Hai Phong, Vietnam

(*Continued*)

Table 10   (*Continued*)

- Ascott secures contract to manage its first serviced residence in Turkey, Somerset Maslak Istanbul
- Ascott marks US expansion by acquiring the 411-key Element New York Times Square West hotel located in Midtown Manhattan for USD$163.5 million.
- CapitaLand expands Vietnam presence with plans for an upscale residential development with approximately 1,000 homes in Ho Chi Minh City. The development will have an estimated total project value of US$150 million
- Ascott marks China expansion with four new management contracts for 583 serviced residence units. Two of the properties are located in Shanghai and one each in Beijing and Dalian, marking Ascott's position as the largest international serviced residence owner-operator in China with over 14,300 units in 80 properties across 24 cities.

2016
- Ascott acquires the 369-unit Sheraton Tribeca New York, its second property in New York, the United States of America, for USD$158.0 million
- Ascott, the largest serviced residence operator in Southeast Asia, clinches seven new management contracts adding over 1,500 apartment units to its portfolio with deals in Thailand, Vietnam, Malaysia and Indonesia

---

Table 11   Ascendas Real Estate Investment Trust (A-REIT)

FY2006
- First to undertake development projects since the amended REIT guidelines allowed such activities — won bids to develop two Warehouse Retail Facilities for Cold Storage and Courts.
- A-REIT acquired 28 properties bringing the total number of properties in the portfolio to 64 and its total assets to S$2.8 billion.

FY2007
- A-REIT completed its first two development projects, two warehouse retail facilities, in this financial year.
- It acquired 13 properties bringing the total number of properties in the portfolio to 77 and its total assets to S$3.3 billion.

FY2008
- A-REIT secures new investments in development projects amounting to over S$270 million
- Goodman sold its 40% stake in Ascendas-MGM Funds Management Limited and its 6.28% direct stake in A-REIT to the Ascendas Group
- A-REIT completed its third development project, Hansapoint @ CBP, Singapore

---

(*Continued*)

Table 11 (*Continued*)

FY2009	• Acquired 8 Loyang Way 1, Singapore in a S$25 million deal
	• Purchased 31 International Business Park, Singapore for S$246.8 million
	• Occupancy of 15 Changi North Way, a logistics and distribution facility launched
	• Pioneer Hub, a logistics and distribution facility in Singapore was completed with 100% occupancy rate
	• Business park at 3 Changi Business Park Crescent, Singapore completed for Citibank N.A.
FY2010	• Completed development of 71 Alps Avenue — customised logistics facility for Expeditors Singapore
	• Completed Plaza8 @ CBP — a business park cum amenity centre at Changi Business Park, Singapore
	• Completed development of 38A Kim Chuan Road, Singapore — a custom-built industrial facility for Singtel
	• Completed acquisition of 31 Joo Koon Circle and DBS Asia Hub
FY2011	• Representative office opened in Shanghai, China to carry out business development.
	• Completed 5 Changi Business Park, a built-to-suit Business Park facility for Citibank N.A. with a revaluation gain of 123.0% (S$42.9 million) over its cost.
	• Entry into the Shanghai market with a forward purchase of a Business Park property for S$117.6 million.
	• Acquired Neuros & Immunos, Singapore for S$125.6 million
FY2012	• Awarded business park site at Fusionopolis, Singapore for S$110.0 million
	• Acquisition of property in International Business Park, Nordic European Centre, Singapore for S$121.55 million.
	• A-REIT's maiden property in Beijing, China acquired with the purchase of Ascendas Z-Link for 300.0 million yuan.
	• Acquired Corporation Place and 3 Changi Business Park Vista, Singapore for S$179.0 million.
	• Completed acquisitions of Cintech I to IV for a total sum of S$183.0 million.
FY2013	• Sold Block 5006 Techplace II, Singapore, for S$38 million.
	• Acquired The Galen, a Science Park property in Singapore Science Park II for S$127.5 million.
	• Disposal of 6 Pioneer Walk, Singapore for S$32 million.

(*Continued*)

Table 11 (*Continued*)

FY2014	• Acquired A-REIT City @Jinqiao, a business park property located in the Pudong New District in Shanghai, China.
	• Completion of Nexus @one-north, business park property in Fusionopolis, Singapore
	• Divestment of No.1 Kallang Place, Singapore for S$12.6 million.
	• Inclusion in the 30-stock FTSE Straits Times Index, Singapore Stock Exchange's main benchmark.
	• Disposal of Block 5006 Techplace II, Singapore for S$38 million.
FY2015	• Acquired Hyflux Innovation Centre for S$193.9 million. Besides Hyflux, other tenants include NEC, Covidien Private Ltd, American Express and Renesas Electronics Singapore.
	• Acquired Aperia, a mixed-use development, for S$463 million. Located in Singapore Aperia houses offices of companies such as Intel, Roche Diagnostics, Audi, Cardinal Health, McDonald's, and retailers like Cold Storage, Tim Ho Wan and Old Town Café.
	• Acquired The Kendall, Singapore in a S$113.7 million deal. The property caters to tenants who are Research & Development and related companies.
	• Merger of A-REIT's sponsor, Ascendas Pte Ltd, and Singbridge Pte Ltd to form the Ascendas-Singbridge Group.
FY2016	• Sold 26 Senoko Way for S$24.8 million.
	• Sale of BBR Building in Singapore for S$13.9 million.
	• A-REIT's maiden Australian buy with A$407.1 million acquisition of logistic properties.
	• Completed second phase of logistics acquisitions in Australia for A$605.9 million.
	• Acquired logistics facility in Sydney for A$76.6 million.
	• Completed S$420 million acquisition of ONE@Changi City, a business park.
	• Sold Four Acres Singapore for S$34 million

Table 12 CapitaLand Mall Trust (CMT)

2006	• CMT gets approval to increase the allowable commercial gross floor area at IMM from 26.8 percent to 40.0 percent, which translates to an increase of approximately 188,000 sq ft of additional GFA at the mall.
	• Signing of a collaboration agreement to jointly acquire Raffles City
	• CMT was granted permission to increase the gross plot ratio of Hougang Plaza from 1.4 to 3.0 for full residential or mixed development. This translates to an increase of around 91,493 sq ft of additional GFA at the mall.
	• CMT completed the acquisition of shares it does not already own in Hougang Plaza to make it a fully owned asset.
	• Retail extension at Funan, measuring over 8,000 sq ft was completed.
	• Asset enhancement plan is announced for Raffles City which can potentially increase Raffles City's retail NLA by between 150,000 sq ft and 200,000 sq ft.
2007	• CMT receives consent from Urban Redevelopment Authority to erect a nine-storey commercial building at Funan to maximise unutilized gross floor area of approximately 386,000 sq ft.
	• CMT gets approval to increase the plot ratio of JEC from 1.85 to 3.0 for commercial development.
	• Phase 1 asset enhancement plan at Raffles City announced to add 41,000 sq ft of retail space at Raffles City Shopping Centre.
	• Acquired remaining shares to own 100.0% of the beneficial interest in the property portfolio which includes Lot One, Bukit Panjang Plaza and Rivervale Mall.
	• CMT gets permission to increase Tampines Mall's plot ratio from 3.5 to 4.2 for full office development. This would create a potential 95,000 sq ft of office space at Tampines Mall, a pure-retail asset.
2008	• CMT acquired from the Government of the Republic of Singapore The Atrium@Orchard (Atrium) at a purchase price of S$839.8 million.
	• Lot One Shoppers' Mall completed building the retail units at its new four-storey retail extension block. The over 50 newly-created shops, are expected to add an annual incremental Net Property Income of S$5.24 million to the CMT portfolio.
	• Sembawang Shopping Centre started operations following major redevelopment works at a cost of S$68.4 million. It is expected that the property will add an annual incremental income of S$3.24 million to the CMT portfolio.

(Continued)

Table 12 (*Continued*)

2009	• Lot One Shoppers' Mall,Riversvale Mall complete their asset enhancement works.
	• CMT commenced asset enhancement works to re-configure the Basement 1 space of Raffles City Singapore and construct a new underground link at Basement 2.
	• CMT commenced asset enhancement works for Jurong Entertainment Centre.
2010	• CMT entered into a sale and purchase agreement with Clarke Quay Pte Ltd, a wholly-owned subsidiary of CapitaMalls Asia Limited (CMA), to acquire Clarke Quay for S$268.0 million.
	• CMT starts construction work on JCube, the new mall on the site of the former Jurong Entertainment Centre
	• Raffles City Singapore completed asset enhancement works at Basement One Marketplace and Basement Two Link
2011	• CMT acquired Iluma for S$295.0 million from Jack Investment Pte Ltd
	• Purchase of land parcel at Jurong Gateway, marked CMT's entry into Greenfield developments with its 30.00% stake in the joint venture. The total development cost of the project was expected to be S$1,565.0 million at the time of the acquisition
2012	• Groundbreaking ceremony for Westgate, an upcoming shopping mall and office tower at Jurong Gateway, commenced. CMT owns a 30% stake in the joint venture.
	• CMT completes sale of Hougang Plaza, to Oxley Bloom Pte. Ltd. for S$119.1 million.
	• JCube was opened after the completion of asset enhancement works.
	• Bugis+ saw the completion of asset enhancement works. The mall is positioned as the retail and entertainment extension of Bugis Junction, with both properties linked by an overhead bridge.
	• Clarke Quay completed asset enhancement works at its Block C.
	• Asset enhancement works for The Atrium@Orchard were completed, with its retail space integrated with Plaza Singapura's.
2013	• Asset enhancement works for Clarke Quay completed. It now has food & beverage and entertainment outlets at Block C and Block E, including a new frontage along River Valley Road.
	• Junction 8 saw the completion of asset enhancement works, with enhanced connectivity to the Bishan Mass Rapid Transit Interchange Station.

(*Continued*)

Table 12 (*Continued*)

	• Phase one of plan to reposition IMM Building as a value-focused mall completed. IMM Building is Singapore's largest outlet mall with over 55 outlet stores. • Phase one of the asset enhancement works for Bugis Junction completed. Along with phase two, now close to 70,000 sq ft of space recovered from an anchor tenant and converted to specialty shops. • Westgate opens its doors to shoppers.
2014	• Options to purchase office units of Westgate Tower granted to a consortium consisting of Sun Venture Homes Pte. Ltd. and Low Keng Huat (Singapore) Limited for S$579.4 million. • Phase two of the asset enhancement initiative for Bugis Junction was completed. Combined with the phase one, completed in 2013, the mall now has more specialty stores with a wider range of merchandise. J. Avenue, a new retail zone in JCube also commenced trading.
2015	• CMT acquires Bedok Mall by acquiring all the units in Brilliance Mall Trust, funded by the issuance of units, with the balance comprising bank borrowings. • Sold Rivervale Mall to a private equity fund for S$190.5 million. • IMM Building, Singapore's largest outlet mall increased its total number of outlet stores to 85 with new designer brands. It also boosted its F&B offerings. • Plan announced to redevelop Funan DigitaLife Mall into an integrated development. • Clarke Quay completed reconfiguration works of Block C, comprising a dance club, F&B and entertainment outlets.

Table 13 Global Logistic Properties

FY2010	• Announces corporate branding of "Global Logistic Properties" ("GLP"). • Becomes the largest provider of modern logistics facilities in China and Japan by floor area with over 250 established customers across Japan and China.
FY2011	• Acquires a stake in the parent company of BLOGIS — the second largest provider of modern logistics facilities in China after GLP. • Lists on the main board of the SGX on 18 October, the largest IPO in Singapore since 1993 as at GLP's listing day. • Expands into Zhongshan, increasing presence in China to 19 cities.

(*Continued*)

Table 13   (*Continued*)

FY2012	• Enters into a 50:50 joint venture with China Investment Corporation to acquire 15 modern logistics facilities in Japan.
	• Commences construction of an advanced healthcare logistics facility at Hangzhou, China.
	• Enters into a strategic partnership with Transfar Road-Port to expand the logistics network in China. The partnership added gross floor area of 951,354 sq m to GLP's China portfolio.
	• Forms a 50:50 joint venture of USD500 million (JPY38 billion) in equity with Canada Pension Plan Investment Board to develop and hold institutional quality, modern logistics facilities.
	• Acquires 90% stake in Vailog's existing property portfolio. GLP has an option to acquire the remaining 10% interest from Vailog.
	• Expands into Xiamen, increasing GLP's presence in China to 20 cities.
	• Commences development of 1.22 million square metres of land and secured 1.3 million square metres of new and expansion leased area.
	• Acquires approximately a 53% stake in Airport City Development Co. Ltd., the sole developer in the Beijing Capital International Airport airside cargo handling and bonded logistics area, adding a gross floor area (GFA) of 273,843 square metres of completed properties and GFA of 513,000 square metres of development pipeline to the portfolio.
	• Included in the Straits Times Index (STI)
FY2013	• Doubles GLP Japan Development Venture, the 50:50 JV with CPPIB to develop modern logistics facilities in Japan, to USD2.2 billion.
	• USD82 million investment of to install solar panels on the rooftops of 22 properties in Japan
	• Sells 33 Japan Properties to GLP J-REIT; Continues to Grow Fund Management Platform.
	• Development of GLP Ayase, a 68,400 square metre facility in Greater Tokyo.
	• Completes listing of USD2.6 billion GLP J-REIT, Japan's largest real estate IPO, on the Tokyo Stock Exchange.
	• Enters Brazil: and establishes two joint ventures with CPPIB, CIC and GIC to acquire logistics platform in Brazil for USD1.45 billion; it is the largest logistics platform in Brazil with most assets located in Rio de Janeiro and Sao Paolo.
	• Increases stake in GLP Park Suzhou, GLP's joint venture with SEALL, to 70%.

(Continued)

Table 13 (*Continued*)

<table>
<tr><td></td><td>

- Sells 16.7% stake in GLP Japan Income Partners I to CBRE Global Multi Manager.
- Partners Haier to develop state of the art logistics network across China.
- Signs 20-year lease for 60,000 square metres with Beijing Aviation Ground Service Co. at Beijing Capital International Airport; GLP's largest lease by value.
- Announces plan to develop GLP Atsgi, a 109,500 square metres logistics facility in Greater Tokyo.
</td></tr>
<tr><td>FY2014</td><td>

- Signs agreement with Chinese SOEs and leading financial institutions in China, investing up to USD2.5 billion.
- Forms strategic alliance with SOE's COFCO, Sinotrans, Bank of China, Guangdong Holdings and Jinbei enhancing access to strategic land and large scale customer leasing needs
- Acquires USD1.4 billion portfolio in Brazil from BR Properties
- GLP Brazil Development Partners expands to USD1.1 billion
- GLP Launches USD3 billion China Logistics fund
- GLP Misato III, completed in May 2013, is the first LEED® Platinum certified logistics facility in Japan.
- GLP Japan Income Partners I to sell seven properties to GLP J-REIT.
- GLP to sell two Japan properties to GLP J-REIT; continues to grow fund management platform.
</td></tr>
<tr><td>FY2015</td><td>

- Plans to acquire one of the largest logistics real estate portfolios in the United States for USD8.1 billion via its fund management platform;
- GLP expands Japan Development Venture and Brazil Development Partners I; forms USD1.1 billion partnership, GLP Brazil Income Partners II
- GLP signs strategic partnership agreement with China Development Bank Capital and CMSTD, China's largest state-owned warehouse provider
- GLP sells nine additional properties to GLP J-REIT
- Completed USD$2.5 billion landmark agreement with Chinese SOEs and leading financial institutions
</td></tr>
<tr><td>2016</td><td>

- GLP signs leases totaling 87,000 square meters ("sqm") (940,000 square feet ("sq ft")) with three industry leaders in China
- GLP signs a new 15,000 sqm (161,000 sq ft) lease with Akachan House, a leading e-commerce retailer for baby products in Japan
- GLP expands its relationship with CEVA, third party logistics customer, in the US with a new 157,000 sq ft (14,600 sqm) lease in Columbus, Ohio, USA
</td></tr>
</table>

Table 14   StarHub

2004	• StarHub launches Singapore's first prepaid broadband service — MaxOnline 2000 FlexiSurf, without registration and monthly bill payment
	• StarHub and Connexion by Boeing sign a Memorandum of Understanding to provide in-flight wireless broadband Internet access to StarHub's customers
	• StarHub launches Digital Cable services
	• StarHub is listed on the Main Board of the Singapore Exchange Securities Trading Limited
	• StarHub rolls out its 3G network and started customer trials of 3G services
2005	• StarHub introduces Digital Terrestrial Television (DTTV) system which offers better quality service and a compelling selection of cable TV channels for corporate customers
	• StarHub launches 3G services and introduced a broad portfolio of mobile video content over its 2G and 3G mobile platforms
	• StarHub launches MaxOnline Ultimate, the highest download speed available for residential broadband access plan in Singapore, at up to 25 Mbps
	• StarHub launches Demand TV, Singapore's first near video-on-demand service on television
	• StarHub included in the FTSE/ASEAN Index
2006	• StarHub launched Voice-over-IP services using a SIP adaptor for homes and businesses
	• StarHub announces the upgrade of its broadband HFC cable network to a DOCSIS 3.0 compliant architecture to deliver ultra-high broadband speeds for customers in the second half of 2006
	• StarHub and six other Asian mobile operators form Conexus Mobile Alliance for global roaming and corporate mobile services
	• StarHub launches Smart TV, a digital recording service to allow customers to 'time shift' so that they have more control when TV programmes are viewed
	• StarHub launches pre-paid cable TV service — FlexiWatch StarHub wins exclusive rights for the next three seasons of the Barclays English Premier League, commencing from the 2007/2008 season, for the Singapore market
	• Singapore becomes the first country in the world to commercially launch 100Mbps (MaxOnline Ultimate) residential broadband services nation-wide — another milestone with its deployment of DOCSIS 3.0 technology
	• Official launch of Conexus Mobile Alliance, Asia's largest alliance of mobile operators, of which StarHub is founding member, has a coverage footprint to over 130 million mobile subscribers in nine countries and regions

(*Continued*)

Table 14 (*Continued*)

2007	• StarHub provides customers free wireless broadband access at all StarHub hotspots in Singapore. They also get free access to Wireless@SG services through a Memorandum of Understanding reached between StarHub and QMax Communications.
	• StarHub launches Southeast Asia's first commercial High Definition Television service
	• StarHub launches HubStation, an integrated device that enables consumers to watch, surf and talk, all at the same time.
	• StarHub commercially launches pfingo, the innovative new mobile Internet service suite.
	• StarHub launches HubStation FlexiWatch, a new prepaid cable TV service that allows non-cable TV customers to subscribe to an exciting line-up of channels and pay only for the duration for which they wish to enjoy the channels.
2008	• StarHub wins exclusive UEFA EURO 2008 rights and broadcasts the content across multiple platforms on cable TV, online and mobile networks.
	• StarHub launches the first nationwide location-based mobile advertising service.
	• StarHub starts expansion and upgrade of its 3.5G mobile network to deliver high quality mobile surfing experience and improved indoor and outdoor coverage.
	• StarHub launches Demand TV, comprising both On Demand Channels and true Video-on-Demand services, allowing viewers to enjoy instant access to content at advanced windows
	• StarHub launches Home Zone, the world's first commercial 3G Femtocell service.
2009	• Launches undersea cable system, Asia-America Gateway, in Singapore
	• Launches Singapore's first pre-paid data plan for BlackBerry service
	• First in Asia to offer free local data access to Windows Live Messenger and Facebook on supported handset models
	• Deploys first solar powered mobile base station in Singapore
	• Launches Singapore's first commercial HSPA+ service
	• StarHub added to the MSCI Singapore Free Index
	• Selected to build and manage OpCo for Singapore's Next Gen NBN
	• StarHub TV goes fully digital
2010	• Introduces Singapore's first solar-powered mobile base station enabled vehicle
	• Adopts world's first smart phone signalling solution to further enhance network performance and improve end-user smart phone experience

(*Continued*)

Table 14   (*Continued*)

- Scores broadcast rights to the 2010 FIFA World Cup
- Commences HSPA+ network upgrade to support up to 42.2Mbps on the downlink
- Launches new mobile TV client to enhance TV viewing on smart phones
- Partners Golden Village and launched Singapore's first movie-ticketing service on television

2011
- StarHub teams up with DBS and EZ-Link to roll out NFC mobile services
- Introduces Singapore's first mobile post-paid plan that offers the sharing of bundled data, airtime and SMS for customers
- Launches Roam Manager — Singapore's first set of tools that provides mobile roaming users with pertinent roaming related information and data usage cost notification feature
- Joins top Asian carriers to build and operate the Asia Submarine-Cable Express, an undersea cable system linking Singapore directly to Hong Kong, Japan and the Philippines

2012
- Launches government public cloud service
- Enhances high-speed mobile broadband network with LTE and DC-HSPA+
- Unveils SmartWallet, an NFC smart phone app for secure payment and lifestyle services
- Asia Submarine-Cable Express starts operations in Singapore
- Launches TV Anywhere, a multi-screen service
- Becomes the exclusive partner of Vodafone in Singapore

2013
- Unveils MediaHub, the new facility for future business and innovations at one-north
- Launches SuperSports Arena, the first free-to-cable channel in Singapore
- Introduces HD Voice for enhanced clarity of mobile voice calls
- Launches StarHub TV on Fibre for commercial customers

2014
- Expanded e-waste recycling programme *RENEW* with partners DHL and TES-AMM
- Commenced production of Public Service Broadcast content
- Launched 4G voice service *HD Voice+*
- Launched market-first integrated fibre and cable home broadband solution Dual Broadband

2015
- ST Telemedia and StarHub Enter Partnership to Develop MediaHub
- StarHub launches Internet Protocol Television (IPTV) for Singapore residences

(*Continued*)

Table 14 (*Continued*)

	• Recognised by global independent network checker Opensignal as the fastest 4G network in the world • Ooredoo Myanmar and StarHub form strategic partnership
2016	• Singapore Press Holdings (SPH) and StarHub sign Memorandum of Understanding (MOU) to collaborate in areas of advertising sales, creation and carriage of content, data analytics and marketing. • StarHub and Netflix announcepartnership to bring Netflix to StarHub customers through their set-top boxes by the early second quarter of 2016. StarHub will also join the Netflix Open Connect programme.

Table 15 Singtel

1988	Singtel launched Singapore's only satellite, ST-1, to support video, data and voice communications through- out Asia
1992	Singtel was corporatised. The erstwhile TAS was renamed Singapore Telecommunications Private Limited.
1993	Singtel issues its Initial Public Offering (IPO), Singapore's largest IPO that year.
1997	Singtel acquires National Computer Systems Pte Ltd (NCS) from the National Computer Board (NCB).
2001	• Singtel makes its largest acquisition — a 100% stake in Australia-based Optus for SSD13 billion. • Singtel buys 22.3% of Indonesia-based Telkomsel
2008	Singtel and Apple jointly announce that Singtel will be the first mobile operator to launch iPhone 3G and allied services to Singapore in June
2010	• Singtel organises a world's first 3D 2010 FIFA World Cup Finals • Singtel provides the world's largest deployment of satellite technology for the Philippines election • Launch of ultra high-speed fibre network of up to 100Mbps — encompasses SingNet eVolve Broadband (Dynamic IP), SingNet eLite Access (Static IP) and Meg@POP eLite.
2011	• Founded Innov8, a venture capital fund, with an initial fund size of SGD200 million.
2012	• Singtel buys digital ads firm Amobee for USD321million

(*Continued*)

Table 15 (*Continued*)

2013	• Singtel and Amdocsopen joint development centre in Israel to identify, nurture and commercialize innovative technologies by Israeli start-ups with the potential to reach more than 470 million mobile customers of the Singtel Group
	• Singtel and Optus Business sign A$530 million agreement with ANZ to provide telecommunication and managed services for a further five years.
2014	• Singtel enters into agreements for total credit facilities of approximately S$3.5 billion for general corporate purposes and refinancing of existing facilities.
2015	• Singtel, Sony Pictures Television and Warner Bros. Entertainment establish joint venture start-up, to offer a regional over-the-top (OTT) video service in Asia
	• Singtel acquires 98% equity interest in US-based Trustwave, a specialist in managed security services, in a USD$810 million deal
	• Singtel launches S$400 million data centre in Singapore to meet growing demand for co-location and cloud services.
2016	• Singtel and Ericsson partnership readies Singtel's 4G LTE network to support the expected rapid growth of connected devices. The collaboration will start with a trial of Narrow Band Internet of Things (NB-IoT) technology beginning in the second half of 2016.
	• Singtel, SubPartners, and Telstra enter into a Memorandum of Understanding (MOU) to build a new international submarine cable, APX-West, connecting Perth and Singapore.

Table 16   ComfortDelGro

2003	• ComfortDelGro and Global East Investment form a joint venture company, ComfortDelGro Insurance Brokers.
	• Forms a new taxi joint venture, Shenyang ComfortDelGro Taxi, with Shenyang Taxi Co., in China.
	• Official opening of Toyota car distribution business in Suzhou, China.
2004	• Formation of four joint venture companies in Chengdu, China — Chengdu ComfortDelGro Yiyou Taxi, Sichuan ComfortDelGro Car Servicing, Chengdu Jitong Integrated Vehicle Inspection and Chengdu CityLimo Auto Services to operate taxi services, an automotive repair and maintenance workshop, a vehicle inspection centre and a vehicle rental and leasing services respectively.

(*Continued*)

Table 16 (*Continued*)

- Acquires 80% stake in Beijing Tian Long Da Tian Vehicle Inspection, a vehicle inspection company in Beijing.
- Acquires F.E.Thorpe & Sons, a bus operator in London.
- Formation of a bus joint venture company, Shenyang ComfortDelGro Anyun Bus in Shenyang, North East China.
- Metroline acquires the E.H. Mundy Holdings, a bus and coach operator in London.
- Computer Cab expands its taxi fleet in London through a licensing agreement with Manganese Bronze Holdings.

2005
- ComfortDelGro Savico Taxi, the Group's second taxi joint venture company in Ho Chi Minh City, Vietnam, is formed.
- Acquires Westbus Group in Western Sydney, Australia.
- ComfortDelGro's Scottish coach operation enters into a joint venture with Stagecoach Bus Holdings
- ComfortDelGro sets up Chengdu ComfortDelGro Qing Yang Driving School, its first driving school overseas.
- Shenyang ComfortDelGro Bus, ComfortDelGro's second bus company in Shenyang, is formed.

2006
- Acquires Onward Travel, a private hire company in Edinburgh.
- Acquires the bus routes and assets of Holroyd Bus Lines in New South Wales, Australia.
- Expands its China footprint with a new driving school investment in Chongqing.

2007
- Introduces its second inter-city coach service in Cork, Ireland.
- Acquires a 70% stake in Your Taxi Ltd, a licensed taxi and private hire company in Birmingham.
- Nanjing ComfortDelGro Dajian Taxi, ComfortDelGro's first investment in Jiangsu Province, is formed.
- Acquires the business and assets of Toronto Bus Services in the Newcastle region of New South Wales, Australia.
- Issues its Green Statement and pledges to cut emissions and increase its recycling efforts

2008
- Increases its stake in Cabcharge Australia Limited, which is listed on the Australian Stock Exchange, and which is a global leader in electronic payment systems for the transport sector, through a share swap agreement.
- Acquires Liverpool's largest taxi circuit operator, Merseyside Radio Meter Cabs, and increases its taxi fleet in UK to 4,500 vehicles.

(*Continued*)

Table 16 (*Continued*)

- Forays into Victoria, Australia by acquiring Kefford Group, the fourth largest bus operator in the state.
- Expands presence in China through the purchase of 100 Jia Run Taxi Co., Ltd in Beijing, thus bringing the Group's total fleet in China to about 13,000 vehicles. Also increases its stake in Chongqing ComfortDelGro Driver Training Co., Ltd.

2009
- VICOM Emission Test Laboratory, Singapore's first state-of-the-art vehicle emission and fuel efficiency test laboratory opens.
- ComfortDelGro Engineering makes its first foray into motorsports. Sparks Motorsports, a partnership between ComfortDelGro Engineering and LTM Performance Limited, caters to the motorsports market.

2010
- Launches the world's first taxi-hotel charge card with The Regent Singapore.
- Makes an AUD38.8 million bid for Perth's largest taxi operator, Swan Taxis Limited and takes over the company.

2011
- Chengdu ComfortDelGro Taxi Co., Ltd awarded 800 new taxi licenses by the Chengdu Municipal Government, making it the second largest taxi operator in the City with 1,050 taxis.
- Moove Media Pte Ltd (Moove Media), ComfortDelGro Group's Outdoor Advertising arm and Singapore's leading Out-Of-Home Advertising media owner, will be making its maiden foray into Sydney through its newly formed subsidiary, Moove Media Australia Pty Ltd.
- Expands its footprint in China with a third driving school located in the Liangjiang New Business District called Chongqing Liangjiang ComfortDelGro Driver Training Co., Ltd.

2012
Expands Australian operations through an AUD53 million acquisition of Deane's Bus Lines Pty Ltd and Transborder Express — both of which are part of Deane's Transit Group (DTG).

2013
- Metroline, which runs 80 routes through an area that extends from North to West London, including Central London and the City, became the first bus operator to be chosen by the Mayor to run Route 24 comprising only of the New Bus for London by mid-year.
- ComfortDelGro, through its wholly-owned subsidiary, Metroline, acquires part of FirstGroup plc's London bus business, comprising 494 buses operating from five West London garages — Alperton, Greenford, Hayes, Uxbridge and Willesden Junction — for £57.5 million (SGD111.1 million).

(*Continued*)

Table 16 (*Continued*)

- Expands its operations in Australia through the acquisition of Driver Group Pty Ltd in Melbourne for approximately AUD22.0 million (S$27.0 million). Established in 1931, the Driver Group operates metropolitan bus routes under a long-term contract with the Victorian Government in the Eastern suburbs of Melbourne.
- ComfortDelGro's subsidiary in Sydney, ComfortDelGro Cabcharge, rolls out five double decks under its Hillsbus brand.
- Launches Singapore's first City Direct service from Jurong West into the City.
- ComfortDelGro, has through its subsidiary, Jilin ComfortDelGro Taxi Co., Ltd, incorporated a wholly-owned subsidiary Jilin ComfortDelGro Driver Training in Jilin City, China.

2014
- Nanning Comfort Transportation won 30 new licenses and rolled out its first-ever Volkswagen Santana Vista Compressed Natural Gas (CNG) taxis.
- ComfortDelGro Bus rolls out second City Direct service from Hillview/Bukit Batok areas into the City.
- Acquires the assets of Blue Mountains Bus Company for about AUD26.5 million.

Table 17 Singapore Airlines

2000
- Becomes the 11th member of the Star Alliance, which provides customers with access to a global route network and seamless service.
- Acquires an 8.3 per cent stake in Air New Zealand and a further 16.7% from Brierley Investments Ltd, raising its total stake to 25 per cent.
- SIA, Lufthansa Cargo and SAS Cargo step up cooperation in the air cargo business by signing an agreement to embark on New Global Cargo, a joint project to enable the seamless carriage of airfreight throughout their combined cargo network.
- SIA subsidiaries Singapore Airport Terminal Services (SATS) and SIA Engineering Company (SIAEC) each list 13% of their shares on the Singapore Exchange following the launch of their respective initial public offers.
- Teams up with International SOS, the world's largest medical assistance company, to introduce the Telemedical Service on board its flights. The service allows cabin crew to consult medical staff on the ground if a passenger becomes ill on board.
- Joins eight other Asia-Pacific airlines to launch Travel Exchange Asia, an Internet portal that offers customers a full range of online travel services
- Introduces Mobile Services to allow customers to access up-to-the minute flight information anywhere and at any time of the day using WAP phones.

(*Continued*)

Table 17   (*Continued*)

	• Joins 12 other leading airlines to launch Aeroxchange, an Internet-driven business-to-business e-commerce exchange that offers the most comprehensive selection of aircraft technical parts and services on the Internet, as well as general business supplies.
2001	• Becomes the first airline to launch global flight alerts via the short message service (SMS).
	• SIA's Cargo Division is corporatized as Singapore Airlines Cargo Pte Ltd, a wholly-owned subsidiary and a designated all-cargo airline of Singapore.
	• SIA and Virgin Atlantic Airways launch their first codeshare service between London and Singapore.
	• SIA's stake in Air New Zealand is reduced to 6.47%following a recapitalization package which sees the New Zealand Government invest NZ\$885 million in new ordinary shares and new convertible preference shares in Air New Zealand.
2002	• Singapore Airlines Cargo launches Securerider, a new freight product designed to meet customer needs for high security in the transportation of valuable and vulnerable goods.
	• Launches a new Internet check-in service that allows customers to choose their seats up to two days before departure.
	• First flight by SpaceBed-equipped aircraft operates from Singapore to London.
	• SIA and Virgin Investments subscribe for additional shares in Virgin Atlantic, amounting to GBP25 million (SGD65.7 million)
	• Official opening of SATS In-flight Catering Centre
	• KrisFlyer announces new partners — Emirates, Starwood Hotels and Resorts, Taj Hotels Resorts and Palaces and the Saville Hotel Group.
2003	• Announces plans to suspend 65 services a week in response to softening demand, caused primarily by the war in Iraq.
	• Announces service cutbacks of up to 19.7 per cent due to SARS and war in Iraq
	• Singapore Airlines Cargo starts direct freighter services from China to the US three times a week
	• Acquires 49% of low cost carrier Tiger Airways, in partnership with Temasek Holdings, Indigo Partners LLC and Irelandia Investments Ltd
2004	• SIA's A345LeaderShip commences daily non-stop services from Singapore to Los Angeles, the world's longest non-stop commercial flight
	• The Group introduced fuel surcharges on all routes to partially offset the impact of higher jet fuel prices.
	• SMS check-in services launched in 12 cities.
	• Sells its 6.3% stake in Air New Zealand.

(*Continued*)

Table 17 (*Continued*)

	• Commences weekly B777-200ER non-stop flights to Cape Town in South Africa. This is the first direct air service between Cape Town and Southeast Asia.
2005	• A tripartite codeshare agreement was signed by Singapore Airlines, SilkAir and Malaysian Airlines.
	• First airline in the region to introduce Connexion by Boeing, an in-flight broadband service that provides passengers with real-time, high-speed and secure internet connectivity in-flight
	• Signs an agreement with Great Wall Industry Corporation and Dahlia Investments to form a joint venture cargo airline, The Great Wall Airlines Company Limited, in Shanghai. SIA Cargo holds a 25% in Great Wall Airlines.
	• Becomes the first airline in the world to introduce live TV on international flights.
2006	• Sells SIA Building, at 77 Robinson Road, for SGD343.88 million.
2007	• Announces plans to outsource some of its reservations call centre functions in Australia, New Zealand, United States and Canada.
	• Ranked as the first non-US carrier, and third in the airline industry, in implementing interline e-ticketing.
	• Singapore Airlines and China Eastern Airlines launch interline e-ticketing.
2008	• Commits globally to advertising fares inclusive of all taxes, surcharges and fees, becoming the first carrier to do so.
	• Launches the world's first all-Business Class service on the Transpacific. The Singapore-New York service is operated by Airbus A340-500 aircraft, configured with 100 of the Airline's award-winning Business Class seats. The re-fitted aircraft is also the first in the world to offer iPod and iPhone connectivity through KrisWorld.
2009	• An 11% reduction in overall capacity, starting from April 2009, is announced. The Airline engages the three staff unions in discussions on ways to best mitigate the impact of the global downturn
	• New SIA Mobile facility introduced, allowing customers to check in for their flights using their Singapore-registered mobile phones.
2010	• SIA Mobile is enhanced to include booking facility and selected KrisFlyer services, for customers using selected mobile phones, BlackBerry and iPhone devices.
	• Partners the Civil Aviation Authority of Singapore in the world's first multi-sector demonstration green flight under the Asia and Pacific Initiative to Reduce Emissions (ASPIRE) programme.

(*Continued*)

Table 17   (*Continued*)

2011	• SIA customers in the US, Singapore and five other Asia Pacific countries and territories pay for their flights with PayPal when they buy their tickets online.
	• Announces intention to launch Scoot, a wholly owned and independently operated low cost airline, operating wide-body aircraft on medium- and long-haul routes.
	• Advance selection of Economy Class seats on the Airline's flights made available through all booking channels, including travel agencies.
	• Joins the Sustainable Aviation Fuel Users Group.
	• The Airline and Virgin Australia commence reciprocal frequent flyer recognition, enabling members of each airline's frequent flyer programme to earn and redeem points on the other's flights. Reciprocal lounge access is also available for eligible customers.
2012	• Acquires a 10% stake in Virgin Australia through a placement of new shares by Virgin Australia Holdings for a total consideration of AUD105.3 million.
	• Sells its 49% in Virgin Atlantic Ltd to Delta Air Lines for USD360 million cash.
2013	• Increase its equity holding in Virgin Australia to 19.9% with the purchase of 255.5 million shares for a total consideration of AUD122.6 million.
	• SIA and Tata Sons announce plan to set up a joint venture airline based in New Delhi with SIA holding 49% equity and Tata Sons 51%.
	• Integrates its website bookings with Google Now to enable customers to have easy access to travel information such as flight status, traffic and weather conditions at destination.
2014	• SIA and Air New Zealand announce a proposed alliance that would enable SIA to fly the A380 to Auckland for the first time and Air New Zealand to return to the Auckland-Singapore route.
	• SIA and Airbus sign a Memorandum of Understanding to establish a flight training joint venture in Singapore called Airbus Asia Training Centre. SIA to hold a 45% equity stake and Airbus 55%.
2015	• SIA which currently owns 55.8% of Tiger Airways, unveils plan to buy the shares it does not own with the intention of delisting Tiger Airways from SGX, and if possible, to privatise it
	• SIA and Lufthansa sign deal to operate flights between Singapore and the European cities of Frankfurt, Munich and Zurich under revenue-sharing agreements.
2016	SIA delists Tiger Airways Holdings Ltd after acquiring 100% stake in Tiger Airways

APPENDIX 2

REGULATORY GUIDELINES FOR SINGAPORE BANKS

Basel III Guidelines

The Basel III guidelines are a set of guidelines laid down by the Basel Committee for Banking Supervision at the Bank for International Settlements (BIS) *to strengthen the regulation, supervision and risk management of the banking sector. These measures aim to:*

* *Improve the banking sector's ability to absorb shocks arising from financial and economic stress, whatever the source*
* *Improve risk management and governance*
* *Strengthen banks' transparency and disclosures.*

The reforms target:

* *Bank-level, or microprudential, regulation, which will help raise the resilience of individual banking institutions to periods of stress.*
* *Macroprudential, system wide risks that can build up across the banking sector as well as the procyclical amplification of these risks over time.*

MAS's Prudential Regulations

Capital Adequacy Ratio: CAR is a measure of the adequacy of a bank's capital. It is expressed as a percentage of the sum of a bank's tier 1 and tier 2 capital to its risk weighted credit exposures. Tier 1 capital can absorb losses without a bank being required to cease trading, and Tier 2 capital, which can absorb losses in the event of a winding-up and so provides a lesser degree of protection to depositors.

The MAS has consistently required Singapore banks to be better capitaliaed than banks in the developed nations of the western hemisphere and has stipulated CARs that are higher than Basel III guidelines. While Basel III guidelines recommend a Common Equity Tier 1 (CET 1) CAR of 7%, the minimum for Singapore banks to be achieved by 1 January 2019 is 9%. The MAS Notice 637 requires Singapore-incorporated banks to maintain the following minimum CARs with effect from 1 January 2015:

- CET 1 of 6.5%,
- Tier 1 CAR of 8%, and
- Total CAR of 10%

A capital conservation buffer of 2.5% above the minimum capital adequacy requirement is to be phased in from 2016 to 2019.

Minimum Liquid Assets (MLA): Banks are required to hold at all times:

- Liquid assets denominated in any currency amounting to no less than 16% of the value of its Qualifying Liabilities denominated in all currencies (*"All currency MLA requirement"*); and
- Liquid assets denominated in Singapore Dollars amounting to no less than 16% of the value of its Qualifying Liabilities denominated in Singapore Dollars (*"Singapore Dollar MLA requirement"*)

Liquidity Coverage Ratio (LCR): Singapore incorporated and head-quartered banks are required to maintain a Singapore Dollar LCR of at least 100% and an all currency LCR of at least 60% with effect from 1 January 2015. Further, all banks should increase their currency LCRs by 10% every year to 100% by 1 January 2019. LCR is defined as the percentage of high quality liquid assets to total net cash outflows. Total net cash outflow is defined as the difference between:

- Total expected cash outflows and
- The lower of total expected cash inflows and 75% of total expected cash outflows

Loan to Value Norms: The MAS has capped real estate exposure by banks at 35% of eligible assets with a loan to value ceiling of 80% for individuals purchasing houses for the first time. Further the total debt servicing ratio (TDSR) which includes payments on all outstanding debt, including motor vehicle loans and credit card balances not to exceed 60% of income. A Mortgage Servicing Ratio (MSR) limit of 30% also applies to housing loans for the purchase of non-private properties (Housing Development Board flats). The LTV cap on motor vehicle loans was set at 60% and 50%, for motor vehicles whose open market value is up to SGD20,000 and more than SGD20,000 respectively. The tenor is restricted to five years.

Counterparty Exposure Norms: The MAS restricts a single counterparty group's exposure (including commitments and contingencies) to 25% of a bank's capital funds. Exposures exempted from this rule include those to the Singapore government and multilateral development banks. The aggregate of large exposures (defined as those that exceed 10% of a bank's capital funds) should not exceed 50% of the bank's total exposures.

Non-performing Loans and Provisioning: In line with global standards and Monetary Authority of Singapore's (MAS) article 612, the loans extended by Singapore banks are categorized into five types:

- ***Pass:*** *"...Repayment is prompt and the credit facility does not exhibit any potential weakness in repayment capability, business, cash flow or financial position of the borrower..."*

- *Special Mention*: "...*Indicates that the credit facility exhibits potential weaknesses that, if not corrected in a timely manner, may adversely affect repayment by the borrower at a future date, and warrant close attention by a bank...*"
- *Substandard*: "...*Indicates that the credit facility exhibits definable weaknesses, either in respect of the business, cash flow or financial position of the borrower that may jeopardise repayment on existing terms...*"
- *Doubtful*: "...*Consumer loans past due for 120 days or more, but less than 180 days fall under this classification...*"
- *Loss*: "...*Consumer loans past due for 180 days or more fall under this classification...*"

NPLs are the sum of a bank's loans categorised as substandard, doubtful and loss.

Also, as per MAS' article 612; banks are required to maintain two types of provisions on their loan portfolio with effect from March 2005:

- A minimum collective impairment provision of 1% of loans and receivables net of collateral and individual impairment provisions, and
- Minimum individual impairment provisions of 10% of substandard loans, 50% of doubtful loans and 100% of loss loans.

Non-credit Exposure Norms: A bank is required to secure MAS approval to hold a stake in excess of 10% in any company. A bank's equity investment in a single company cannot exceed 2% of the bank's capital funds. Banks are prohibited from owning immovable property in excess of 20% of their capital funds — properties for the banks' business use are excluded from this limit. Moreover, banks are not allowed to engage in property development or management activities, unless it involves properties that are foreclosed or used for the banks' business use.

Corporate Governance: The MAS requires independent directors to constitute a majority in the Board of Directors. The independence of a director must be reviewed in light of his length of service. A director who has served for a continuous period of nine years or more is no longer deemed independent. Board-level committees should include nominating, remuneration, audit and risk management committees. Remuneration should be aligned with the long-term interest and risk policies of the bank, with input from the board risk committee. The nominating committee should review the nominations and resignations of key personnel such as directors, the CEO, deputy CEO, CFO and CRO.

BIBLIOGRAPHY

Curtain Raiser

1. http://www.doingbusiness.org/rankings
2. https://www.transparency.org/cpi2014/results
3. http://www.kpmg.com/global/en/services/tax/tax-tools-and-resources/pages/corporate-tax-rates-table.aspx
4. fDi Magazine December 2014 issue "Singapore leads global city ranking for greenfield FDI"

Temasek Holdings

1. Temasek Review, 2006 to 2016
2. Business Times dated 6 March 2015 "Redefining Reserve Returns"
3. Business Times dated 15 April 2015 "Temasek is singe-largest foreign investor in Chinese banks: report"
4. Business Times dated 22 May 2015 "Global public sector investors favour real estate, infrastructure"
5. Temasek's Statement dated 3 March 2015 "NIR has no impact on Temasek investment strategy and dividend policy"

Golden Agri Resources

The following documents were downloaded on 13 March 2015 from http://www.goldenagri.com.sg/

1. GAR IPO Prospectus dated 30 June 1999
2. Sustainability Report 2011
3. GAR Annual Reports: 2005 to 2015
4. Media Release dated 21 December 2012 titled "SMART and GAR take responsibility for land cleared without IPK process"

Other Reports

5. http://www.sustainablepalmoil.org/consumers-retailers/ consumers/environmental-and-social-impacts/ downloaded on 13 March 2015
6. The World Bank Commodity Pink Sheet downloaded on 16 March 2015 from http://econ.worldbank.org/
7. "How Sinar Mas is expanding its empires of destruction" dated 29 July 2010 downloaded on 13 March 2015 from http://www. greenpeace.org/
8. "Golden Agri scheme gains traction" Financial Times dated 6 March 2015 downloaded on 13 March 2015
9. "Palm Oil Facts & Figures" downloaded on 13 March 2015 from http://www.simedarby.com/

Wilmar International

1. Green Rankings: 2012 downloaded on 21 March 2015 from www.newsweek.com
2. The World Bank Commodity Pink Sheet downloaded on 16 March 2015 from http://econ.worldbank.org/
3. Wilmar Annual Reports 2006 to 2015
4. Wilmar Fact Sheet downloaded on 21 March 2015 from www. wilmar-international.com
5. "Palm Oil King Goes From Forest Foe To Buddy In Deal With Critics" published on www.bloomberg.com on 13 March 2015 and downloaded on 21 March 2015

Olam International

1. Olam International IPO Prospectus, 2005
2. Olam International Annual Reports FY2005 to FY2015
3. Bunge Limited Full Year 2015 Results
4. Noble Group Full Year 2015 Results
5. Muddy Waters Research Report downloaded on 21 February 2015 from http://www.muddywatersresearch.com/wp-content/uploads/2012/11/MW_OLAM_11272012.pdf
6. Muddy Waters current stance on Olam: http://www.muddywaters-research.com/track-record/ downloaded on 21 February 2015
7. Olam's response to MW downloaded on 21 February 2015 from http://49tmko49h46b4e0czy3rlqaye1b.wpengine.netdna-cdn.com/wp-content/uploads/2014/05/OlamRespondstoMW-ReportFindings_28Nov2012.pdf
8. Bloomberg dated 25 April 2013 "Olam Survives as Short-Seller Block Proves Investors' Friend"
9. Africa Business Magazine dated 13 August 2013 "Olam's Blueprint for Success"

The Banking Troika

1. DBS Annual Reports: 2000–2015 downloaded from www.dbs.com.sg
2. OCBC Annual Reports: 2002–2015 downloaded from www.ocbc.com.sg
3. UOB Annual Reports: 2002–2015 downloaded from www.uob.com.sg
4. ICBC, Maybank and Bangkok Bank: 2015 Annual Report
5. Coping with the Asian Financial Crisis: The Singapore Experience, by Ngiam Kee Jin, Institute of Southeast Asian Studies ©2000
6. Downloaded from http://eresources.nlb.gov.sg/history/events/: Establishment of the Development Bank of Singapore, Oversea-Chinese Banking Corporation is Incorporated and United Chinese Bank Opens
7. Downloaded from the Monetary Authority of Singapore website, www.mas.gov.sg: MAS Notices 612, 637 and 649 and Financial Stability Review 2014

8. Financial inclusion: http://datatopics.worldbank.org/financial-inclusion/country/singapore
9. Financial Stability Board: Global Shadow Banking Monitoring Report 2015
10. Safest Banks 2014: https://www.rabobank.com/en/images/Safest_banks_2014_sept2014.pdf
11. The Straits Times "What to expect for Singapore property prices in 2015?" published on 2 January 2015
12. Bank for International Settlements for Basel 3: http://www.bis.org/bcbs/basel3.htm

SGX

1. Singapore Exchange Limited Web site www.sgx.com
2. SGX Annual Reports 2000–2015
3. Singapore Infopedia, "Stock Exchange Of Singapore Ltd Is Incorporated" downloaded on 7 January 2015 (http://eresources.nlb.gov.sg/history/events/4bf4d698-2616-4614-937f-30fcc5652763)
4. World Federation of Exchanges, Annual Statistics 2003 to 2015 downloaded from http://www.world-exchanges.org/statistics/annual
5. Thomson Reuters News

2015 Annual Reports of

6. ASX Limited
7. Hong Kong Exchanges and Clearing Limited
8. Japan Exchange Group Inc
9. London Stock Exchange Group Annual Report plc
10. Intercontinental Exchange Inc

Keppel Corporation

1. The Singapore Economic Development Board (EDB) Website: https://www.edb.gov.sg/content/edb/en/industries/industries/marine-offshore-engineering.html. Downloaded on 5 February 2015

2. "Tough Men Bold Visions: The Story of Keppel" by Richard Lim downloaded on 5 February 2015 from http://www.kepcorp. com/en/content.aspx?sid=59

3. Keppel Corporation Annual Reports 2006 to 2015, Keppel Corporation Milestones and Offshore & Marine Orderbook downloaded on 5 February 2015 from http://www.kepcorp. com/en/

4. Keppel Corporation Announcement dated 23 January 2015 "Keppel Corporation Limited Launches Voluntary Unconditional Cash Offer For Keppel Land Limited" downloaded from http:// www.kepcorp.com/en/news_item.aspx?sid=4970

5. Keppel Land Annual Reports 2010 to 2015 downloaded on 5 February 2014 from http://www.keppelland.com.sg/IR-Financial-Results.asp

6. The World Bank Commodity Pink Sheet downloaded on 20 July 2015 from http://econ.worldbank.org/

Fraser & Neave

1. Singapore Infopedia, Fraser & Neave (F&N) downloaded on 7 January 2015 (http://eresources.nlb.gov.sg/infopedia/articles/ SIP_1792_2011-03-04.html?s=Fraser%20\%26%20Neave)

2. Singapore Management University Case Collection 3-2014: "*Asia Pacific Breweries: A Big Gulp for Heineken?*" by Stephen Wyatt and Sarita Mathur

3. Reuters dated 22 January 2013 "*Thais set to win F&N battle after Overseas Union bows out*"

4. Asian Legal Business dated 1 Feb 2013 "*Of F&N and Other Deals*" by Ranajit Dam

5. Fraser & Neave 2008, 2010, 2012 and 2013 Annual Reports downloaded from http://www.fraserandneave.com/

6. "*Asia Pacific Breweries History*" downloaded on 7 January 2015 from http://www.fundinguniverse.com/company-histories/ asia-pacific-breweries-limited-history/

7. Frasers Centrepoint Limited: http://www.fraserscentrepoint. com/html/company_history.php

Sembcorp Industries

1. Sembcorp Annual Reports, 2006–2015

ST Engineering

1. ST Engineering Annual Reports, 2006 to 2015
2. ST Engineering Results Presentation, 2011 to 2015

SIA Engineering Company

1. Frost & Sullivan
2. SIA Engineering Company Annual Reports, FY06 to FY16
3. SIA Engineering Performance Review FY16

The Gaming Duopoly

1. 2010 to 2015 Annual Reports: Genting Singapore and Las Vegas Sands
2. Jan 2010 edition of the National Geographic: Lee Kwan Yew's interview with Mark Jacobson
3. Macau Statistics and Census Service: www.dicj.gov.mo
4. World Tourism Organization, UNWTO Tourism Highlights 2015

CapitaLand

1. CapitaLand Annual Reports 2005–15
2. The Business Times dated April 20 2015 "S'Pore still seen as a major Asia Reit hub"

City Developments Limited

1. City Development Limited, Annual Reports 2006 to 2015
2. Thomson Reuters
3. Nihon Keizai Shimbun

Global Logistic Properties

1. Global Logistic Properties Annual Reports, FY11 to FY15
2. Forrester Research
3. Economist Intelligence Unit
4. ChannelNews Asia

StarHub Limited

1. StarHub Annual Reports, 2006 to 2015
2. StarHub Fourth Quarter & Full Year Results Presentation, 2006 to 2015
3. www.referenceforbusiness.com
4. www.investopedia.com

Singtel

1. Singtel Annual Reports: FY05 to FY15
2. www.bloomberg.com

ComfortDelGro

1. ComfortDelGro Annual Reports, 2006 to 2015
2. Singapore Land Transport Statistics In Brief, 2004 to 2015
3. SMRT Corporation Ltd FY15 Annual Report
4. "Joint release by the Land Transport Authority & PTC — Some Parts Of Taxi Fare Structure To Be Standardised To Prevent Further Fare Complexity" dated March 31 2015 downloaded from http://www.lta.gov.sg
5. "From Third World To First: Singapore And The Asian Economic Boom" by Lee Kwan Yew

Singapore Airlines

1. Singapore Airlines Annual Reports, FY06 to FY15

2. The following documents were downloaded from IATA's website, www.iata.org

   - IATA Fact Sheet: Industry Statistics — December 2015
   - IATA Safety Fact Sheet — June 2016
   - IATA Fuel Fact Sheet — December 2015

3. Singapore Airlines downloaded from http://eresources.nlb.gov. sg/infopedia/articles/
4. The World Bank Commodity Pink Sheet downloaded on 7 June 2016 from http://econ.worldbank.org/
5. The Business Times dated May 16–17, 2015 *"SIA adopts multipronged approach to keep its edge"*
6. The Business Times dated 10 June, 2015 *"Record profits for aviation industry this year, but challenges remain"*

And The Curtains Fall...For Now

1. Press release dated 17 January 2014 titled *"Entrepreneurship Review Committee (ENRC) Unveils Eight Recommendations to Enhance Entrepreneurship Landscape"* downloaded from http:// www.spring.gov.sg/NewsEvents/PR/Pages/
2. The Business Times dated 17 April 2015 *"Women directorships make some headway among S'pore firms"*
3. The Business Times dated May 2–3 2015 *"Singapore slips in investment rankings"*
4. The Business Times dated June 9 2015 *"Job outlook better elsewhere in region than S'pore"*
5. The Business Times dated June 16 2015 *"Singapore's quarterly total employment falls for the first time in 5 years"*
6. The Business Times dated June 16 2015 *"Developers' sales slump amid lack of new major launches"*
7. Singapore tourist arrival data downloaded from https://www.stb. gov.sg/statistics-and-market-insights/Pages/statistics-visitor-arrivals.aspx

GLOSSARY

Acquisition	Purchase of an ongoing business, unit or an asset
AFC	Asian Financial Crisis of 1997
Balance Sheet Leverage	The loan to value (LTV) ratio is a measure of balance sheet leverage. It is no indicator of repayment capacity. But indicates how much debt a company has raised to funds its asset purchases. A lower (say 30% to 40%) LTV indicates that banks would be willing to extend more loans to the company as it can offer its unencumbered assets as collateral to the banks
Capital Expenditure	Asset purchases to expand a business' capacity or output or to the diversify business
Capital Gains	The difference between the share price at the end of a period and the beginning of the period, expressed as a percentage of the share price at the beginning of the period. A positive value indicates that the company's share price has increased while a negative value indicates that the share price has decreased

Cash Flow Leverage	There are multiple measures of cash flow leverage. A commonly used measure is the ratio of net lease adjusted debt to EBITDA, which captures a company's debt repayment capacity
Current P/E	Current share price divided by the last twelve months EPS
Debt	Borrowed capital which has to be returned at the end of a fixed tenor to the lender. Repayment may either be amortized over the tenor or a bullet at the end of the tenor of the loan or some combination of the two
Debt equivalent of lease	Companies have the option to either purchase assets outright or lease the assets used in the normal course of business. Based on reported financials, it would appear that companies which lease their assets have lower debt levels. To assess the 'true' level of borrowings, the debt equivalent of leases is computed. There are multiple methods to compute the debt equivalent of leases. This book uses the common industry practice of multiplying the lease rental payable in the next twelve months by a factor of eight
Derivatives	An instrument that derives its value from an underlying asset. Popular derivative instruments include options, futures, forwards, swaps and asset backed securities
Depository	A business unit that holds and facilitates the exchange of securities on behalf of clients
Dividend Payout	The percentage of cash dividends paid to net income. Dividend payout indicates the percentage of net income distributed to shareholders and the (balance) percentage that is re-invested in the business

Dividend payout should not be confused with dividend yield. A high dividend payout does not automatically translate into a high dividend yield. If a company's net income and consequently its dividends is low (despite the high dividend payout) is low and/its share price is high, the dividend yield will be low

Dividend Per Share (DPS)
In this book, DPS has been defined as total dividend including special dividends paid divided by a company's outstanding shares

Dividend Yield
The sum of dividend per share (DPS) paid by a company over a period of time, expressed as a percentage of the market price of 1 share at the beginning of the period, assuming the dividends are not reinvested

Earnings Per Share (EPS)
Net income divided by a company's average outstanding shares

E-commerce
The general term used for business conducted online or electronically

EBIT
Earnings/profit before incurring interest and tax expenses but after incurring manufacturing costs, selling, general and administrative expenses and depreciation of fixed assets and amortization of intangible assets (D&A)

EBIT Margin (%)
EBIT expressed as a percentage of total revenue

EBITDA
The sum of EBIT and D&A. As D&A is a non-cash expense, the EBITDA provides an estimate of the 'cash' earnings of the company before paying interest and tax expenses

EBITDA Margin (%)
EBITDA expressed as a percentage of total revenue

Exchange Traded Fund	A marketable security that tracks an index, a commodity, bonds, or a basket of assets like an index fund. Unlike mutual funds, an ETF trades like a common stock on a stock exchange. ETFs experience price changes throughout the day as they are bought and sold. ETFs typically have higher daily liquidity and lower fees than mutual fund shares, making them an attractive alternative for individual investors.
Fair Value Gains/ Losses	Increase or decrease in value of as asset when making an unbiased estimate of its market price
GDP	Gross domestic product — a measure of the size of an economy that aggregates the total value of goods and services produced by it over a specific period of time
GFC	Global Financial Crisis of 2007–08
Lease adjusted debt	The sum of total debt reported by a company and the debt equivalent of its leases
Loan to Value Ratio (%)	Loan a lender is willing to extend as a percentage of the market value of an asset
Logistics	The business of managing the flow of goods and services from its origin to the ultimate consumer, thereby connecting consumers and producers
Mark to Market Value of Derivatives	Adjusting the book value of a derivatives instrument to reflect its current price
Market capitalization	The total number of equity shares of a company multiplied by its stock price. It is the approximate market value of the business, presuming that all its assets and liabilities are taken over
Merger	The process of combining separate companies and businesses so that the resulting enterprise operates as one entity

Net Income	The post-tax profit or earnings of a company. EBIT Less Interest Expense Less Tax
Net lease adjusted debt	Lease adjusted debt less cash
Net lease adjusted debt/EBITDA (x, Times)	This ratio is an indicator of a company's debt repayment capacity and is an estimate of the number of years a company would take to repay its debt using cash earnings. A lower ratio of net lease adjusted debt to EBITDA indicates lower financial risk, all other factors remaining unchanged.
Portfolio	Collection of assets, shares or investments
Price Earnings Ratio (P/E)	Stock price of a company divided by its EPS. It indicates what price an investor is willing to pay per dollar of a company's earnings
Retailer	The business unit selling consumer goods or services to the ultimate consumer
Stock index	Benchmark comprising various bellwether stocks whose function is to give a broad sense of the health of the market or economy
Total Return	The sum of dividend yield and capital gains
Utilities	A collection of services provided by organizations that are consumed by public including electricity, natural gas, water, and sewage
Working Capital	Liquidity that is required for running a firm's day to day operations. Key components of working capital include current assets such as trade receivables and inventory and current liabilities such as trade payables. Working capital is expressed as the excess of current assets over current liabilities

Printed in the United States
By Bookmasters